Legends of Blood

Legends of Blood

The Vampire in History and Myth

WAYNE BARTLETT
AND
FLAVIA IDRICEANU

PRAEGER

Westport, Connecticut
London

Library of Congress Cataloging-in-Publication Data

Bartlett, W. B.
  Legends of blood : the vampire in history and myth / Wayne Bartlett & Flavia
  Idriceanu.
      p. cm.
  Originally published: Stroud, U.K. : Sutton, 2005.
  Includes bibliographical references and index.
  ISBN 0–275–99292–6 (alk. paper)
  1. Vampires.   2. Vampires in literature.   3. Vampire films.   I. Idriceanu,
  Flavia. II. Title.
  GR830.V3B37   2005
  398.21—dc22   2006026799

Originally published in English by Sutton Publishing under the title **Legends of
Blood** copyright © Wayne Bartlett and Flavia Idriceanu, 2005

British Library Cataloguing in Publication Data is available.

Library of Congress Catalog Card Number: 2006026799
ISBN: 0–275–99292–6

First published in 2006

Praeger Publishers, 88 Post Road West, Westport, CT 06881
An imprint of Greenwood Publishing Group, Inc.
www.praeger.com

Printed in the United States of America

The paper used in this book complies with the
Permanent Paper Standard issued by the National
Information Standards Organization (Z39.48–1984).

10 9 8 7 6 5 4 3 2 1

Copyright Acknowledgments

The author and the publisher gratefully acknowledge permission for use of the
following material:

Excerpts from The Lord of the Rings by J.R.R. Tolkien. Copyright (c) 1954, 1955,
1965, 1966 by J.R.R. Tolkien. Copyright (c) Renewed 1982, 1983 by Christopher
R. Tolkien, Michael H.R. Tolkien, John F.R. Tolkien, and Priscilla M.A.R. Tolkien.
Copyright (c) Renewed 1993, 1994 by Christopher R. Tolkien, John F.R. Tolkien,
and Priscilla M.A.R. Tolkien. Reprinted by permission of Houghton Mifflin Company. All rights reserved.

Every reasonable effort has been made to trace the owners of copyright materials
in this book, but in some instances this has proven impossible. The author and
publisher will be glad to receive information leading to more complete acknowledgments in subsequent printings of the book and in the meantime extend their
apologies for any omissions.

Dedicated to our mothers, for their love and support in our decisions, and through the consequences!

Contents

Introduction

Mention Transylvania to most Westerners, and the image created in their minds will be of Bram Stoker and his mythical Count Dracula. Mention Dracula to a Romanian from Transylvania, however, and the name will, in many cases, elicit a defensive response and a frustrated shrug of the shoulders. This book has been stimulated by these contrasting responses, which hint at a more complex phenomenon than vampirism is usually perceived to be. It combines the experience of a Westerner with a lifelong interest in history and that of a Romanian philologist, and attempts to trace the various "qualities" that make a vampire. During the course of our research, it became clear just how deeply rooted are the beliefs on which the phenomenon relies for its impact.

It is important to state at the outset that this is not merely a "vampire" book. The subject is too complex to be taken as a completely discrete unit in the history of ideas. Vampires are an interesting mental construct, bringing together myth, legend, history, and literature. What we will examine in the chapters that follow are the various themes that underlie the effectiveness and longevity of the vampire myth.

Fear of vampires has been with us for almost as long as written records exist, and we find these threatening figures of the undead in the oldest of myths. The legend grew across time and space, so that in fairly recent times, one writer, the Reverend Montague Summers writing in 1928, described the feelings of many when he said that "throughout the vast shadowy world of ghosts and demons there is no figure so terrible, no figure so dreaded and abhorred, yet dight with such fearful fascination, as the vampire, who is himself neither ghost nor demon, but yet who partakes the dark natures and possesses the mysterious and terrible qualities of both."[1]

But even in the modern world, the vampire still has the power to shock. In the era of computers and space travel, this terrifying creature, which frightened the ancients and spread panic in the villages of Eastern Europe several hundred years ago, still has an unexpected effect on us, though in a changed form. The myth has evolved and appeals to our fears in a different manner than that experienced by our ancestors. The mechanisms of fear have not lost their impact with the advance of technology.

Our world is still, in many ways, the threatening place that it was to our ancestors, and the principles of good and evil still have an impact on our imagination. This explains the contemporary popularity of vampire filmography, from *Buffy the Vampire Slayer* to *Van Helsing*. We are, to an extent, prisoners of a mental whirlpool, where fear of and fascination with the unknown and the supernatural still exist. This is what lies at the heart of the effectiveness of the vampire myth: there is a narrower dividing line than we would like to think between the everyday world and the land where "myriads of horrible fancies began to crowd in upon my mind—all of them connected with death and vampires; with blood, and pain, and trouble."[2]

Our fears can make fantastic stories seem true. Humanity has often believed that we share our world with good or evil spirits, fabulous beings and strange creatures, sometimes helpful, sometimes menacing and vengeful. For centuries, pain and illness were thought to be caused by evil spirits, which could be summoned by a witch or a wizard (beliefs that still exist in some parts of the world). Fear of death, and of the souls of the departed being "trapped" on earth, was at the origin of burial rituals. When these were not respected and something went wrong, the dead would not find peace and would come back to punish the living. And the frontier between life and the world beyond was easy to cross at the right moment or with the correct password.

This may be one explanation for the way in which events that had a natural cause were perceived as interventions into our world by these spirits. The localized outbreaks of "vampire" activity that terrorized communities in the seventeenth and eighteenth centuries were probably the result of plague and other natural phenomena. But there is no doubt that those who witnessed and felt themselves threatened by what seemed like supernatural epidemics genuinely believed that they were being visited by some malignant and evil force.

Rumor played an important part in the evolution of the vampire image. It was a mentality similar to that which lay behind the witchcraft trials of slightly earlier times. An accusation half a millennium ago that a neighbor was a witch might have had flimsy evidence to support it, but that often did not stop the subsequent execution of the poor unfortunate who was so charged. What may start off as historical fact may soon lose its shape as it is distorted by interpretation, elaboration, or just plain error into a shadowy reflection of the reality. The plagues that decimated Eastern European villages during the time of the great "vampire epidemics" were real enough, even if the supernatural explanations offered as a cause no longer seem plausible.

Vampirism is an amalgam of a number of different motifs and symbols. To associate the phenomenon with what has come to be regarded as its two major traits—the association with blood and a state of being "undead," neither truly alive nor dead—is to ignore a number of other attributes that help to explain its hold over the imagination. Further, because it is linked to so many other manifestations of the supernatural, it cannot be looked at in isolation. These concepts are ancient, and as a result, they have a history of their own. Yet in all this diversity, there are common elements that go further back in time than might first appear. There are a number of recurrent images, easy to recognize in the latest Dracula movie, in the oldest of myths, in the accusations against the witch who was about to be burned, and in the scary legends which have been told on stormy nights for centuries.

The phenomenon is also an amalgam of historical record, legends, and literature. Sometimes it is difficult to identify where one ends and another begins. The boundaries between them become blurred, as is often the case with historical personalities around which stories grow. One example pertinent to vampires is the man who gave his nickname to Count Dracula, the medieval prince known as Vlad the Impaler. This historical figure was (and still is) a hero in his own land, but in the eyes of many others is (erroneously) associated with a vampire. Who is the "real" Dracula: the warrior who fought a heroic losing battle against the Turks, or Bram Stoker's Transylvanian Count?

This is where our book begins. It looks at the mechanisms behind these famous stories (and histories) of blood, examining their development in mythology, legend, and literature, and their effects on history and imagination. A huge amount has been written on the subject, and a multitude of films continue to be churned out at an impressive rate. Space prevents us from considering more than a representative sample of these, and because of this, we have attempted to identify a literary core from which we will illustrate the key themes that, taken as a whole, make the vampire phenomenon such an effective one. The themes are many and link into different areas of the occult—witchcraft and wizardry, for example. Or they may take us in a different direction, such as the association of the vampire with animals like bats and wolves. Even the landscapes in which the vampire tales are set often help to deepen their impact.

We will analyze these themes and trace their development across the centuries. We will examine the features that make a vampire story effective.

Our quest will take us deep into dark forests, into the medieval village, to the sanctuary of the church, and to the graveyard, or on a broomstick towards the witches' sabbat, and to deserted country mansions. We will follow the animals of the night, the wolf, the bat, and the cat; we shall peek into the cauldron of the witch, and into the tomes of the magician. We shall see how dark legends turned into an even darker history. We shall discover novels, short stories, and films, and take a look at what lies behind their success or failure. Our journey will lead us to discover a combination of images, each touching a certain chord in our sensibility. Fear, curiosity, defiance of the norms, all of these combine to exercise a vice-like grip over the imagination.

NOTES

1. Summers, p. xiii.
2. Dr. Seward's journal in *Dracula,* p. 287.

CHAPTER 1

Origins

Consider, too, how deep the abyss between life and death; across this, my power can build a bridge, but it can never fill up the frightful chasm.
—Johann Ludwig Tieck, "Wake Not the Dead!"

Like all products of the imagination, the vampire has taken many shapes, each mirroring the customs, beliefs, and fears of different cultures. It is difficult to find one definition for it, as all the aspects which vary from one manifestation to another cannot be encapsulated in a few words. One attempt to define the core features of a vampire is "a dead person believed to come from the grave at night and suck the blood of living people" (*Penguin English Dictionary*). This definition includes the two classic elements that we have already alluded to: the physical appearance of death combined with the ability of returning to a kind of existence, and the need for a diet of blood. The same dictionary offers an alternative description, which can be seen in a more "politicized" sense: "a person who lives by preying on and exploiting others." This second definition is also accurate: vampires exist by using their victims as a source of blood, and the meaning of the word has evolved so that it is applied to any exploitative person. But neither tells the whole story, as we will reveal.

The vampire is a "revenant," a being from beyond the grave, which destroys life in order to continue its own unholy and unnatural existence. Besides the need for blood and the state of being "undead" (neither a departed spirit, nor a living person, and therefore in a kind of spiritual no-man's-land), there are other attributes that we should consider, such as magus-like qualities, sexuality, links with nature. This definition underlines the fact that a "vampire" should be distinguished from a "ghost." Both, in a way, are undead, and thus there is a connection between the two, but in our definition a ghost returns in a spiritual, immaterial form, whereas a vampire is very much a real, physical presence, in every way flesh and blood—and partaking of the blood of others.

In the era of *Buffy the Vampire Slayer*, it is perhaps difficult to understand the vampire phenomenon in a literal sense. But previous generations certainly did.

To many communities, vampires were not a mythological flight of fantasy, they were a reality. Rulers from Charlemagne to the princes of nineteenth-century Wallachia have felt the need to forbid their subjects from taking the law into their own hands, as fear of vampires was causing the population to impale or burn corpses. Written accounts of vampires are found right back at the beginning of recorded history.

Not only is the vampire a creature which, in the past, was considered a genuine phenomenon, it is also a universal presence. The implication of the development of this myth in different parts of the globe, in so many unconnected cultures, and its ancient origins, is that the fears that it arouses are deep-rooted in the human psyche. To list all the regions of the world where the vampire appears in one form or another would be tedious, so the examples that follow are a sample from what is a very large corpus.

Transylvania was once the "classic" vampire location, thanks in the main to Bram Stoker, and it does indeed have many accounts of vampire activity. But Stoker had plenty of illustrations to choose from far closer to his Irish home.[1] A particularly interesting tale comes from the splendidly named Slaughtaverty in Co. Derry. This is the legend of a local chieftain named Abhartach, renowned for his cruelty. He was killed in battle and buried, as was traditional, standing up. However, it seems that this wasn't enough to keep him in the grave. The day after his burial, he reappeared, seeking fresh blood to nourish him. He was killed again and reinterred. When he returned once more, a local druid advised that he should be dispatched with a sword made of yew. Then he should be reburied, this time with his head at the foot of the grave. Mountain-ash sprigs were then buried in the earth above his corpse, and a large rock was placed on top to prevent another escape. Thus the evil chieftain was forever imprisoned in his grave.

Another tale, this one from Co. Antrim, is a variation on the femme fatale theme. Here, a beautiful woman who becomes a vampire can only be released from her half-life when another replaces her. Tales from Waterford speak of enchantresses enticing unwary young men and then sucking the lifeblood out of them. These accounts present different elements that are commonplace in vampire lore: the return of one apparently dead, the dependence on blood, the seduction of the unwary, and frequent attempts to find a cure for the visitation, initially unsuccessful, until by a disturbing process of trial and error a solution is (usually) found.[2]

These bloodthirsty creatures from the grave haunted all corners of Europe. They were the more frightening as they were a representation of the birth of evil in the midst of the community, a fearsome break in the normality of everyday life. A vampire is usually the result of a transformation where the innocent become corrupted; a mere accident or the breaking of a social or moral taboo would unleash the powers of hell. The ways in which somebody could become such a creature differed from one region to another, mirroring the specific cultural traits of each area. Incest was the cause in Croatia (where the undead were known as *pijavica*) and Serbia (*vlkoslak, mulo,* or *dhampir*), while in Romania *strigoiul* or *moroiul* were the illegitimate children of parents themselves born out of wedlock. In Macedonia, the vampire was known as a *vrykolakas* and was created when various taboos were broken, such as when an unbaptized child died or when burial rituals were not properly respected. Werewolves would become vampires in Serbia, as they did in Russia. Occult activity could also create such a monster: witchcraft was the cause in Portugal and another explanation in Russia.

These different causes demanded different ways of dealing with vampires according to regional lore and wisdom, which perhaps explains the variety of methods for killing them in literature. Driving a stake through the heart is the classic way of doing this, of course—though anyone reading *Dracula* for the first time may be surprised to learn that this is not how the Count is finally destroyed: he is stabbed in the heart with a knife and his throat is cut. This is the remedy in Albania, Russia (no room for fear or a shaky hand here, strike it more than once and the vampire comes back to life), and Romania. Cutting off the head is also popular, and this is the tactic in Bavaria, Croatia (where it should afterwards be put between the legs), Greece, and Crete (where it should be boiled in vinegar).

Driving a nail into the head, neck, or navel also seems to be an effective method for disposing of a vampire. This is the remedy in Macedonia, Hungary, and Serbia, and an alternative solution in Romania. In Poland (where being born with teeth was a sign that the individual would become a vampire), the creature would be buried face downwards, presumably so that it was confused and spent an eternity digging the wrong way! However, if the dead subsequently returned as vampires, then they would be destroyed in their coffins. The blood of the revenant was then baked in bread and eaten by the living, an infallible way of protecting themselves from further attacks. In Ireland (where the *dearg-dul* comes to suck the blood of the living), stones were piled high on top of its grave.

This list has been presented to demonstrate that there are many regional variations in terms of the detail of European vampirism. But broad general features of the phenomenon may be identified, typically the fact that the vampire is "undead" and needs human blood. And there are enough regional similarities to hint at a common mythological origin in certain areas, particularly in parts of Eastern Europe, in spite of the different customs linked to it.

The realm of the vampire reaches far beyond the frontiers of Europe, though. In Africa, for example, the *adze*—found in Ghana and Togo—assumes the form of a firefly and lives off blood, palm oil, and coconut water. It is particularly attracted to children. Another form from Ghana is known as the *obayifo*. Again, this is especially fond of infants, but can also damage crops. From Madagascar comes the *ramanga*, which drinks spilled blood.

Asia also adds its variants to the list. India had a particularly large number of different types of vampire.[3] There is the *bhuta*, normally found in cemeteries, and the *brahmaparush*. The latter is especially nightmarish. It drinks its victims' blood through their skull and then eats the brains. The *gayal* is also interesting, as this vampire is created when the burial rites of a funeral are not properly performed, a common theme in European lore, too. There are Chinese vampires (*kuang-shi*), Japanese (*kasha*), and some from the Philippines, where the *aswang* lives off blood, preferably that of infants. Also from these islands, the *danag* has an interesting story. It was once an ally of man. However, one day a woman it was working with cut her finger. The *danag* sucked her blood and was so enthusiastic about the taste that it proceeded to drain it all from her body.

The New World, too, has its vampires. The *lobishomen* is from Brazil. It does not kill its prey, but instead takes small amounts of blood at a time. This has interesting side effects, for if the victim was a woman, this dramatically increased her sex drive. From Mexico, there are witch-vampires (*tlaciques*), a recurrent theme of dark magic and sensuality entwined. Even Australia has its own variant, the *talamaur*. This is a living vampire, which could extract any residual life force trapped in the body from a recently dead corpse (an interesting case of role reversal).

Historical records mentioning vampires date back to the beginnings of recorded history. The *ekimmu* is found in Assyrian and Babylonian mythology during the third millennium B.C. This creature was the soul of someone who had died but could not find peace. There were several ways the *ekimmu* might be brought into existence. Two methods are similar to those often used to explain the presence of ghosts: unrequited love or a violent or premature death. But a third is particularly important in the light of later vampire lore, as it was also believed that failure to follow the correct burial rites was responsible for creating a vampire. It is also from this era that we find the first written evidence of the vampire—a reference to one on the seal of a cylinder from ancient Babylon.

The terrible Babylonian female demon, *labartu*, was particularly fearsome. She was a hellish creature who feasted on the blood of humans and animals alike, but she preferred to drain the life force of young children. She would ask mothers to entrust their babies to her, pretending that she wanted to breastfeed them. Instead, she would drink their blood. One of the remedies against her was the *ittamir* stone, which was also a protection against miscarriage. This is a double metaphor, the demonic preying upon the innocent and the breaking of a bond of trust. This theme migrated, and is found in Judaic culture, where the *estrie* is also a female demon that takes on human form. It lives among men, feeding on their blood to sustain itself, and again, particularly likes the blood of young children.

In the first millennium B.C., vampires found their way, first into the Greek, and from there to the Roman, pantheon of monsters. The Greeks called them *lamiae*, the Romans *lamiae, striges*, or *mormos*.[4] The *striges* were a combination of witch and vampire. She could transform herself into a crow, which would then drink the blood of humans. The *mormos* were servants of Hecate, goddess of the witches. Horace wrote about vampires, describing how they ate children (an allegation frequently made against many different groups that broke the conventions of society, including early Christians and Jews, as well as witches) or drank their blood: the abuse of innocents (and innocence) already forming a key part of the vampire imagery. Ovid stated that these demons could assume the form of ravenous birds (shape-shifting again is a timeless quality of vampires), which sucked the blood of children and ate them.

The *lamiae* inspired terror among the Greeks. These creatures were said to ensnare unwary young men. They were invariably beautiful, voluptuous young women (an unmistakable forerunner of the so-called vamps of more recent times)—though an unfortunate habit of removing their eyes must have done something to lessen their attractiveness. The creature is sometimes argued to be a close cousin of the better-known Gorgon.[5] One story, given by Philostratus in the *Life of Apollonius*, could have come straight from Bram Stoker's pen. It tells of a striking-looking young man, Menipus Lycius, who falls in love with a foreign-looking girl, "good-looking and extremely dainty." Apollonius, an ancient precursor of Professor van Helsing, sees through her at once and warns Menipus that she is a vampire. In the end, she tells all to Apollonius, admitting that she was just fattening Menipus up before eating him, because "it was her habit to feed upon young and beautiful bodies, because their blood is so pure and so strong." This early vampire tale made a great impression on readers of all eras, and was the inspiration behind Keats' poem, "Lamia."

Keats (1795–1821) wrote two millennia after the initial tales of Apollonius and the *lamia*, which serves to demonstrate just how strong the ability was of these ancient accounts to inspire writers in the Gothic era, thirsty as they were for stories from Classical times to thrill and shock their readers. In the poem, Keats describes how Lamia was a woman who was transformed by magic into a serpent. In return for her assistance, Hermes agrees to metamorphose her once more into a woman (an example of shape-shifting, i.e., the ability to change from an animal into human form and vice versa—a phenomenon we will return to later). She meets and entrances Lycius, and they marry. But on their wedding night, she transforms herself back into a serpent. The following morning:

> Lycius' arms were empty of delight,
> As were his limbs of life, from that same night.
> On the high couch he lay!—his friends came round –
> Supported him—no pulse, or breath they found,
> And, in its marriage robe, the heavy body wound.[6]

Keats's poem demonstrates the dangers inherent when boundaries are crossed, in this case between demons and humans. Lamia is, literally, a demon, and the serpent is a traditional Christian representation of Satan. It is interesting that the serpent in ancient times was not necessarily a representation of evil, but was often associated with magical powers (the link between snakes and medicine in ancient Greece and the healing powers of the brass serpent that the Children of Israel look upon in the desert so that they may be healed[7] are just two examples).

Some characteristics of the vampire in Philostratus' story are worthy of comment, as they foreshadow those of later examples of the genre. First of all, she is foreign, a stranger, a figure that was often a target for suspicion in many eras. Her beauty is also a feature of many classic literary vampires, making her a seductress as well as a supernatural creature. The association between youth, purity, and strength is also significant. In purity, there is a reference to the corruption of innocence, while the connection between youth and strength hints at the restorative powers of young blood. There is transferability in the power of this blood: by drinking it, the vampire herself will retain vitality and also beauty (Lycius himself is an attractive young man, and the implication is that his lifeblood will give beauty as well as strength).

The *Odyssey* makes overt statements about the power of blood. In Limbo, which lies between the land of the living and the Underworld (a symbolic place of transit neither in this world nor the next—the approximate state of a vampire), Odysseus meets with the spirits of the departed. They are, however, deprived of the gift of speech; they have no blood, their life force—which gives them the ability to talk—no longer exists. So, when Odysseus needs to speak with them, he digs a pit which he fills with the blood of sheep. As a result, one of the spirits of the dead, that of Tiresias of Thebes, is able to give Odysseus the information that he desires, also telling him that the blood given to the spirits in Limbo— the undead trapped between two worlds—will invest them with at least some of the attributes of the living.

Another account, this time Roman, written by Phlegon of Tralles, tells how a young girl, Philinnion, died but refused to give up her lover. She returned to spend the night with him on a number of occasions. She was, however, seen. In an attempt to verify the frightening accounts for themselves, the "undead" girl's parents waited for and confronted her. On seeing them, she promptly dropped down dead once more. When her coffin was examined, it was found to be empty, but in it was a ring that her lover, Machates, had given her on one of her recent visits. The authorities ordered that her body should be cremated on a pyre outside the city walls—a precursor of remedies a millennium and a half later—which was duly done. The nocturnal visitations stopped at once.

Christianity appeared to do nothing to alleviate the fears implicit in all these vampire beliefs. On the contrary, the importance of blood as a symbol in its theology strengthened it. During the medieval period, accounts of vampires continued. Many of the legends are continental, but there are several interesting accounts of vampire-like activity in Britain written by William of Newburgh between 1196 and 1198.[8]

An early twentieth-century writer, Montague Summers, who became infamous as a defrocked priest who specialized in studies of the occult, wrote several detailed accounts of vampirism and the occult, such as *The Vampire, His Kith and Kin* (1928) and *The Vampire in Lore and Legend* (1929). He made much of Newburgh's descriptions. These do not evince all the attributes of vampirism, but some features are common to later manifestations of the creature.

Newburgh gives an account of the Squire of Alnwick, on the borders of England and Scotland. Here, a man had lived a wicked life and, as a result, the Devil made sure that he rested uneasily in his grave. The scene painted by Newburgh is a nightmarish one. In the hours of darkness, the squire returned to the town and roamed its streets. His mere presence made the dogs of the town go wild, howling as he passed them. In one crucial respect, though, the story follows a different path from that of the traditional literary vampire: rather than the body remaining uncorrupted, it is in a state of decay. The resulting description could have been lifted straight from Poe's "Masque of the Red Death":

The air became foul and tainted as this foetid and corrupting body wandered abroad, so that a terrible plague broke out and there was hardly a house which did not mourn its dead, and presently the town, which a little while before had been thickly populated, seemed to be well-nigh deserted, for those who had survived the pestilence and these hideous attacks hastily removed themselves to other districts, lest they also should perish.[9]

Terrified by this horrific creature, the townspeople resolved that they would take matters into their own hands. Understandably nervous, they made their way to the cemetery where they dug the squire's body up. They expected to have to dig a fair way down, but were surprised and, no doubt alarmed, when his corpse was discovered just below the surface, "gorged and swollen with frightful corpulence, and its face was florid and bloated, with huge red puffed cheeks, and the shroud in which he had been wrapped was all soiled and torn."

So incensed was the crowd, that they felt no fear. Instead, one of them struck the cadaver with a sharp spade. From here on in, the story follows classic vampire lines, as "immediately there gushed forth a stream of warm red gore." They dragged the corpse from its shallow grave and built a large pyre. When the body was consumed by the flames, the plague stopped at once.

This is a remarkable account, which presages in many ways tales of vampirism that were related by populations cursed by vampire manifestations in the seventeenth and eighteenth centuries.[10] The state of the body, for one thing, is uncannily like later so-called real life accounts—by which we mean those from historical records rather than literature—particularly the swollen body and the puffed cheeks, while the torn shroud implies that the creature had not been lying easy in its grave. Similarly, the effect of this horrific visitation mirrors that of later historical accounts: the latter often do not mention the drawing of blood from the victims, but describe a feeling as if of suffocation, and symptoms that strongly resonate of an outbreak of the plague.

Newburgh's most chilling account is that of the revenant at Melrose Abbey, Scotland. This concerned a cleric who had, in life, demonstrated a very unpriestly passion for hunting. When he died, he returned to the abbey, but could not cross its sacred boundaries. So he turned his attention to the chambers of a woman he had known in life, groaning terribly as he did so. She asked the abbey for help. Two monks took on the disturbing task of watching his grave. He rose once more, though unfortunately one of the sentinels had fallen asleep. The other managed to fight him off with an axe and chased him back to his tomb. As he approached it, the ground opened up and swallowed him. When they dug up the earth of his grave, they found that his body had a gaping, fresh wound—caused by the watchful monk's blows—and the tomb was filled with black blood. They removed the corpse from the grave, took it outside the abbey grounds, and burned it. The undead cleric was seen no more.

This account introduces several other elements that would be found in the later evolution of the vampire. It is about a man who claimed to be holy, but implicitly was not. As such, his sin is all the greater. A specifically Christian element is introduced, too: the iconic power of the abbey, symbol of goodness, the threshold of which the restless priest cannot cross, and an impenetrable barrier against the forces of evil. There is also the wound on the body—this is no ghost that has come back from the grave, it is a physical resurrection as evidenced by the blood and the wound, a grotesque parody of the Christian version.

As time went on, various writers came to be regarded as authorities on vampires. The first to make his mark on a large scale was the sixteenth-century writer Louis Lavater, who was also a Protestant theologian. He wrote, for the time, the classic study on the creature. His work was translated into English in 1572 in a book entitled, *Of Ghosts and Spirits Walking by Night*. He believed that some men and women were too easily influenced by any sudden movement during the hours of darkness, "things that go bump in the night," so to speak. Such people were quick to ascribe even natural events to supernatural intervention. He stated further that they believed them to be "souls of dead men, which crave help of them that are living, to be delivered out of the torments of most cruel pain in Purgatory." In his view, they were wrong. Where a vampire existed, it was not the soul of a dead person, but "either good or evil angels, or else some secret and hid operations of God."

This was very much in keeping with late medieval attitudes, where divine intervention was a part of everyday life. God had a hand in everything. In vampirism could be seen divine judgment, a punishment for sin. It did not stop Lavater from asserting that many cases of supernatural activity were hoaxes, occurring when people dressed themselves as devils or even put on white sheets to frighten their neighbors. He was in no doubt as to the cause of such pranks: young men overindulging themselves at inns, egged on by "harlots and whoremongers."

Rogue priests were not above suspicion either, an unsurprising suggestion from a Protestant theologian of that time. This explanation for vampirism would be used on a number of occasions over the centuries. Lavater accused some of them of consorting with the spirits of the dead: "To these things may be added that there have been in all ages certain priests, which practising strange devices, and giving themselves to necromancy, have bewitched foolish men that highly esteemed them, to the end that they might thereby increase their riches, and follow their lustful pleasures."[11]

In Lavater's era, there was no real consensus about the spiritual status of a vampire. Some asserted that a vampire was created when a demon entered into a corpse, effectively "borrowing" the body to indulge in unholy activities. More popularly, it was the spirit of the man or woman who has died that resides in the body, unable to find peace. There are various explanations for this belief. Again, one of the most common is that some element of the funeral rites was omitted during the committal of the body. Failure to follow the correct process could therefore have catastrophic results, which meant that the rules of burial were normally scrupulously complied with. Another explanation offered was that the departed had led a particularly sinful life, in the context of which vampirism assumed the form of a divine punishment, whereby the soul of the deceased could find no peace.

That belief in the existence of vampires goes back a long time and is found in cultures all over the world is evident. But this on its own does not explain why it is such a familiar, and still disturbing, phenomenon even now—a creature so widely recognized that it can be seen in areas as diverse as advertisements for batteries to children's cartoons. This is because something happened that took the legends and the historical accounts that existed and made them seem so real, that stories of vampires would appear in newspapers as if they were as factual as reports on a war or records of parliamentary proceedings. The event that created this lasting effect was a series of localized epidemics that seized the imagination of Western Europe, which, in its turn, acted as a catalyst for a remarkable literary and cinematographic development.

NOTES

1. This theme is developed by Haining and Tremayne in *The Undead*.

2. For further references, ibid., chap.5.

3. A now defunct website, *The A–Z of Vampires* (http://www.vampireaz.com), listed nine different types of vampire from India.

4. These words have been transferred to modern Romanian as *strigoi* and *moroi,* respectively. The former is a kind of ghost, the latter a form of vampire.

5. Summers, p. 8.

6. Keats, *Selected Poems,* p. 181.

7. Numbers 21: 8.

8. Historia rerum Anglicorum, Book V.

9. Newburgh's accounts are quoted in full in Summers, pp. 80–88.

10. See Chapter 2, below.

11. In Ronay, pp. 20–22.

CHAPTER 2

The Vampire Epidemics

If the return of the vampires is real, it is of import to defend it, and prove it, and if it is illusory, it is of consequence to the interests of religion to unde-ceive those who believe in its truth, and destroy an error which may produce dangerous effects.
　　　　　　　—Dom Augustin Calmet, "Treatise on the Vampires…"

The closing years of the seventeenth century were marked by epidemics in parts of Europe, and these outbreaks continued well into the follow-ing century. This time, however, it was no Black Death or Bubonic Plague that decimated local populations. It was something very different which, rather than being a mere physical illness, also had very marked psycho-logical effects. To those directly involved, it was more sinister, frightening, and inexplicable than any previous epidemic. It was, in short, a plague of the undead. It was concentrated in Eastern Europe, and was particularly prevalent in Hungary, Bohemia, Silesia, Poland, and Greece. There were not a huge number of cases, but the few reported incidents had an impact across Europe.

It is worth saying at the outset that the limited number of accounts might give the impression that these outbreaks were isolated. This may not nec-essarily be the case. A common feature of the various historical records that we will shortly consider is that they were written by foreigners. This phenomenon was witnessed mainly in areas that had recently passed into the sphere of the increasingly powerful European empires, particularly Austria, from a disintegrating Ottoman Empire. The cultural mix here, where vampire legends formed part of everyday beliefs, was novel and extraordinary to Westerners, and their enthusiasm to commit such stories to print only increased the curiosity of the public to discover more about these extraordinary events.

But the victims of the epidemics did not write about them. Their way of recording strange events like these was through folklore and oral tradition, much harder to verify, and much less likely to leave a traceable footprint in historical accounts. And the large numbers of legends that exist, even into modern times, suggest that, to them, such events were not as amazing as they were to, for example, a Walloon officer stationed in Hungary. So we cannot say with confidence that the seventeenth and eighteenth centuries saw the peak of the outbreaks. What we *can* say is that they were reported in Western Europe on an altogether larger scale than was previously the case. It was during this period, in 1732, that the word "vampire" first entered the English language.

Even in those far-off times, the media played an important part in the relaying and evolution of the vampire myth. The seventeenth century saw a significant expansion in newsletters and news broadsheets which helped to communicate tales of extraordinary happenings to a much wider audience. So the impact of the vampire myth at this time was due to a combination of two factors: the "discovery" of lands that, although known about, were previously inaccessible and mysterious, and the development of wider methods of access to an interested public, both through newsletters and books.

Early accounts thus appeared and quickly became conversation pieces in the coffee shops of Paris and London. For example, the French newspaper *Mercure galant* ran an article on the phenomenon in 1694. The reports thrilled its readers; they were horrifying, but also a little bizarre: "The vampires appeared after lunch and stayed until midnight, sucking the blood of people and cattle in great abundance. They sucked through the mouth, the nose but mainly through the ears. They say that the vampires had a sort of hunger that made them chew even their shrouds in the grave."[1]

The image of vampires sucking blood through their ears, or chewing their shrouds in their graves, is, to say the least, an incongruous one—but no doubt the readership examined these accounts with barely suppressed horror and wonder. The imagery was so vivid that one serious attempt to look at the vampire phenomenon by the German professor Michael Ranfft was called *Treatise upon the Dead who Chew in their Sepulchres*.

The newspaper account in *Mercure galant* followed closely upon the publication of a book called *Die Ehre Herzogthums Krain*, which appeared in Lübeck in 1689. This told the story of a peasant who died suddenly. Soon afterwards, his friends and relatives started to be pestered by him. His appearances became so troublesome that the church authorities felt that they had no option but to exhume the corpse. They did so and found to their horror that, although he had been buried for several months, there were no signs of decomposition. Deeming this to be conclusive proof that he was a vampire, they ordered the public executioner to decapitate him. He did so. To the shock of those present, as the blade struck home, the "corpse" went into spasm as if he were still alive.

The frequency of reported outbreaks increased. There were well-attested infestations in Istria (1672), eastern Prussia (1710, 1721, and 1750), Hungary (1725–1730), Silistria (1755), Wallachia (1756), and Russia (1772). Some of them led to detailed reports being prepared and even public commissions set up by the state to investigate the circumstances. They still make fascinating reading.

One account was given to a Freiburg University professor in 1730. The professor later passed it on to Fr. Calmet, who published it in 1746. The time delay in transmitting the account makes its accuracy suspect, but it is nevertheless a good illustration of the stories that were extant in Europe at the time, as it possessed a number of the features common to many of them. The story concerns a soldier who was billeted with a peasant family on the borders of Hungary. One day, he:

saw as he was at table with his landlord, a stranger come in and sit down by them. The master of the house and the rest of the company were strangely terrified but the soldier knew not what to make of it. The next day the peasant died, and upon the soldier's inquiring into the meaning of it, he was told that it was his landlord's father, who had been dead and buried for over ten years, that came and sat down at the table and gave his son notice of his death.

The account so far is typical of vampire reports of the time. The vampire visits a relative, essentially as a harbinger of death, which follows closely in its footsteps. The soldier was, naturally enough, somewhat amazed at this turn of events, and enthusiastically told his comrades-at-arms what had happened. News travels fast, especially when it concerns a subject as interesting as this, and before long, the regiment was positively buzzing with reports of the incident. The gossip attracted the attention of the authorities, and a captain in the regiment, the Count of Cabreras, was commissioned to undertake an inquiry into the happenings.

He cross-examined a number of people who claimed to have seen the vampire. They all swore that it was the father of the landlord. The investigation led to inquiries into other supposed cases of vampirism, with the forces of the law being called upon to exterminate the menace: "In consequence of this, the body of the spectre was dug up and found to be in the same state as if it had just been dead, the blood like that of a living person. The Count de Cabreras ordered its head to be cut off and the corpse to be buried again."[2]

The count then went on to obtain evidence that other vampires had been seen, and in particular, learned of one man who had died 30 years before but had still appeared at mealtimes in his old house several times subsequently. During his first appearance, he had bitten his brother on the neck and sucked his blood. On his next visitation, he had done the same to one of his children, and on the third occasion, he had bitten a servant. All three victims died at once. Faced with these accusations, the count ordered that the body of the supposed revenant should be exhumed. Those given the unenviable task found that the blood of the corpse was still fluid. They drove a large nail through his temple and reburied him. Another man believed to have returned from the grave to kill two of his children by sucking their blood was dug up and burned. The commission subsequently reported back to the court of Emperor Charles VI, who was so intrigued by the events that he sent some clergymen to investigate them further.

Very soon after, another case hit the headlines. This concerned a vampire that had created terror in the village of Medreyga near Belgrade. The emperor set up a commission to investigate the stories that emanated from the region. The preamble to the official report sets the scene: "Having heard from various quarters that so-called vampires have been responsible for the death of several persons, by sucking their blood, I have been commissioned by an Honourable Supreme Commander to throw some light on this question" [the inquiry was headed by Regimental Field Surgeon Johannes Fluckinger].

Fluckinger was told that, five years previously, a man named Arnold Paole had fallen from his wagon and broken his neck. He had told people before he died that he had previously been bitten by a vampire. What followed was to become something of a cause célèbre of the genre. Paole had tried several traditional remedies before he died. One was to eat earth taken from the grave of the vampire, another to bathe himself in a vampire's blood. However, it did not have the desired effect. Within a few weeks of his death, Paole had been seen wandering the neighborhood. Worse still, he was supposedly responsible for the deaths of four others. In order to put a stop to this, it was decided that Paole should be disinterred. This

was duly done, forty days after his death, and he was found to be perfectly preserved. His flesh had not decomposed, his eyes were filled with fresh blood, which also flowed from his ears and nose, soiling his shirt and funeral shroud.

His fingernails and toenails had dropped off, as had his skin, and others had grown through in their place, from which it was concluded that he was an archvampire. So according to the custom of those regions, a stake was driven through his heart. But as this was being performed, he gave a great shriek and an enormous quantity of blood spurted from the body. The body was burned that same day and the ashes cast into his tomb.

This was, again, not the end of the affair—far from it. This was truly an epidemic. Those who had come into contact with the vampire had themselves caught, and died of, his disease, so they too must be "cured."

So the four others killed by Paole were also exhumed and dealt with in a similarly undignified manner. But the so-called archvampire had been accused of attacking cattle as well, and these had passed into the human food chain. Anyone who had eaten the flesh of these cattle was at risk. A few years later, there was another outbreak of the infestation. It turned out that, in the space of three months, 17 people had died mysteriously, and it was considered likely that these too might have become vampires.

There were disturbing accounts of strange deaths explicitly suggesting vampire involvement. One woman had "gone to bed a fortnight before, in perfect health, [and] had woken up screaming horribly; terrified, she claimed that she had been touched on the neck by a man who had been dead for more than nine weeks…" From that moment, she became weaker and weaker from pains in the chest, and died within three days.

As a result of these stories, further corpses were dug up. They revealed a catalog of signs of vampire infestation. One was a woman who had died in childbirth, having previously washed in the blood of a vampire (a traditional protection, this, among those who believe they are potential victims). When she was cut open, there was a good deal of fresh blood, her stomach and intestines were fresh, and she had fresh skin and living fingernails and toenails. The corpse of a child of eight days of age was also deemed to look vampiric. There was a woman named Miliza who was 60 when she died, who actually looked much plumper in the grave than she had during life. Eight other corpses were found to exhibit signs of vampirism.

Having exhumed no less than 11 of these presumed revenants, the authorities took "the appropriate action, [and] we ordered the heads of all these vampires to be cut off by some wandering gypsies, their bodies were burned and their ashes scattered in the River Moravia, while the corpses found in a state of decomposition were returned to their coffins."[3]

Another case was described by the writer Charles Ferdinand de Schertz in *Magia Posthuma*. This was a terrifying story which still managed to retain an element of black humor. The events he spoke about took place in the village of Blow in Bohemia in 1706. Here, the vampire summoned people to him from his grave—an interesting example of the theme later found in literature where the undead exercise control over the minds of their victims. Many died as a result, and the villagers decided that something needed to be done to put a stop to his activities.

They marched to the graveyard and dug the vampire up. They then drove a post through his corpse. But, rather than having the desired effect of consigning him at last to oblivion, he thanked them: "How friendly you are to give me a stick with which I can drive away the dogs."

The remedy clearly didn't work in this case, for the same evening, he rose once more from his grave and killed five more people. The next day, the public executioner had his corpse disinterred again and stabbed him repeatedly with a stake. He was then carried away on a cart to be burned, still kicking and screaming. The fire at least worked, for after he was burned, the village returned to its former state of tranquility.

Calmet also quotes the story of a vampire in Liebava, Moravia. In this case, the attacks had taken place over a period of four years. The perpetrator was a man who had died and returned to the village. A visiting Hungarian worked out a way to stop them. He climbed the clock tower of the church, taking with him the shroud of the vampire which the creature had left behind during his visits. When the Hungarian saw the vampire, he shouted down from the top of the tower, waving the shroud at him. The enraged creature climbed up to get it back, and when he reached the top, was struck a heavy blow. While stunned, he was decapitated.

This is probably a source used by Sheridan Le Fanu in his late nineteenth-century novel *Carmilla*. His description brings together several elements which became part of vampire symbolism. The following extracts from *Carmilla* prove how close the link was between the historical accounts of the seventeenth and eighteenth centuries and the inspirations of the literati of the nineteenth. In Le Fanu's story, it is a Moravian rather than a Hungarian who deals with the infestation. He chose a moonlit night, and took guard in the tower of a chapel from where he could see the churchyard. He carried with him the shroud that the vampire left behind when it came up from the grave.

When the vampire returned from his prowlings and missed his clothes, he cried furiously to the Moravian, whom he saw at the summit of the tower, and who, in reply, beckoned him to ascend and take them. Whereupon the vampire, accepting his invitation, began to climb the steeple, and as soon as he had reached the battlements, the Moravian, with a stroke of his sword, clove his skull in twain, hurling him down to the churchyard, whither, [he] cut his head off, and next day delivered it and the body to the villagers who duly impaled and burnt them.[4]

This is the classic scenery of the bloodthirsty revenant: the moon and its occult symbolism, the haunted churchyard, and the chapel tower. The impossibility of the vampire returning to its grave without its shroud hints at the links that keep it suspended between two spheres—the blood of its victims give it a sort of half-life in the world of the living, while the paraphernalia of death, here the shroud, chain it to the world of the dead and allow it to return to the grave. The invitation is a recurrent theme in folklore, where there is a prohibition against pronouncing the names of evil spirits, as the simple uttering of the name may summon them. This was successfully borrowed in literature, as we shall see later. Finally, the author brings together several ways of destroying a vampire: decapitation, impaling, and burning.

An interesting account from about the time of the Paole case (it was published from a letter in 1732) comes from Hungary, and tells how a vampire was hunted using local traditions. It was written by a Walloon officer stationed in Hungary:

As for these Hungarian spectres, the thing generally happens in this manner: a man finds himself fallen into a languid state, loses his appetite, decreases visibly in bulk and, at eight or ten days' end, dies without a fever or any other symptom of illness save anaemia and loss of flesh and a dried, withered body.

In Hungary they say that a vampire has attacked him and sucked his blood. Many of those who fall ill in this way declare that a white spectre is following them and sticks to them as close as their own shadow.[5]

He goes on to say that several officers in the regiment had been victims of vampire attacks and were dead. Several more were injured and would have died if traditional remedies had not been adopted to bring an end to the assaults. He then describes the vampire hunt that followed in these terms:

They select a young lad who is innocent of girls, that is to say who has never performed the sexual act. He is placed upon a young stallion who has not yet mounted a mare, who has never stumbled and who must be pitch-black without a speck of white. The stud is ridden into the cemetery to and fro among the graves, and the grave over which the horse refuses to pass in spite of blows liberally administered to him, is where the vampire lies.

The tomb is opened and they find a sleek, fat corpse, as healthily coloured as though the man were quietly and happily sleeping in calm repose. With one single blow from a sharp spade they cut off the head, whereupon there gushes forth a warm stream of blood of rich red colour, filling the whole grave. It could easily be surmised that they had just decapitated a big brawny fellow of most sanguine habit and complexion.

When this business is done, they refill the grave with earth and then the ravages of the disease immediately cease, while those suffering from this malady gradually recover their strength, just as convalescents recuperate after a long illness.

This account "from life" is particularly interesting as it builds on several other motifs which are characteristic of classic vampire literature. Just as a spirit of hell cannot cross the threshold of the church, pure beings cannot pass over a place where evil dwells. The disinterred corpse is robust and healthy looking, just as it was with Arnold Paole and the 60-year-old woman he had killed, and indeed would be the case with Lucy, the count's first victim in *Dracula*. The belief that the infestation stops when the vampire is killed and victims who are still alive recover their health would also be borrowed by writers and filmmakers, where characters like Stoker's Mina Harker are saved once Count Dracula is destroyed.

These historical accounts present the first substantial body of written evidence about so-called real cases of vampire activity. There are other common features in them which would find their way into works of literature, such as the way in which the vampires often attacked members of their own family. This increases the horror of already terrifying stories by having the vampire prey on those who are inclined to trust them, a betrayal of innocence.

The climax of these accounts, the final encounter and the destruction of the creature, is the more fascinating as it can take a number of forms. Driving a stake into the corpse was only one way of doing so, and has become to the classic remedy to the modern world, thanks in part to the efforts of writers like Bram Stoker, but more to an assortment of film directors, and even through modern heroes and heroines such as *Buffy the Vampire Slayer*. Other methods, such as driving a nail through the temple or burning the body, are reflections of accounts from folklore, and indeed from earlier beliefs—Philinnion, for example, was burned, as we have already seen. The act of biting that the creature indulges in has become the classical "signature" of the vampire in works of fiction. Not all victims of the seventeenth- and eighteenth-century epidemics mentioned this though, some describing the sensation of being attacked as more like a feeling of suffocation.

These cases collectively demonstrate that one of the core reasons that people believed in vampires was the appearance of "unnatural" phenomena. Dead bodies are supposed to decompose, and the cadavers in these examples did not. Their blood flows as freely as it does in life. It has been shown convincingly, in a twentieth-century work by Paul Barber,[6] that what actually happens to a corpse is quite different from what is commonly supposed to be the case, and could easily be misinterpreted for classic signs of vampirism when witnessed by an audience without the benefit of scientific knowledge.

But the seventeenth- and eighteenth-century inhabitants of remote rural areas did not have this knowledge. Local traditions of vampirism were part of their cultural inheritance, and these represented the normal reference point in such cases. The physical state of the corpse when disinterred "proves" to the witnesses that what they are looking at is a vampire—because the cadaver actually looks to them as if it is still, in many ways, alive. So in the case examined by Cabreras, the first vampire, when dug up, is "found to be in the same state as if it had just been dead, the blood like that of a living person," while the second is discovered with "his blood in as fluid state as if he had been alive." In the Paole case, "his flesh had not decomposed," whereas other bodies in the same example were deemed to be nonvampiric because they *had*.

These stories, and others like them, gripped the imagination of Western Europe. The location of the tales, in these newly accessible and as yet barely known regions, no doubt added to the air of exoticism which imbued them with even more sinister undertones. A large number of vampire publications was produced as a result of the accounts, with the vivid imaginations of a seemingly insatiable public providing very fertile ground for ambitious publishers. These books, though, were not typically literary works exploiting the vampire theme, but academic treatises attempting to analyze the phenomenon.

Germany proved a particularly productive source of new publications, especially around the time of the Paole case, for example Rohlius's *Dissertatio de hominibus post mortem sanguisugis, uulgo dictis Uampyrea* (Leipzig, 1732), reprinted in the same year in Jena. This was followed by *Dissertatio de Uampyris Serviensibus* by John Heinrich Zopfius, published in Duisburg in 1733. Ranfft, quick to jump on the vampire bandwagon, published an expanded version of his work in Leipzig in 1734. Not all of them postulated a supernatural explanation for events; among theories suggesting the reasons for the outbreaks were food poisoning and the effects of opium!

The discussions concerning the validity or otherwise of these accounts became very heated. Some writers saw the phenomenon as an example of the survival of outdated superstitions among uneducated peasants whose beliefs held no place in the "modern" world. This was, after all, the Age of Reason, when King Science ruled. But it was also the Age of Contradiction. For, despite the technological advances of the time, many people were still superstitious. If it were not so, then the advent of Gothic literature would not have been so enthusiastically received. It was popular precisely because people still thrilled to tales of the supernatural and the unexplained. Despite the barely suppressed fury of the rationalists who castigated the gullible masses, superstition simply refused to go away.

Whatever the reasons behind these outbreaks, they were serious enough for Dom Augustin Calmet, the abbé of Senones in Lorraine and one of the foremost biblical scholars of the eighteenth century, to pen his *Treatise on the Vampires of Hungary and Surrounding Regions* in 1746. It was a well-balanced attempt to look for scientific explanations for the phenomenon. All the standard scientific explanations were examined and, in the end, Calmet concluded that "'the stories told of these apparitions, and all the distress caused by these supposed vampires, are totally without solid proof."

Calmet (1672–1757) was a particularly important writer on the subject because he was a prominent theologian, so much so that two and a half centuries after his death he still merits a detailed biographical note in the *Catholic Encyclopaedia*. He became a brother at the Abbey of St-Mansuy at 16 years of age, and by the time he was 24, he was a teacher of philosophy and theology. He completed a commentary on the Bible, the first volume of which appeared in Paris in 1707. Second and third editions followed. These works were widely, though not universally, acclaimed. His works were translated into a number of languages, and his promotion through the ranks of the Catholic establishment saw him become a prior in 1715, an abbot in Nancy in 1719, and finally Abbot of Senones in 1729.

But there were some contemporaries who were furious that this widely respected theologian would deign to write a book on a subject like vampirism. To these so-called rationalists, such matters were not worthy of comment. To them, the best way to rid the world of superstition was to rob it of credibility and ignore it. Admittedly, Calmet stopped short of saying that there were not vampires; he merely said that there was no "solid proof" of their existence. But in the Age of Reason, his slight reserve in condemning vampirism was seen as nothing more than a psychological hangover from a bygone age, leading to a storm of protest in some quarters. De Jacourt wrote of "this absurd book ... a book one would not have considered [Calmet] worthy of writing." Dufresnoy called it an assemblage of secondhand stories— "the true, the doubtful and the false are all put together, without any coherent principle for distinguishing them."

And in fairness, even Calmet himself accepted that some of the evidence could appear to the casual observer to be quite convincing:

We are told that dead men return from their tombs, are heard to speak, walk about, injure both men and animals whose blood they drain, making them sick and finally causing their death. Nor can the men deliver themselves unless they dig the corpses up and drive a sharp stake through their bodies, cut off their heads, tear out their hearts, or else burn the bodies to ashes. It seems impossible not to subscribe to the prevailing belief that these apparitions do actually come forth from their graves.[7]

So widespread did discussion of the vampire phenomenon become, that it was deemed worthy of consideration by some of the greatest philosophers of the time, including Voltaire and Rousseau. Voltaire, naturally enough, managed to turn the outbreak into a comment on the political environment of his day, giving full vent to those he saw as the real vampires:

What! Vampires in our Eighteenth Century? Yes .... In Poland, Hungary, Silesia, Moravia, Austria and Lorraine—there was no talk of vampires in London, or even Paris. I admit that in these two cities there were speculators, tax officials and businessmen who sucked the blood of the people in broad daylight, but they were not dead (although they were corrupted enough). These true bloodsuckers did not live in cemeteries, they preferred beautiful places .... Kings are not, properly speaking, vampires. The true vampires are the churchmen who eat at the expense of both the king and the people.[8]

Voltaire, indeed, was prompted by the volume of so-called evidence from vampire outbreaks to remark, quite caustically, that "if there ever was in the world a warranted and proven history, it is that of vampires; nothing is lacking, official reports, testimonials of persons of standing, of surgeons, of clergymen, of judges; the judicial evidence is all-embracing."

The idea that there was an overwhelming corpus of evidence for vampirism—although all rational men surely agreed that it did not exist!—was picked up as a theme by Le Fanu in *Carmilla*, a century after

Voltaire's remarks. The author, speaking through his heroine, boldly asserts that "if human testimony, taken with every care and solemnity, judicially, before commissions innumerable, each consisting of many members, all chosen for integrity and intelligence, and constituting reports more voluminous than exist upon any one other class of cases, is worth anything, it is difficult to deny, or even to doubt the existence of such a phenomenon as the vampire."[9]

Scientific efforts to explain the outbreaks were made by some writers; for example, in *Lettres Juives* (1738), Jean Baptiste de Boyer, the Marquis d'Argens, argues that the blood found in the bodies of supposed vampires was in fact a substance produced in the putrefying body by chemical reaction which looked like blood, though it wasn't. He helpfully published a recipe which allowed the would-be investigator to produce their own quasi-blood substance (basically a combination of milk and oil of tartar which, when boiled, changes color).

The rationalists produced a list of likely causes of the phenomenon. These included natural explanations, such as the chemical properties of particular types of soil which could inhibit decomposition. The shrieking sound heard when vampires were pierced with a stake was air being emitted from the body when it was struck. A particular favorite was the argument that bodies had been buried prematurely, when in a state of catalepsy, rather than death.

Natural diseases were also offered as an explanation. Plague was one disease blamed for the epidemic. The pallor, lethargy, the nightmares and the fevers of the victim were common symptoms. The classic features of vampirism were outlined in *The Jewish Spy* by the Marquis d'Argens (1729), and were described as "complete exhaustion and a faintness as though from excessive loss of blood"—something that could as easily be applied to diseases with a mundane rather than a supernatural cause. The contagious nature of vampire epidemics, so well illustrated by the Paole case, closely mirrors that of the plague, where the only reliable cure in the eyes of many people was to isolate those with the disease from the rest of the community until they had died. A later explanation was that rabies was the cause, given the fact that the disease often produced animal-like behavior in its victims.

The concept that outbreaks of pestilence could be stopped by destroying the corpse of someone who had recently died is regularly found in folklore, and continued into much more recent times. One later example, from 1848, concerns a young Russian woman, Justina Yuschkov, who had died of cholera. Others died soon after, not altogether surprisingly given the epidemic nature of the disease. However, the local medical officer advised the peasants that they should disinter the girl and see if she had been pregnant, as this might be a supernatural cause of the pestilence. When they did so, they found the corpse of a baby buried with her. As her mouth was open—a telltale sign of vampirism—they reburied her but drove an ash stake into her. They then returned to their business, confident that the cholera would now end.

The eighteenth-century rationalists also postulated psychological and theological explanations. Some said that mass hysteria in the community brought about by collective superstition produced an atmosphere in which such epidemics could thrive. In many ways, this argument sees the vampire outbreaks as the last knockings of the mass psychosis that produced the great witch hunts of earlier centuries. In these, a whole community appeared to be gripped by hysteria, and in these cases, anyone who exhibited traits that were unconventional could be the target of an accusation of witchcraft.

Theology also had an important part to play. It is interesting that the majority of European vampire cases occur where two religious worlds meet: those of Catholicism and Orthodoxy. The Orthodox Church argued that the corpses of those who were not of its faith would not decompose in the grave. Unlike the Catholic Church, where such an event would be a sign of sanctity, this was regarded by the Orthodox Church as something unnatural and against the laws of God.

For its own reasons, the Catholic Church would not be averse to talking up the incidence of vampirism. It was in relative decline in the west after several centuries of Protestant expansion had weakened its hold there. It had also often come into conflict with Orthodoxy in Eastern and Central Europe, and was eager to avail itself of opportunities to restore its fortunes in the region. One of the ways it could do this was to take the lead in a new Crusade, against, not an earthly enemy, but a supernatural one. Giuseppe Davanzati, Archbishop of Trani, wrote *Dissertazione sopra I Vampiri* in 1744, examining contemporary outbreaks of vampirism and attributing them to the influence of demonic spirits. At a local level, corruption within the Church may also have encouraged the outbreak. No less a person than Pope Benedict XIV, echoing the views expressed by Lavater in the sixteenth century, had declared that the real problem was not a supernatural pestilence but "those priests who give credit to such stories, in order to encourage simple folk to pay them for exorcisms or masses."

Another leading ecclesiastical writer, Pierre-Daniel Huet, bishop of Avranches and Soissons, included a section on vampires in his *Memoirs*, partly relying on information provided by Father François Richard, for many years a priest on Santorini. He gave an account of how the Greeks dealt with outbreaks, such as the burning of corpses. He also spoke of their belief that a vampire was created when a soul had been evil in life. A strange remedy was prescribed, involving cutting off the feet, nose, hands, and ears and hanging them around the neck of the corpse.

Sometimes a combination of causes was blamed for outbreaks of vampirism. Joseph de Tournefort was botanist to the Sun King Louis XIV of France. In 1700, he sailed to the east to collect specimens for the royal gardens, and found himself right in the middle of a vampire epidemic. His ship put into Mykonos, already the location for reported vampire activity a few decades before. What he found was written up in *A Voyage to the Levant* (1702). This would assume importance for later writers, such as Polidori, who would, to some extent, be inspired by the story.

Tournefort wrote that a man of ill repute had been murdered, though no one knew why. Within two days, he was seen walking through the streets of the town. The priests advised that nine days must pass before anything could be done. On the tenth, the body was disinterred and taken into a chapel where mass was said. Then the priests called in a butcher, who cut him open and pulled out his heart. Tournefort said that the corpse stank, leaving him in no doubt that the supposed vampire was well and truly dead.

Despite his cynicism, the locals were convinced that they were in the presence of a vampire. They swore that smoke came out of the body, though the Frenchman was sure that this was because of the incense that the priests had burned. Several of the crowd declared that they had seen blood come forth when the butcher had cut open the body, while the butcher himself said that the corpse was still warm when he touched it. Others said that the cadaver had not stiffened at all, but was still loose and supple. In short, the supposedly dead man exhibited a number of symptoms that suggested he was still alive.

Tournefort was dismissive when asked what he thought. He averred that he was "almost poisoned with the intolerable stink that issued [from the body]." There was no surprise that parts of the body were still warm when the insides were rotting. As for the blood, it was "nothing but a very stinking nasty smear."

The certainty of the Frenchman that the vampire was nothing save a figment of the collective imagination cut little ice. The locals decided to burn the vampire's heart on the seashore, but this made no difference; he continued to terrorize the population. Tournefort was convinced he knew the reason for all this: "all the inhabitants seemed frightened out of their senses: the wisest among them were stricken like the rest: it was an epidemical disease of the brain, as dangerous and infectious as the madness of dogs."

Some of the more thoughtful citizens reasoned that the vampire was still around because the ritual to dispose of it had not been conducted correctly. By saying mass before the heart was cut out, they assumed that they had driven the Devil away, so evil had fled the body too soon. Other rituals were followed, they processed around the town, they sprinkled holy water, all in a vain attempt to drive the evil spirit away. They "took up the corpse three or four times a day" in their efforts to exorcise the demon. Eventually, they decided that the only option was to dig up the body and burn all of it (one wonders why they had not adopted this as the first option). They prepared a pyre of wood and pitch and the corpse (or what was left of it) was quickly consumed. This did the trick; the vampire was seen no more.

Tournefort noted that only the Greek (Orthodox) Christians of the island were believers in vampires, adding that the residents of the nearby island of Santorini were terribly afraid of their own particular brand of the creature. In his view, responsibility for the obsession with the vampire was clear enough: "After such an incidence of folly, can we refuse to own that the present Greeks are no great Grecians; and that there is nothing but ignorance and superstition among them?"[10]

No less a person than Empress Marie Thérèse of Austria–Hungary was involved in the vampire controversy, coming down firmly on the side of science over superstition. A renewed outbreak of vampirism in Silesia was the cause. The Empress was profoundly shocked at the mutilation of corpses believed to be revenants in her territories. She herself was convinced of the explanation—"the dark, disturbed imagination of the common people." In order to prove her hypothesis, she sent her physician, Gerhard Van Swieten, to investigate.

Interestingly, he came down firmly in favor of a theological cause for the problem, saying that it was found "where ignorance reigns" and was the fault of "Greek schismatics," that is, the Orthodox Church, presumably news that was manna from heaven for the very Catholic Empress. Exaggeration also had its part to play, as the so-called gullible masses were quick to play up the significance of minor incidents into major proofs of vampirism: "One of the vampires 'executed' was said to have been swollen with blood, since the executioner, a thoroughly reliable man, no doubt, in matters concerning his trade, claimed that when he cut up bodies which were sentenced to be burned, a great quantity of blood gushed forth. Nevertheless, he afterwards agreed that this great quantity was about a spoonful—and this is a very different matter..."[11]

The learned doctor continued to describe how the bodies of innocents, including children, had been handed over to the executioner for destruction. Such sacrilege and loss of dignity was more than he could bear. He ended his report with a statement that he could write no more, for he was on the point of completely losing his temper.

This is another example of the importance of religious beliefs in the myth of the vampire. The emphasis that the Church places on burial rites, and on the fact that the dead should not be disturbed in their sleep, encourages legends to evolve. The superstitions that grew around the dogma often made the rites so complicated that it was not difficult to look back and find that something had been done incorrectly if any abnormal phenomenon followed the funeral.

It is no wonder that many vampire stories have in common a breach of a ritual. It was often said that people who had led an evil life would become vampires. But if these were thieves, murderers, women accused of witchcraft, prostitution (see the example of the Russian unmarried girl, Justina Yuschkov, who was pregnant when she died), incest, people who committed suicide, they would not be buried in "holy ground" and would not have sacred rituals performed at their death. They were, therefore, often believed to return as vampires.

Van Swieten's report was exactly to order as far as the Empress was concerned. She was determined to stamp out posthumous magic in her territories, and this was firm justification for doing so. A series of proclamations was duly enacted. The major practical implication was that, in future, investigations of outbreaks would not be the responsibility of the Church, but of the civil authorities—hardly the result that the Catholic Church desired, as it seriously undermined its authority, but something that the scientific community would have welcomed enthusiastically. In future, legal proofs would be needed to allow the desecration of the graves of the dead. In fact, although in some ways the vampire trials represent a continuum from the great witchcraft trials of the late medieval period and the werewolf trials of the sixteenth century, this is only true in part, as it was the secular authorities that conducted the investigations into vampirism and not the Church.

The outcome was less final than the Empress would have wished. The debate continued, with some commenting that vampirism was clearly a form of disease, while others agreed that it was indeed very strange that only the common man witnessed vampire activity, but men of substance (and by implication intelligence) did not. But some were not convinced that a rational explanation would do. The Berlin correspondent of the *Gazette des Gazettes* looked at the evidence on offer and attested that he at least was convinced that the philosophers could not so easily wheedle their way out of the problem with glib explanations of mass hysteria: "[vampirism] is proved by so many facts that no one can reasonably doubt its validity, given the quality of the witnesses who have certified the authenticity of those facts."

The article, published on November 1, 1765, threw down the challenge to the scientific community to provide conclusive counterevidence against all the eyewitnesses that attested to the reality of vampirism. Rousseau, while not refuting the claims of the Berlin correspondent, referred to his article. He did not really express much interest in the concept of vampirism, but did find it useful as a way of discussing weaknesses in the way that the law functioned: "For some time now, the public news has been concerned with nothing but vampires; there has never been a fact more fully proved in law than their existence, yet despite this show me a single man of sense in Europe who believes in vampires or would even deign to take the trouble to check the falseness of the facts."[12]

So to Rousseau, as to Voltaire, vampirism was little more than a way to contemplate the inadequacies of human testimony as a way of proving facts one way or another. His barely concealed criticism is that those who enthusiastically attest to the reality of the phenomenon are simply gullible—no "single man of sense" could believe that vampires were real.

But despite the protestations of the scientific and philosophical establishment, vampirism continued to fascinate.

In a way, vampirism epitomized the spirit of the age. The scientists might consider this the Age of Reason, when superstition, even God, might be consigned to the dustbin of history, but others were not so sure. It was the age, after all, that spawned men like the Count of St. Germain, 2,000-years-old, and apparently looking the same age all the time. It was said that there were people who saw the Count in the middle of the eighteenth century who had last met him 50 years previously, in which time he had not aged a bit. Some said that he had lived in Ancient Chaldea and Egypt millennia ago. Annoyingly for rationalists, his friends were kings, princes, and aristocrats, people who should know better, not common peasants.[13] It was also an era when Freemasonry, with its rituals, symbolism, and mysteries of the Ancients, boomed in Western Europe. The old beliefs would not, it seemed, die as quietly as the scientists wished them to.

But the debate did eventually become more subdued. The volume of publications indicates that the heyday of academic consideration of the phenomenon occurred in the period around 1720 to 1770, after which they tailed off. Any thoughts that t he decreased ferocity of the debate would bring an end to the interest in vampirism were well off the mark, though. Not long after the intensity of the arguments lessened, the vampire was about to make its mark again, this time through the medium of literature.

NOTES

1. In Ronay, p. 24.
2. Ibid., pp. 27–29.
3. In Barber, pp. 16–18.
4. Sheridan Le Fanu, *Carmilla*.
5. *Les Lettres Juives*, 1732. This is quoted extensively in both Ronay, pp. 37–39, and Barber.
6. *Vampires, Burial and Death. Folklore and Reality.* It is also useful as it quotes extensively from original source documents some of the major vampire cases from historical records.
7. From Calmet, *Treatise on the Vampires of Hungary and the Surrounding Regions*, Paris, 1746. Extended extracts of Calmet's work are included in Frayling, pp. 92–103.
8. From *Dictionnaire Philosophique*, in Frayling, p. 31.
9. *Carmilla*, p. 88.
10. In Barber, pp. 21–24.
11. In Frayling, p. 30.
12. Ibid., p. 32.
13. Perhaps unsurprisingly, Germain was transformed into a vampire in literature, appearing in the novel *Hotel California*, by Chelsea Quinn Yarbro, published in 1978.

CHAPTER 3

The Myth Evolves

The vampire live on and cannot die by mere passing of the time.
—Bram Stoker, *Dracula*

The vampire legend still continues to develop in an age of high technology and supposed sophistication. New elements continue to be added as the volume of films and books about the subject increases. So, in *Interview with the Vampire*, for example, the crucifix is no longer powerful enough to counteract the undead—a comment on the increasing secularization of society and the decline of religion. This evolution has been a continuous process ever since preexisting myths were given a new impetus by literary developments, particularly in the nineteenth century. This in its own turn was perpetuated by the production of numerous films in the twentieth century, and on into the twenty-first.

There were some key works, and some key moments, in the life of the vampire in literature that are particularly important in light of the thematic study of the phenomenon that we will consider throughout this book, and we will give the background to them here. We will also look at how this process has been carried on by cinematography.

We have already looked at "academic" interest in vampirism in the eighteenth century. The creatures of the night also found their way into the literature of the time. The German writer and theater manager (a profession shared with Bram Stoker), Johann Wolfgang von Goethe (1749–1832), is most famous for his *Faust*, a work with some relevance to our investigation given the pact with the devil which is the bedrock of the story. *Faust* was a monumental undertaking by Goethe: it took him 57 years to write, and he finally finished it when he was 81 years old. Goethe was influenced by elements of the vampire story, and the legend of the Bride of Corinth (the story concerning Apollonius) was employed by him.

Other German writers also used the theme. Ludwig Tieck (1773–1853) wrote a number of works which used fantastic themes and had an important effect on the direction of the German Romantic Movement. "Wake Not the Dead!" which was attributed to him, appeared in about 1800. Another writer, Ernst Hoffmann (1776–1822) was an author who mixed the fantastic with elements of irony in his work. He too used themes based on the vampire, with the Baroness Aurelia appearing as a seductress luring victims to their doom in *The Serapion Brethren* (published in 1820).

In Keats's "Lamia," the plot employed by Philostratus in his story of Menipus and the *lamia* evolves to suit the spirit of the Gothic era. The poem is based on the Ancient Greek tale, but is different in one crucial respect. In the old version of the tale, Apollonius warns Menipus, and the *lamia* vanishes before she can harm him. But in Keats's verse, he fails to heed the danger signals and, as a result, dies a terrifying death on his wedding night, an end which mirrors almost exactly that employed in "Wake Not the Dead!" when a young lord marries a vampire who changes into a serpent. Such melodramatic and frightening conclusions are an element of many Gothic tales (see also "The Vampyre," discussed below). Writers such as Keats adapt very old tales to suit the mores of their times—so the myth of vampire-like creatures lives on but it also evolves.

In England, full-scale employment of vampire motifs in literature took a while to arrive. Lord Byron had an interest in vampirism, best evidenced by his poem, "The Giaour," which appeared in 1813. However, his most famous encounter with the creatures from hell was when he was at the heart of a real-life controversy. This involved his personal physician, John Polidori, who wrote a short story, "The Vampyre," which first appeared in 1819. It concerned a young gentleman, Aubrey, who comes into contact with the sinister Lord Ruthven. Realizing that the nobleman is a vampire, Aubrey breaks free of his influence. He later falls in love with a young Greek girl, Ianthe. Ruthven catches up with him and kills Ianthe. Not realizing that the lord is responsible for her death, when Ruthven nurses the broken Aubrey back to health, he manages to reingratiate himself.

Soon after, the two men are attacked, and Ruthven is mortally wounded. As he is dying, Ruthven makes Aubrey swear that he will keep all knowledge of his crimes and his death to himself for a year and a day. Aubrey goes for help to bury him, but when he returns, the corpse is gone. Aubrey then returns to England, where the story builds to a terrifying and tragic finale. He is horrified to find that Ruthven has returned and is making advances to his sister. Unable to break his oath, Aubrey attempts to delay the forthcoming marriage of his sister and Ruthven. Fate intervenes, Aubrey is taken ill at the crucial moment, and the marriage goes ahead. Dying, he relates his tale to his sister's guardians. They rush to save her but, as

Polidori immortally puts it: "Too late. Lord Ruthven had disappeared, and Aubrey's sister had glutted the thirst of a VAMPYRE!"

The story was written when Polidori and Byron had had a serious personal disagreement. Byron had just dismissed Polidori after a tour of Europe which had, in terms of their relationship, been a disaster. The character of the dilettante Lord Ruthven is based on Byron. The genesis of the short story is itself interesting, connected as it is with the most famous late night storytelling session of all time. Mary Shelley, who reputedly wrote *Frankenstein* as a result of this session, tells how she journeyed to the shores of Lake Geneva, along with Lord Byron, Shelley, and Polidori. They were prevented by bad weather from leaving their villa. Short of something to do—this is hard to believe considering the company she kept—the party amused itself by reading ghost stories.

It was, according to Mary, Lord Byron's idea that the party should hold a ghost-story writing competition. The rest, as they say, is history. Shelley wrote her magnum opus, and Polidori made his own contribution. Subsequently, commentators have suggested that her memory was playing tricks on her,[1] or that she invented the story of the ghostly soirée in a marketing initiative designed to increase the sales of her book.

The inspiration for "The Vampyre" was a disastrous love affair involving Byron. Lady Caroline Lamb, on the wrong end of it, had written a book in which the antihero had clearly been based on Byron. Polidori used the contemporary image of Byron, and his own difficult relationship with him (which swung between detestation and hero worship), to mold his leading character on the poet. Ruthven was a shadowy, sinister figure, waiting to feast on the blood of innocents. He is aristocratic, haughty, and superior. Those that came into contact with him fell under a spell, as they were hypnotized by the sheer evil that emanated from his presence. This Byronic prototype of a vampire was to form one of the key elements in the literary corpus that later developed. Count Dracula was a metaphorical grandson of Lord Byron.

Often, the story within the story is as fascinating as the fiction itself, and this is certainly true of Polidori's "Vampyre." He wrote it in 1816 and then forgot about it. When it was published in 1819 it created something of a sensation. Many members of the public refused to believe that the humble doctor could have written it. They therefore ascribed it to Byron himself. Goethe, who held a very low moral opinion of the lord, stated with some sarcasm that it was his finest work. Even publishers were confused. The story was sometimes included in early editions of Byron's works, only to be taken out of later ones and then reinserted.

It was undoubtedly Polidori's story, or at least his words, that we read (though the idea might have emanated from Byron, he is hardly likely to write a work that is so overtly hostile towards himself!). It has not always received the attention it deserves. It is well written and provides many of the prototypes of the vampire in later literary developments. Not that it did the doctor much good. He had fallen from grace with Byron long before it was published. The figure of Lord Ruthven was entirely uncomplimentary to Byron, and the fact that the vampire had been modeled on him was an indication of how completely the relationship had broken down. But the doctor was involved in a serious accident, which broke his health completely. He died soon after in 1821, aged only 25, reputedly as a result of drinking prussic acid.

The arrival of "The Vampyre" laid the foundations for what was to come. The impact of Lord Ruthven was particularly important, enabling Professor Leonard Wolf to claim in his book *The Annotated Dracula* (1975) that "Polidori gave us a prototype vampire ... that is to say, as a nobleman, aloof, brilliant, chilling, fascinating to women, and coolly evil."

The publication of the story inspired several plays in its wake, and the vampire became an established star of the stage a century before its Hollywood debut. Writers such as Dumas wrote accounts of visits to the theater to watch examples of the genre. Continental authors also continued to use the myth as the basis for their literature. Count Alexis Tolstoy, cousin of the famous writer Leo, wrote a real chiller called "The Family of the Vourdalak" (it was written in the 1830s/1840s, but not published until 1884). It is based on a classic Eastern European vampire theme, that of a creature returning to haunt and devastate his family. In a shocking conclusion, the whole hamlet becomes a "Village of the Damned," where all the inhabitants are vampires and where the living cannot journey without losing their lives.

Gogol, a writer best known as the creator of the modern Russian novel and the author of short stories and plays of great literary force, used both strong realistic elements and fantastic images inspired by local folklore in his work. In *Viy* (1835), he employs the theme of the vampire. She appears as a witch on a phantom horse, and is able to control other creatures. A dog, capable of transforming itself into a beautiful girl, also appears. This snatches babies and turns them into vampires, a nightmare scenario if ever there was one. The master of horror, Edgar Allan Poe, also employs vampires in "Berenice" (1833); his creature can be made powerless by the removal of her teeth!

Poe's tale represents the other key strand that vampire literature developed—that of the femme fatale, the seductive temptress who would lure her would-be victims into her clutches and then, like a black widow spider, devour them in a contorted, gross distortion of the act of love. This, "the tempestuous loveliness of terror," as it has been described,[2] was to be the other dominant characteristic of the genre. This model was to be fused with the first, Byronic variation, as epitomized in Polidori's "Vampyre" in the ultimate creation of Stoker's Count. Throw a large dash of folklore into the cocktail and you have a potent mix indeed.

The Byronic image of the vampire was reinforced in *Varney the Vampyre* (1847). In this story, the revenant preys on innocent young girls, a successor to Polidori's Lord Ruthven and a forerunner of Count Dracula. The book remained a best seller for over a decade. There was again a debate over its authorship. For a while, it was thought that Thomas Preskett Prest, who wrote the spine-tingling story of Sweeney Todd, was responsible. It was not until 1963 that Louis James showed that it was the creation of James Malcolm Rymer. Those who liked horror certainly had it in abundance, as it was published at a length of 850 pages, appearing in 220 weekly parts in one of the penny dreadful magazines of the day. Written in a style that milked the essential "creepiness" of the vampire myth to the full—and in so doing, took all possible advantage of the Victorian obsession with melodrama—it continued the tradition of the evolving vampire literature splendidly. Spooky locations, the exploitation of innocence, thunder and lightning, the mesmeric qualities of Varney, all combined to paint a sensational canvas that, despite the work's great length, must have enthralled the reader.

It proves impossible for Rymer's antihero, Sir Francis Varney, an English lord, to kill the creature. All the traditional remedies are ineffective. Hanging does no good, shooting and drowning don't work, even the stake is ineffective. In this case, it is moonlight that restores life to him. In the end, Varney—a surprisingly conscientious vampire—realizes the harm that he is doing and takes his own "life" by throwing himself into the fiery depths of Mount Vesuvius. This is an interesting reversal of some traditions where suicide creates a vampire; this time it destroys one!

A half-forgotten genius of horror literature was the Irish writer, Sheridan Le Fanu. In *Carmilla* (1872), Le Fanu added another important building block to the evolution of vampire literature. This time, the antihero is not an aristocratic lord, but a beautiful young girl, systematically taking advantage of other adolescent females. It is an important example of "the tempestuous loveliness of terror," in this case with barely concealed lesbian tendencies.

The heroine lives in an isolated chateau in Styria, a region of Austria, with her father. They come across Carmilla, who has been injured in an accident, and take her into their home. Carmilla is a mysterious figure, excessively coy about her past, but she becomes ever closer to the daughter. Before long, it is noted that Carmilla wanders abroad at night, that apparently healthy members of the local community are dying, and that the daughter herself appears to be unwell. A doctor is called in, but it becomes clear that only supernatural remedies will suffice. Eventually, Carmilla disappears, and the story becomes a race against time to find and destroy her and save the young girl.

Carmilla turns out to be an incarnation of the Countess Millarca, who had died several centuries previously, but whose grave has been lost. It is eventually traced to a ruined chapel in the forest, and in a gripping finale, her would-be destroyers uncover her tomb. The opening of the coffin could have been a description lifted straight from the accounts of the vampire commissions of the previous century:

Her eyes were open; no cadaverous smell exhaled from the coffin. The two medical men, one officially present, the other on the part of the promoter of the enquiry,
attested the marvellous fact that there was a faint but appreciable respiration, and
a corresponding action of the heart. The limbs were perfectly flexible, the flesh
elastic; and the leaden coffin floated with blood, in which to a depth of seven
inches, the body lay immersed.[3]

There then follows a scene of pure overkill; the heart is pierced with
a stake, at which point the "corpse" lets out a blood-curdling scream.
The head is cut off, which causes blood to spurt forth from the neck. The
body is then burnt to ashes, which are scattered on the nearby river. After
this, unsurprisingly, there are no further outbreaks, though ominously,
it is obvious from the introduction to the book that the heroine dies
prematurely anyway.

When Bram Stoker wrote *Dracula*, which first appeared in 1897, he was
heavily influenced by previous works in the vampire genre, especially
Carmilla. Whatever literary commentators may say about the quality or
otherwise of the writing, it would be a myopic critic who would deny that,
as a work of literature, the novel is stunningly effective and atmospheric.
Stoker's tale concerns a count in Transylvania who invites a young solici-
tor, Jonathan Harker, to his castle to conclude some property deals in London. The English guest soon discovers that he is a prisoner. Some young
women try to trap him, and he is saved from their vampiric advances in
the nick of time by the count, who wants him for himself. Jonathan eventually manages to escape, but the count has meanwhile made his way to
England, where he lands at Whitby. His first victim on British soil happens to be a friend of Jonathan, Lucy Westenra, who becomes a vampire
herself.

Lucy is "killed" soon afterwards, but Jonathan's wife, Mina, is also
attacked by the count. A desperate battle against the clock ensues to save
her, in which a band of men, led by the redoubtable van Helsing, a professor and expert on vampirism, traces all but one of the count's London lairs
and destroys the boxes of earth from his grave that he requires to survive.
Before they find the last one, the count flees back to Transylvania. In the
final scene, the count is caught just outside his castle. There is a last fight,
in which the count is killed; so too is one of the heroic would-be rescuers,
the American Quincey Morris. Such are the bare bones, cruelly reduced, of
the story. They do not do justice to the power of the tale, which is increased
by the author's vivid use of language and just about every piece of occult
imagery available.

The power of myth evolves over time, and Stoker's *Dracula* illustrates
the point perfectly, as myths have grown up about the book itself. Stories
have been developed about, for example, the places that inspired Stoker
to write the novel and the personalities on whom he may have based the
characters—many of them, frankly, with little evidence to support them.

We do know something, however, of the influences that did have an impact on the author. First, the places. Whitby is a crucial setting in the story; it was also a holiday spot where Stoker went to relax. It is hard to think of a more atmospheric place than the ruined medieval abbey, standing sentinel on the clifftop, overlooking the cemetery with its wind-eaten tombstones (both abbey and cemetery play key roles in the book). Much of the novel, however, was written at Cruden Bay in Scotland. There is less evidence that this plays any part in inspiring any of the places in the novel, although some have attempted to suggest that a castle there might have been the place on which the count's was based.[4]

Stoker did undertake a fair amount of research, and his working papers have survived and are now housed in Philadelphia. From these, we can obtain a very good idea of what material he used and where it came from. It should be noted that he was not above using his own initiative; Dracula having to be buried in the earth from his grave wherever he goes is a good example, and another illustration of how new imagery is added to the vampire myth over time. But the research was done from a distance; Stoker never went anywhere near Transylvania, except in his imagination. But that proved to be a particularly productive way of writing for him, and very effective for his readers.

From his working notes, we can form a thorough understanding of the themes that inspired Stoker. Before we consider what they were, we should eliminate one red herring from the start. There is very little evidence, despite assertions to the contrary, that the medieval Wallachian prince known as Vlad the Impaler contributed anything to Stoker's Count Dracula, other than his name and the barest of historical details. Nevertheless, the tourist industry continues to make great capital out of the supposed connection. In Transylvania, Bran Castle is trumpeted as the home of Dracula; this, despite the fact that it was not the base of Vlad the Impaler and there is no evidence at all that Stoker used it as the home of his fictional count.

Vlad was a cruel and ruthless ruler, few people would argue with that. Yet, even his enemies—and there were a fair number of them—never accused him of being a vampire. Bloodthirsty yes, but in the same way that, for example, Genghis Khan was, and nobody has ever, as far as we know, suggested any vampiric tendencies for him. Local legends are in distinctly short supply as far as evidence of any supernatural powers are concerned.

Stoker did use Vlad's nickname in his book, and we even know exactly where he got it from. William Wilkinson, the British consul in Bucharest in 1820, wrote a book called *Account of the Principalities of Wallachia and Moldavia*. In this, he wrote a very short account of the historical Dracula (a name which was, confusingly, also used as a sobriquet for several other Wallachian princes). Vlad the Impaler's father (also Vlad and also nicknamed Dracula by Wilkinson, though this is an error on his part) is discussed briefly in the book, not altogether covering himself in glory.

His son, the Impaler, is then described, with brief reference made to his heroic but ultimately futile campaign against the Turks in 1462.

It is likely that the references in the novel *Dracula* to the count's illustrious warrior ancestors owe their genesis to this brief passage (in alliance with the efforts of the librarians in the public lending library at Whitby where Stoker found the book). However, it is in a footnote to this brief description that we can find evidence of Stoker's greatest debt to Wilkinson. This gives the origin of Vlad's nickname: "DRACULA in the Wallachian language means Devil. The Wallachians at that time, as they do at present, used to give this as a surname to any person who rendered himself conspicuous either by courage, cruel actions or cunning." Here we have a perfect explanation for the attraction of the name Dracula. The name was synonymous to Stoker with cruelty, cunning, courage, and is linked with the Devil. What better title for the antihero of his novel?

That is all that exists in Stoker's working papers to give evidence of a link to Vlad the Impaler (his notes suggest that it is unclear which Dracula he was actually talking about, but this is unimportant; it was the name that interested the author). Of Vlad's historically attested atrocities, there is no mention in the novel. Is it really likely that a novel based on blood makes no mention of these if the author intended his count to be based on the medieval ruler? There were plenty of them, enough to satiate the most bloodthirsty reader. Tales of men, women, and children impaled on stakes while Vlad enjoyed his breakfast in the midst of them as they writhed in their last agonies; stories of arrogant ambassadors who had their caps nailed to their heads; accounts of thousands of Bulgarians and Turks slain and decapitated as the ruler numbered their dead by an all-too-literal head count.

But the association, we believe largely unwarranted, between Vlad and Count Dracula is an example of how myths mutate. During the course of our research for this book, we came across another evolving myth. A report on the BBC Web site[5] stated that "it is estimated that 17 million people—including the British Royal Family, Iranian Royalty, and the family of Dracula—are direct descendants of Genghis Khan." We had not previously come across claims that such a link existed, and of course they can only refer to the "historical" Dracula. But the article does not make this clear, and to the uninitiated, reading the article without knowledge of Vlad the Impaler, the most likely inference is that Count Dracula was a descendant of Genghis Khan (not as strange as it might sound, as the literary count does claim descent from Attila). It will be very interesting indeed to see whether this particular variation, the original source of which is unknown to us, becomes an established part of the revised "Dracula myth."

Three main sources of inspiration can be identified as the genesis of *Dracula*; with a nicely alliterative feel, they are literature, legend, and landscape. Stoker picked up on a well-established literary trend following on from Polidori's work, *Varney the Vampire,* and *Carmilla. Carmilla* had a special part to play, so much so that some commentators have suggested that the work, which later appeared as the short story "Dracula's Guest" (published posthumously, years after he wrote it, as a stand-alone story on the instructions of his widow), was originally the first chapter of the novel but was eventually dropped at the insistence of the publisher who thought that it was too similar to Le Fanu's work. In any event, it was originally set in Styria, the same place as *Carmilla,* but Stoker dropped the idea and replaced this location with Transylvania, something of a masterstroke as it transpired. What Stoker did was to invent a bloody cocktail of horror, throwing just about everything into the melting pot that he could think of. The result was a book that was in a different league from anything else he—or most other writers for that matter—ever wrote, not necessarily in terms of quality, but certainly in terms of impact.

Stoker was also an important player in the world of theater, as he was manager of the most famous of all thespians, Henry Irving. In this role, he came into contact with influences that had a profound effect on him. Irving was renowned as a Shakespearean actor, and the works of the Bard resonate through the novel, *Hamlet* in particular (one of Irving's greatest roles). The actor had performed the title role in *Faust,* and the demonic undertones of that particular tale also find a strong echo in *Dracula.* His circle of friends, too, played a part, particularly Arminius Vambery, a Hungarian expert on Eastern Europe and its legends, who has a walk-on role in the novel.

The legendary base of *Dracula* is obvious. The long tradition of vampire legends gave Stoker a perfect foundation for the novel. His Irish background also had an effect. He was brought up in an environment where he was surrounded by legends, myths, and superstitions. His mother was a remarkable lady who told eerie tales of people buried alive during cholera epidemics. As he grew up, he was very close to the parents of Oscar Wilde, avid collectors of folklore with several books published on the subject.

Just a few years before the appearance of the novel, the splendidly named Madame E. de Laszowska Gerard wrote a book called *Transylvanian Superstitions.* Volume XVIII of this publication contains several references that Stoker felt were important enough to include in his research materials. The following is particularly significant: "[In Transylvania] it would almost seem as though the whole species of demons, pixies, witches, and hobgoblins, driven from the rest of Europe by the wand of science, had taken refuge within this mountain rampart, well aware that here they would find secure lurking-places, whence they might defy their persecutors yet awhile."

In other words, here was a land where all the supernatural beings imaginable had found their last bastion of defense against the predations of the world of science. It was a place that, Gerard goes on to describe, as being notable for its associations with the Devil, with prominent landmarks often named after him.

As well as providing him with a country infested with these strange beings, there were more specific references that Stoker found useful. For example: "More decidedly evil however is the vampire, or nosferatu, in whom every Roumenian [*sic*] peasant believes as firmly as he does in heaven or hell."[6]

She goes on to describe two types of vampire, the living and the dead. The former occurs when an illegitimate child is born to illegitimate parents. However, everyone killed by a vampire would become one when they died. They would continue to suck the blood of the living until their spirit was exorcised, either by driving a stake into them or by a pistol shot. If the infestation continued, then the head should be cut off and put back in the coffin with the mouth filled with garlic. Alternatively, the heart could be cut out and then burned, and the ashes scattered over the grave.

There is another detailed reference which is the obvious source of information for one particular scene in the novel. Gerard describes how on St. George's Eve (the eve of April 23) a great deal of occult activity takes place. It is a great night for finding buried treasure, an occupation referred to in the opening chapters of *Dracula*. She mentions how on Easter Eve, such treasure is revealed by a glowing flame. The same beliefs were referred to by Charles Boner in "The Land Beyond the Forest" from *Transylvania: Its Products and its People*, also a work that formed part of Stoker's research.

It was the location that clinched the effectiveness of the book, a region little known to the West, shrouded in legend and mystery. Transylvania was the perfect spot, precisely because so few people knew much about it. To those who have visited it, it is indeed a place of awe-inspiring majesty. Its sheer mountains reaching up vertically inspire terror in anyone with the merest hint of vertigo, and it is blanketed in thick forests where wolves and bears still roam (though sadly in much smaller numbers than they used to). Even if it wasn't though, Stoker created an image that could not fail to chill his readers.

Stoker was also indebted to a work called *On the Track of the Crescent*, written by Major E. C. Johnson in 1885. This is essentially a travel guide, sprinkled with anecdotes from the major's own experience. It is rich in atmosphere; the major stayed at a "grand old castle. Perched up on a height, its frowning battlements and grim old towers presented a perfect picture of a medieval stronghold." His descriptions tell of old towers, formerly torture chambers. There are references to a funeral service at the church of St. Demeter (the name of the ship in which Dracula arrives in England is the *Demeter*—a coincidence or more a direct quotation?). It is the funeral of a young child, with the whole village turning out to pay their respects, "some kneeling and smiting their breasts, others standing, and throwing their arms aloft, and all groaning and wailing."

The references to landscape made by the major are especially evocative. He describes a scene where in front of us, as far as the eye could reach, was an interminable stretch of forest, right up to the base of the mountain range, brilliant in numberless shades of green, blue and brown, and melting into a dusky purple as it became more stunted, and was lost in the haze surrounding the rocky crags. These towered range above range till they were crowned by the mighty "Isten-Szek" (God's Seat), the abode of eternal snow.

He describes the mountains in the following terms: "The Carpathians, towering aloft in their savage grandeur, are a spectacle not readily to be forgotten. They are almost inaccessible, and their steep and rocky sides are cut by numerous chasms, through which descend the waters which fertilise Transylvania."[7]

Reading the descriptions of these legends and the unique landscape (which were used virtually verbatim in *Dracula*), and allying them to the literary legacy of previous writers, Stoker was hooked. His masterstroke was in the personality of the count, who is always a shadowy enigma, waiting to pounce and grab the reader's attention without any prior warning. The effect is spectacular.

When it was published, the novel was enthusiastically received. Three thousand copies were produced in the first print run. It was the start of an amazing life for this extraordinary work, which has never been out of print. Ironically, it did not make Stoker a rich man. The big earnings for the Dracula brand would arrive only with the interest of Hollywood. Neither has the book always received the critical credit that it deserves. At the time, though, the critics were kind. No less a person than Arthur Conan Doyle said that "I think it is the very best story of diablerie which I have read for many years." (An interesting speculation is whether or not the novel might have influenced him to a small extent. In *Dracula*, the count jumps ship at Whitby in the form of a dog and disappears on to the moors. Conan Doyle was about to produce a "dog on the moor" story of his own, with spectacular results, in *The Hound of the Baskervilles*.)

The development of the myth went beyond the realm of literature. In the age of technology, it is technology itself that has helped perpetuate and enhance the impact of vampirism on our imagination via the silver screen. If it is a thankless task to go through all the literature that has ever been written about vampires, it is even more the case with the films that have been produced. One appeared in 1896—the year before *Dracula* was published—called *The Haunted Castle*, a two-minute film that sees a vampire driven off by a crucifix. Although by no means the first vampire movie, the most famous early picture is *Nosferatu*, made in Germany in 1922 and released in the United States in 1929. The film created a scandal.

It was blatantly based on Stoker's novel, and the feeble attempts to disguise the fact fooled nobody, least of all the law courts. Stoker's widow sued the producers for breach of copyright and won. Copies of the film were seized and destroyed.

Fortunately, a couple escaped, and the film can still be seen. In it, Jonathan Harker is sent to Transylvania after the count (called Orlov in the film) asks for help in buying a house. When Jonathan returns to Germany, the count follows him and attacks Mina. The final scene shows a departure from the novel, when the count is overcome because he does not return to his coffin before daybreak and the sun's rays destroy him—an important evolution in the vampire myth. The star of the film is Max Schreck, a name which in idiomatic German means "maximum terror." Shreck, who plays Orlov, gives a performance that sends a chill down the spine—with his rat-like features the count is grotesque. The director, F. W. Murnau, adds a twist by associating the count with rats rather than bats or wolves (though in the novel *Dracula*, rats do have a significant role). The film inspired later directors: when Coppola made his own version of the Dracula story in 1992, the count rises from his coffin in much the same way as Murnau's equivalent did 50 years earlier.

The Dracula theme was also developed on the stage, where Hamilton Deane made the role famous. He was an Irish actor and producer who penned a dramatic version of the novel; the play opened in 1924 in Derby, with Deane taking the part of van Helsing. He later took the role of the count himself. He played an important part in the development of the Dracula image, using a cape and evening dress for the first time. He also took the precaution of having nurses in the audience who would be able to deal with anyone who was overwhelmed by the horror of the storyline. The first dramatic performance, however, was arranged by Stoker himself in 1897, possibly to protect the copyright on the book. Even Henry Irving was in attendance. He walked out long before the end, muttering that the story was quite dreadful.

Bela Lugosi was the first actor to make Dracula really famous on the silver screen in the 1931 film of that name (the first choice for the leading role had been the equally famous Lon Chaney). Lugosi was an extraordinary actor, a Hungarian who did not speak English (and, incidentally, never felt the need to learn it—he merely learned the words he needed for the films he appeared in). Professionally, it was a role from which Lugosi could never escape. So successful was his performance as Dracula that he was typecast in the role (or similar ones) for life, and even in death, as he was buried in the cape he had worn in the film—a small example of how legends and fantasy can affect real life.

Christopher Lee was the most famous successor to Lugosi (and, interestingly, wore the same ring that Lugosi had used in earlier films). Hammer Films and Lee in many ways created the film image of Dracula that is still so prevalent today; the Byronic figure of the count, seductive and mesmeric, the Transylvanian backdrop, complete with thick forests, incredibly creepy Gothic castles, Peter Cushing's van Helsing, a curious combination of academic and folklorist who outsmarts the count in a dramatic final scene. The first Hammer "vampire movie'" was *The Horror of*

Dracula (1958). Lee's last performance as Dracula was in *The Satanic Rites of Dracula* (1974).[8]

Some films have made a greater impact (certainly on the authors) than others. So, *Bram Stoker's Dracula* (1992) is interesting because, although it takes the novel as its starting point, it introduces new features. Particularly intriguing is the explicit link the film makes with the historical Vlad the Impaler and the way in which Mina is a reincarnation of Vlad's wife. It gives the count feelings that are impossible to read into the love-drained character of the novel, and changes the emphasis of the storyline considerably while still incorporating many of the key details from the book, but inserting and overemphasizing others.

Gary Oldman played Dracula, and many other stars appeared in the film, including Winona Ryder as Mina, Anthony Hopkins as a rather quirky van Helsing, and Keanu Reeves as Jonathan Harker. So much of the film is overstated; in many ways, it is a cinematographic reflection of Stoker's novel which takes a vast array of symbols and almost overwhelms the reader with a torrent of them. But the film uses different ways of achieving the effect. The Transylvanian skyline is permanently tinged with red, and the accent of some of the actors portraying foreign characters is almost laughable. The film adds its own twist to the Dracula legends: Vlad's wife commits suicide, and her soul is therefore damned by the Church for which her husband dies fighting (though it should be pointed out that the myth concerning her dramatic end echoes that included by McNally and Florescu in *In Search of Dracula*).[9] As a result, Vlad swears to return from the grave and, driven by the powers of evil, live a terrible vampiric existence.

Coppola, at times, almost seems to go out of his way to out-caricature Stoker. Lucy mostly appears to be almost nymphomaniac in her flirtations, while at another point in the film, she is dressed in an outfit that looks very similar to the kind of dress that the "Virgin Queen," Elizabeth I, would wear. On the other hand, Mina, before her encounter with the count in the film, is prudish to the point of being sanctimonious, though Coppola does show her taking sly looks at pictures of various sexual acts in a book. But when she falls under the influence of the count, she gives herself, heart and soul, to him. The count, while he is in his Transylvanian guise, cuts an extraordinary figure, wearing what looks like a cardinal's cloak, as well as being the owner of an impossibly bouffant hairstyle. On occasion, the end product will, to some, verge on the ridiculous, but—like it or not—it is hard to ignore. And it could be argued that, in its exaggeration of stereotypes, the film is very much in keeping with the original novel, in spirit if not in content.

Vampire literature still has a wide circulation, too. The American writer, Anne Rice, is the most prominent modern vampire author (though famous names such as Stephen King—*Salem's Lot*—have also produced notable books in the genre). Her *Interview with the Vampire* (1976), subsequently made into a powerful movie, also has innovative approaches, such as the ineffectiveness of the crucifix previously mentioned. But it also has traditional vampire images at its core (such as sunlight destroying the creature). The most terrifying aspect of all is that, at the heart of the story, is a young child, Claudia. Apparently a beautiful, innocent girl, the fact that she is actually the most voracious of vampires creates a horrifying picture.

The movie, starring Tom Cruise as the archvampire Lestat and Brad Pitt as his willing victim Louis, also includes Antonio Banderas and Christian Slater in the cast. Neil Jordan directed the film, and Anne Rice herself was responsible for the screenplay. The plot is interesting as it spans several centuries, and much of it takes place in modern America, giving it a very contemporary feel. Louis's so-called fall begins in 1791 in the American South when he loses his wife and child and longs for nothing except death. But instead of this, the vampire Lestat offers him a choice of a life free of death and sickness as a creature like himself. Louis accepts, and the two become close friends. To seal the pact between them, not only does Lestat take blood from Louis, but the reverse also happens (not a unique development this, as several other films have used a similar approach—Coppola's *Dracula* for example). These are interesting variations which show how vampire mythology has evolved, for many "traditional" stories present the victim as helpless in the presence of a vampire who has hypnotic powers over them, and such tales normally present the taking of blood as a one-way process.

Louis turns out to be a vampire who cannot entirely kill his humanity. He and Lestat transform the girl, Claudia, into one of their kind. But Louis is filled with regrets. Claudia longs for a normal life and to grow up; her state means that she always stays the same age. She turns on Lestat and kills him by use of another innovatory technique—tricking him into drinking "dead blood," that is, from corpses that have been dead for some time; Rice's vampires need to drink fresh blood. But Lestat survives, drinking the blood of alligators, snakes, and frogs from the swamp where they place his supposedly dead body. Louis and Claudia flee to Europe, where they come across an underground commune of vampires in Paris. Finding out that she has killed another vampire, a cardinal sin in their world, they destroy Claudia by exposing her to sunlight.

Behind her death is the archvampire of the commune, Armand, who lusts after Louis for himself. But Louis sees this and rejects Armand and the Old World, returning to America. His final vestiges of humanity are obliterated by the death of Claudia. In the New World, he finds that Lestat has survived. Louis tells his story to a reporter, but he refuses to bite him, even when the reporter declares his wish to become a vampire. At the conclusion of the film, though, Lestat does attack the reporter and appears to offer him the choice of whether or not to join him in his nightmare existence.

This is a clever and complex plot. One of the subthemes within it concerns the death of Christianity in a secular society. Not only do the crucifixes not work, but Armand says specifically that "God does not exist." It is the oldest "God" of all, the Sun, which kills Claudia. The way in which Louis's story evolves is like a confession but, in a world where priests no longer seem to be effective, it is given to a reporter instead.

Another subplot concerns subliminal connections to *Dracula*. Louis describes Stoker's novel as "the vulgar fictions of a demented Irishman." In another scene, one of the creatures in Paris appears to parody Count Dracula by climbing up a wall in vaudeville fashion, his cape flapping over him as he does so, making him appear like a bat. On their trip to Europe, the ship on which Claudia and Louis are sailing suffers a number of deaths, just as in Stoker's novel. More subtle hints at the *Dracula* connection come with *Interview*'s links to *Hamlet*, traces of which can also be found in Stoker's work. One quotation by Claudia (whose name is close to that of Claudius in *Hamlet*) gives an obvious link—when Lestat is apparently dying before her, she mockingly bids him farewell: "Goodnight sweet prince, may flights of devils wing thee to they rest."

In the same way that Shakespeare's work has a play within it that reflects real life, when Prince Hamlet arranges for the murder of his father to be acted out, there is a reverse image in *Interview*. In a horrific scene, a girl is murdered onstage by vampires who are, as Louis describes it, pretending to be humans pretending to be vampires. They are very real creatures, and the onstage murder of the girl is all too obvious to us, the distant audience, but to the crowd watching all this happen within the film, it is all part of a very realistic and well-acted play.

The film, and the book on which it is based, is full of horrifying images. There is little of the, admittedly, lethal charm of Lugosi or Lee in this film. It is full of horrifying images, intended to shock and make the watcher feel distinctly uncomfortable. Drinking the blood of rats, a child vampire that looks like a doll, the way that Lestat toys with his victims as a cat might with a dying mouse, these are powerful and deeply disturbing images. But this is a plot with its lighter moments: the vaudeville vampires in Paris, or the way that Claudia, still "learning" to be a vampire, cannot resist the lure of blood, even when the victim is her overbearing piano teacher, give a hint of the ridiculous, too.

The best-known recent development of the mythology of the undead phenomenon is *Buffy the Vampire Slayer* and its spin-off *Angel*. *Buffy* first appeared in 1992 as a film that was not very highly regarded by the critics. Its real success arrived when it was turned into a long-running (1997–2003) TV production which ran for seven seasons. Sarah Michelle Gellar plays Buffy Summers, a 16-year-old girl with extraordinary powers. In a world that is overrun not only by vampires, but all kinds of other demonic creatures as well, it is her destiny to be the "slayer": the one person in each generation with the power to destroy all the agents of evil that stalk the earth. She is taken under the wing of Rupert Giles (played by Anthony Stewart Head), a librarian who has magus-like knowledge which enables him to help Buffy in her so-called mission.

Buffy tries to be a "normal" teenager, but she cannot reject the mission given to her—the destruction of evil—no matter how hard she tries. Strange events follow her around as if by magnetic attraction: she is thrown out of one of her schools for burning down a gymnasium that she says is full of vampires, for example. She has a sexual relationship with a vampire, Angel (David Boreanaz) —who would later have a series of his own, set in Los Angeles (produced between 1999 and 2004), and who is himself an extraordinary being: a vampire with a soul due to a gypsy curse placed on him by the distraught relatives of one of his victims. This gives him some terrible dilemmas, as his vampire nature drives him to destroy human beings, but his conscience creates remorse and compassion within him. At one stage, Angel tries to commit suicide. Haunted by an evil spirit who takes the form of his victims, he resolves to expose himself to sunlight and "kill" himself. But as he waits for the sun to rise, snow falls in Sunnydale, blotting out the sun and miraculously saving him.

Buffy is interesting because it brings vampirism into a very contemporary setting, a small American town called Sunnydale. One of the most striking features of the show is the very ordinariness of some of its aspects. Buffy suffers all the traumas of a teenager growing up: sexual emotions, problems at school, uncertainty about her role in life, for example. The setting is prosaic: no Transylvanian castles, but a stereotypical late twentieth-century U.S. high school. But alongside this ordinary world exists something extraordinary: a land populated with some of the most unspeakable monsters imaginable. The show is something of a spoof; one hint is given by Buffy's band of helpers, known collectively as the "Scooby Gang," a reference to the cartoon character Scooby Doo who gets involved in fights against all kinds of "spooks" in regular entanglements with the supernatural world. Buffy herself is an enigma. A slightly built girl, she nevertheless has superhuman strength, and her approach to the elimination of vampires is part traditional (staking through the heart) and part martial arts.

Why do vampire movies, books, and TV series such as *Buffy the Vampire Slayer* continue to fascinate? We believe that there are a number of reasons. Partly it is because "horror" has always had an attraction for human beings. That it continues to do so is evidenced by the large number of horror movies that continue to appear and the considerable market for books of this nature that exists.

But there are several other specific characteristics that appeal to the subconscious in vampire filmography and literature, some core themes which strike a chord with our deeper emotions. Sexuality is one aspect which has become more overt over the years. This particular theme in Polidori's "Vampyre" (where Lord Ruthven may be a supernatural seducer, but he is a seducer nevertheless) or *Dracula* was more subtle than that, for example, in Coppola's version of *Bram Stoker's Dracula,* where it is anything but. But the sexuality has always been there; it was, and remains, an important part of the vampire's fatal fascination.

Aging and death play a part too—these have still not been conquered by man, despite all our technological advances. Both produce fears that are as great as they have always been because we cannot avoid them. The vampire is caught in a nightmare world, neither dead nor alive, and reminds us of our vulnerability and mortality, but is also often seen as an attractive man or woman in the prime of life when it materializes (though not invariably). They seem to turn back the tide of time, but only at the awful cost of their soul, as well as the souls of their victims. It is only by preying on the blood of others that they can survive. It is to the examination of these themes in more detail that we will now turn.

NOTES

1. See Frayling, pp. 10–17.
2. Ibid., p. 67.
3. *Carmilla,* p. 89.
4. See Haining and Tremayne, chap. 10.
5. "Genghis Khan DNA Test is Offered," 3 July 2004.
6. In Frayling, pp. 319–326.
7. Ibid., pp. 335–342.
8. For a very detailed list of vampire movies, refer to the appendices in *In Search of Dracula.*
9. Ibid., p. 56.

CHAPTER 4

The Path of Blood

The blood is the life.

—Bram Stoker, *Dracula*

Blood is one of the central images of human frames of thought, associated with both life and death, with ritual sacrifice, and with violence. It is also a symbol of power and youth, and so it has a very close connection to the vampire myth of everlasting life—or death. The essence of the vampire myth is contained in the words "the blood is the life," with which the deranged Renfield outlines his topsy-turvy philosophy in the novel *Dracula*. One of the factors that makes this comment particularly relevant is its direct biblical origin, especially as it is taken out of context. In the words of a madman, this statement suggests that the vampire myth is sometimes a dark interpretation of the core images of Christian thought.

The Old Testament is awash with images of blood in many formats. In the story of Cain and Abel, it is associated with innocence, sin, and the afterlife. The blood shed is the witness of the crime, from beyond death, leading God to ask, "What hast thou done? The voice of thy brother's blood crieth unto me from the ground."[1] In the vampire myth, blood is the demonic link between the dead and the world of the living, and legends speak of the undead crying out from the graves the names of their victims.

When the enslaved Israelites in Egypt are rescued by God during the Passover, it is this mark of sacrifice that must be shown to God: "And the blood shall be to you for a token upon the houses where ye are: and when I see the blood, I will pass over you, and the plague shall not be upon you to destroy you, when I smite the land of Egypt."[2]

Blood often appears as a manifestation of sacrifice. Biblical injunctions are given that the sacrifice should be "without blemish" and the priests should "sprinkle his blood round about upon the altar."[3] Blood contains the very life force of the entity through whose veins it flows. It is sacred and precious, and therefore must be treated with due reverence "for it is the life of all flesh: the blood of it is for the life thereof: therefore I said unto the children of Israel, Ye shall eat the blood of no manner of flesh: for the life of all flesh is the blood thereof: whosoever eateth it shall be cut off."[4]

The New Testament added new aspects to the Old with regard to blood, as with many other facets of religion. It brought a religion rooted in love and forgiveness, of the accepted sacrifice which is able to open the doors of everlasting life for humanity. The sacrifice of Christ was a blood offering, in the same way that a lamb or an ox was in the Old Testament. The New Testament is replete with references to the substance, which would have a huge effect on the psychology of Christendom. The Crucifixion made the old ritual sacrifices redundant; for if animals were effective, then "how much more shall the blood of Christ, who through the eternal spirit offered himself without spot to God, purge your conscience from dead works to serve the living God."[5]

The blood of the pure sacrifice brings new life to those who are spiritually dying, symbolism that would create some interesting side effects during the medieval period. Christ established the importance of this philosophy when he said, "Except ye eat of the flesh of the Son of man, and drink his blood, ye have no life in you. Whoso eateth my flesh, and drinketh my blood, hath eternal life; and I will raise him up at the last day."[6]

At the Last Supper, the symbolism reached its ultimate expression, one that was to sear itself into the psyche of a later age that took many biblical injunctions, literally. "And he took bread and gave thanks, and brake it, and gave unto them, saying 'This is my body which is given for you: this do in remembrance of me.' Likewise also the cup after supper, saying, 'This cup is the new testament in my blood, which is shed for you.'"[7] The Communion rituals that developed from this became the very core of Christian belief. Later theologians would argue enthusiastically about whether or not the wine used during Communion was only symbolically transformed or if it literally became the blood of Christ.

Christian symbolism found its most evocative expression in the allegorical development of the Grail legends. These, the ultimate fusion of pagan Celtic and Christian imagery, seized the imagination of medieval man. The Grail became the repository of wine as Christ's metaphorical blood. But it was also the cup in which Joseph of Arimathea collected His physical blood.

The blood of Christ endowed the Grail with great power. Those who drank from it would taste whatever they wished—a clear variation on Celtic mythology.[8] The lance that pierced Christ's side also had magical powers. In the Grail legends, Galahad visits the Maimed King who has been incapacitated for many years, having been injured by this same spear. Galahad is given the lance and told that he should first take "some blood of this lance and anoint his legs with it: for this and this alone can bring him back to health." Galahad then goes to the lance and, "touching the blood with his fingers, he walked across to the Maimed King and anointed his legs with it .... And immediately the king put on a gown, and springing hale and sound from his bed, he offered thanks to Our Lord for looking so graciously upon him."[9]

Robert de Boron was the first writer to make the connection between the Grail and the blood of Christ in around 1190. By so doing, he tapped into reverential feelings towards the power and nature of Christ's blood that were a symbol of the age. As one commentator has remarked, "in the medieval mind, [it] contained both the soul and possibly even the Divinity of the Saviour. It possessed unlimited powers of healing, and it was a means of transmitting a direct apprehension of God. A spiritual essence, and one which was beyond price." The same writer notes that illustrations of the heart of Christ exist, complete with the stigmata showing the wounds of Christ letting forth blood and water: "The blood, which being symbolically shed 'for all men,' was also seen as an individual life-giving source." The similarity between the words "Saint Greal" (Holy Grail) and "Sang Real" (Royal Blood) is also suggestive.[10] Given such vivid and unmistakable links between blood, power, and the life force, it is easy to see some images of vampirism, particularly its concentration on blood, as an ironic parody of Christianity.

Blood has had a significant role in many cultures, as can be seen in some of the oldest cosmogony myths. Some of them seem to follow certain patterns, each defining human nature from a different perspective. One of the recurrent symbols is constructed around the concept of blood as a vital substance, the spring of life. Early mythologies often describe the Creation as a violent and cataclysmic upheaval which placed the entire material world under the dual sign of life and death, of good and evil. From its very genesis, matter therefore has a dual nature: as it is born from the sacrificed god's being, it is partly divine, but the dark shadow of violence is cast upon it. The mark of Death is imprinted on the Living.

The Sumerian cosmogony poem, "Enuma elis," mentions the sacrifice of the two gods Lakhmu and Lakhamu as being responsible for the birth of mankind. The Mesopotamian variant of the Creation myth is the story of Marduk, son of Ea, the All-knowing. From the primordial waters Tiamat, the sea, was born, along with Apsu, the freshwater rivers and lakes of the earth. The other gods were born from the union between the fresh and salty waters. Soon after, the cries of the young gods disturbed Apsu's peace and he decided to destroy them. But hearing of it, Ea used magical incantations to make Apsu fall asleep, then "steals his brightness and clothes himself in it"[11] and subsequently kills him.

In the war that followed, Marduk defeated Tiamat in a fierce battle. He cut Tiamat's body in two, creating the earth and the sky and the whole world from it. Finally, he decided to punish Kingu, Tiamat's son, as the instigator of the conflict. Kingu's end matched the violence of his deeds: his veins were cut open and from his blood Ea made mankind. Man's creation was his doom. Partly god, as he was created by Ea, he would always sense his divine nature, but would never be able to reach it, as he was made from the blood of Kingu, the demon-god,[12] the fallen deity who rose up violently against the other gods.

A similar Creation myth was outlined in Greek thinking. Uranus, the Sky, and Gaea, the Earth, were the first entities born out of Chaos. They gave birth to twelve Titans, the three Cyclopes, and the three Hecatoncheires (monsters with 100 arms and 50 heads), but Uranus hid his offspring in Gaea's womb. At Gaea's request, the youngest of the titans, Cronus, castrated his father. Drops of his blood were spread across the earth, and from them sprang the three Furies (the goddesses of Revenge), the Giants, and the Nymphs. Aphrodite, the goddess of love and sexuality, was created when his genitals fell into the sea and his semen touched the foam of the waves.

An Indian epic, *Purushasukta*, describes how the gods sacrificed the primordial giant Purusha ("Man"). They cut his body into pieces and so created the world and its elements. His head became the sky, his legs the earth, his conscience became the moon, the sun was born from his eyes, and the wind from his breath. From his mouth were born Indra and Agni, and the human beings who were created from different parts of his body were bound to their status forever—born from his mouth was the Brahman, from his arm the Warrior, from his hips the Craftsman, and from his legs the Servant.

Purusha's sacrifice has a cosmic dimension, as it is the source of the universe and, even more important, of the order that governs the new creation which differentiates it from the chaos. This order has to be preserved, and the act of creation has to be ritually reiterated. Here is the source and justification of ancient rituals of blood: the original sacrifice must take place again and again. An intrinsic aspect of it is connected to fertility; the rebirth of nature, of man, of the universe.

While considering India, we must mention the figure of Kali, goddess of death and destruction, and one of the most frightening figures of any religious pantheon. She is normally shown as a creature drenched in blood, naked save for an assortment of skulls draped around her. Her greatest battle was against the demon Raktavija. Every time she drew blood, it struck the ground and produced a thousand new versions of the demon—the substance was, in this case literally, the source of new life. To destroy him, she pierced him with a spear and drank his blood. Her latter-day followers were the infamous Thugees, who made blood a key part of their worship of the goddess.

The early Germanic poem "Völuspá" includes the symbolic story of Ymir, an anthropomorphic being, created at the beginning of the world by the union of fire and ice. A cow born from the melting ice licked the creature until it took the form of a man, Buri. He married the daughter of a Giant and she bore him three sons: Odin, Vili, and Ve. The three brothers killed Ymir, and his blood flooded the earth and drowned all the Giants except two. The brothers then cut Ymir's body into pieces, and made the earth from his flesh, the rocks from his bones, the sea from his blood and the sky from his skull.

Some of the most violent rituals of the Aztecs originated in a similar myth of Creation. In order to create the sun and the moon, two gods were given to the fire. But their sacrifice was not enough. The sun and the moon, though they had been created, could not move, and the other gods understood that a sacrifice of blood was further required. They gathered with the intention of giving an offering from their own veins. The god Xolotl, however, was a coward. He hid, subsequently becoming the god of evil beings and of all that is dual, such as twin brothers. This is an interesting aspect of Aztec thinking: duality is placed under the sign of evil (duality as a literary undercurrent is also a feature of vampire literature). As the sun was the center of Aztec religious belief, the sacrifice had to be made every year, to strengthen the sun for its annual journey across the skies. It was the only way to preserve the integrity of the world and of the community.

For ancient peoples, a myth was not merely a story. It contained a universal and sacred truth. And the acts of the gods had to be symbolically reiterated in order to ensure that the essential order of the world, and therefore its entire existence, was preserved. Ritual sacrifice was the repetition of a primordial divine act, as Holy Communion for Christians is a reiteration of the Last Supper. But new myths came along and pushed the old ones into oblivion, new religions were born and spread, and what was once holy ritual and belief became so-called pagan lore and superstition. The ancient myths lost their essential quality of truth, but the old rituals did not disappear, even if the deep symbolism behind them was in some cases forgotten or twisted.

Christianity, for example, sees the world as a creation of the holy Word, the *Logos,* and therefore initially involves no divine sacrifice, though Christ of course became one. Yet some pre-Christian myths survived for centuries in Christian Europe. One of the most impressive legends of Orthodox Eastern Europe is that of the sacrifice needed in order to build something, such as a house, a bridge, or a church. The house is an *imago mundi,* an image of the universe, and its creation, just like the primordial one, needs blood. Such a legend describes the way in which the monastery of Curtea de Arges, one of the most beautiful sixteenth-century churches in Romania, was built.

A Wallachian prince, Neagoe Basarab, wanted to build a church. He chose nine builders and a renowned master mason, Manole. They searched for the right place along the river banks. Finally, the prince chose a spot that the shepherds said was haunted by evil spirits:

> In hazel brush hid,
> There's a wall all rotten,
> Unfinished, forgotten.
> My dogs when they see it
> Make a rush to bite it,
> And howl hollowly
> And growl ghoulishly.

Work started, but everything built during the day would fall apart at nighttime. Manole had a dream in which God told him that the church needed human sacrifice, and that they should inter in the walls the first woman who came with food for her husband or brother. But to his own despair, the first to arrive was Ana, his young and beautiful wife. Seeing her, he prayed to God to send strong winds and a fearful storm to stop her, but in spite of the fury of nature, she made her way to her husband. When she arrived, Manole, with heavy heart, told her that they were playing a game. He said that the builders would only pretend to build the wall around her. She accepted, but as the wall grew, she started to cry and, frightened, told her husband to stop, or else she and her unborn child would die. The masons did not spare her, and her sacrifice made it possible to finish the church. When the prince came to see it, he asked the masons if they could build something as beautiful as this again. They answered yes, and the prince, angered by their reply, ordered that the scaffolding should be taken away. They were left to die on the church roof. Manole made himself wings, but as he was trying to fly, he heard Ana crying from the walls and he fell to the ground:

> And, lo, where he fell,
> There sprang up a well,
> A fountain so tiny,
> Of scant water, briny,
> So gentle to hear,
> Wet with many a tear![13]

Different variants of this legend can be found across Eastern Europe, and they demonstrate that there have always been myths associating blood with the creation of the universe and life. There are fairly modern accounts of children being kidnapped in order to be buried near the foundation stone of a building. Even early twentieth-century masons would bury a small animal, a dog or a cat, in the foundations. "Stealing a person's shadow" was also a way of protecting a building. Somebody's shadow would be nailed to the wall when the sun reflected it against it. This might seem harmless enough, but was often deemed to cause the so-called victim, on death, to become a vampire. The practice reflects an age-old belief, common to many cultures, that the shadow contains the soul of a person. The vampire, too, appears as a shadow, with no reflection in the mirror.

The concept of sacrifice, particularly human sacrifice, is constructed around the premise that blood is the vessel of life, or as Summers calls it, "vampirism regarded from an entirely different angle."[14] A common motif is the sacrifice offered to encourage the gods to send good harvests and protect the community from evil. The offering can be of fruit or vegetables, or in the form of slaughtered animals. Sacrifices that require human life are also frequent in many religious beliefs, such as in the Old Testament, where Abraham is asked to sacrifice his son Isaac on the altar as a sign of obedience and submission. But the symbolism continues to be used in literature and cinematography, most notably in the well-known British horror movie, *The Wicker Man,* the plot of which is based on ancient Celtic practices according to which humans would be forced inside a huge wicker man that would then be set alight.

Another type of sacrifice is that of the scapegoat. Vengeful gods would often punish an entire community if one member of it had offended them. Therefore, the offender is dangerous, their presence jeopardizes the well-being of the community. Killing them earns forgiveness and allows normal life to resume. In the medieval period, the witch became the scapegoat (and the vampire was also later regarded as one, deemed responsible for epidemics such as plague). Without realizing it, medieval man repeated the ritual gestures of his "pagan" ancestors.

Killing the witch meant ultimately that the community made a sacrifice of blood in order to please the divinity, in the hope that God would restore the normal order of life disturbed by sin.

Perhaps the most famous practitioners of the "art" of human sacrifice were the Aztecs. One version concerned "the Stone of Tizoc," named after an Aztec king. It has a hollowed-out center, in which the heart of the sacrifice would be placed. Blood would run down the side of the stone, a gift to the gods. In Tibetan Buddhism, the yogi offers his blood symbolically, which is then placed in a skull cup. This is transformed into nectar, which is offered to the gods.

Belief in the power of human sacrifice still exists. In 2003, Harold Keke, a rebel leader from the island of Guadalcanal in the Solomons, was reported to have "slaughtered a boy nephew in a ritual sacrifice, praying to the mountain gods for strength and drinking the victim's blood." Whether the story is true or not is largely irrelevant. The fact that such accusations can be made even in our times shows that the world has not changed as much as we sometimes like to think it has. Acceptance of the efficacy of blood as a sacrificial offering to some superior being persists in the imagination and paradigms of different cultures.[15]

The modern mind is still influenced by magical thinking. A vampire book or film, although seen as fiction, remains strangely fascinating. Such accounts are typically constructed of those images that, over time, have been connected to duality and the ambivalent nature of existence, encompassing the concepts of life and death. What makes them sell is the construct of symbols and icons they use that manage to access our deepest ancestral fears together with the devices of the gothic novel and of the easy-to-read melodrama that ensure their success with the general public. A good vampire book is a nicely written dictionary of eerie symbols. And the one which becomes most obsessive and grim is that of blood as the source of life.

Magical qualities have often been attributed to blood as a way of alleviating suffering and illness. Pliny records that the pharaohs used to bathe in it to ward off leprosy. The association is interesting, as it is not the only case in history where blood was believed to fight off the disease. It is a classic case of sympathetic medicine: good blood replaces bad, and therefore cures the illness. Constantine the Great was urged to use this cure for his leprosy even after conversion to Christianity. Nicephorus Gallistus[16] says that the Emperor was counseled to use the blood of children by pagan Greek advisers. The association with innocence is important—it is as if the blood of the pure can restore the spiritual and physical health of the sinful (and the link between the purity of the victim and the vampire who preys on them is a strong image in both vampire legend and literature). It was assumed that illness was God's punishment. Pure blood must be used to cure the sufferer.

The advent of Christianity did nothing to reduce this fascination with blood. An interesting example of this from modern times is that, on her death, some of the blood of Mother Teresa was retained as a relic. This obsession reached its ultimate macabre zenith during the medieval period, the age of supreme paradox and symbolism. The chivalric code had some very strange by-products. It proved to be particularly dangerous for virgins, whose blood was deemed to be pure, carrying as it did the life force of chaste and virtuous maidens who were believed to be free of sin.

There are several references in Arthurian literature to the efficacy of virgins' blood as a cure for disease. In one episode of Malory's Morte d'Arthur, Galahad and Perceval are traveling with Perceval's sister when they come to a castle. It is the custom of this castle that no maiden may pass without giving of her blood. As they approach the gates, a knight duly rides out to challenge them, asking them whether the "gentlewoman" with them is a maid. When they answer yes, the knight refuses to let the entourage pass without the custom being complied with.

Perceval and Galahad, good knights of the Round Table that they are, refuse to let blood be taken from the girl. However, this is not the end of the matter. The girl hopes that, if she willingly offers herself as a sacrifice, then the eternal well-being of her soul will be assured. She does this, so that the lady of the castle—whose poor health is the reason for the bloodletting ritual—might be restored by her actions. The act is duly performed and as the girl grows progressively weaker, she "lifted up her hand and blessed the lady of the castle, and said to this lady, 'Madam, I am come to my death for to heal you. Therefore, for God's love pray for me."[17]

There are several key motifs here. There are the personal characteristics of the donor. She is a virgin, pure, chaste, sinless. She is also a gentlewoman; in fact, the custom demands that she must be a king's daughter. Royal blood is deemed to hold more power than common blood. It is a variation of the tradition of "scrofula," the healing of "the king's evil," whereby the touch of a monarch is deemed to heal. The king is God's appointee and has been given his place by His authority. He therefore carries the seal of approval of the Almighty and, by implication, some of His power. It is not that the king himself is spiritually superior; it is his position that is so.

There is another aspect in all this to consider; the attitude of the donor. In this instance, the girl offers herself freely, in a form of martyrdom, recognizing that spiritual life is more important than physical. Christianity, as well as being a religion of love, is also one of sacrifice. The example of Christ inspires others to give freely of themselves, even to the ultimate, renouncing their lives so that others might live (and so that they too, of course, might live eternally in Paradise). By this offering of blood willingly given, the survival of the Soul is assured.

In the Grail legends, Perceval's sister dies and is taken by Perceval, Galahad, and Bors to the island of Sarras, where the sacred vessel resides. Although she is dead, her body does not decompose. So she achieves both spiritual immortality and, in a way, physical survival, too. Vampire literature often contains a perverted parody of this theme. The innocent young virgin gives of her blood so that another might live. But she is normally an unwilling accomplice, her mind enslaved by the vampire who controls her. She achieves immortality, but it is a curse rather than a blessing, doomed as she is to wander the earth and ensnare others into a half-life of evil, neither living nor dead, with no hope for her soul unless and until someone kills her and at last gives her peace.

The medieval Grail stories may reflect real-life practices. In France, the physicians of Montpelier and Salerne were held in high regard for their skill, and they employed blood as a healing ingredient. The twelfth-century German poet, Hartmann von Aue, was essentially a romantic writer, closely connected to chivalric literature, and his literal accuracy therefore cannot be assumed. However, there is no reason to doubt that he was drawing on a symbolism that would be widely understood in contemporary society when he wrote. He described how a virgin's blood was drawn by the physicians of Salerne as a treatment for leprosy. Again, the sacrifice was a voluntary, one and the physician given the task questioned the donor thoroughly to ensure that she fully realized the implications of her actions.

The robust questioning was accompanied by an admonition that the donor would also lose her dignity in the process. The maiden was proud of her chastity and discretion, and she would suffer much in the ordeal that was to come for, the physician warned her, "I will undress you so that you will stand naked, and your shame and hardship will be great which you will suffer because you stand naked before me: I will tie up your arms and legs. And if you don't feel mercy for your own life and body think of this pain: I will cut to your heart and tear it out live from your breast." If these threats were not enough to dissuade the maid, she would be tied up on a table. Then the physician, armed with a sharp knife to make the donor's end quick and painless, would strike. The blood shed would subsequently be administered to the patient, with the hope that a recovery from leprosy would ensue.[18]

Blood is not only associated with healing, it can also be an instrument of death, a closer image to the vampire myth. Greek legends tell that Hercules killed the Hydra of Lerna, a monster with nine heads which could not be destroyed as two heads grew when one was cut off and one was indestructible. Helped by Iolaos, Hercules killed the Hydra and buried the indestructible head under a great rock. Finally, he dipped his arrows in her poisonous blood so that they became lethal. Years later, as Hercules was traveling with his wife, Deianeira, the centaur Nessos tried to kidnap her. Hercules killed him with one of his poisoned arrows. With his dying breath the centaur told Deianeira to dip Hercules's tunic in the blood that was springing from his veins and had been mixed with the venom from the arrows, because this would make Hercules love her forever. She gathered it in a vessel which she kept hidden from the sun and the fire of the hearth, as Nessos had advised her.

Years later, she found out that her husband had fallen in love with another woman, Iole. Deianeira was half afraid to use the magic blood, but she believed that this was the only way to keep Hercules's love. She made a beautiful tunic, spread the blood over it, and sent it to Hercules. After a while, she noticed that the piece of wool-cloth that she had used had turned into ashes, and around the place where it had been there was now a venomous foam. She became afraid, but it was too late. Hercules was sacrificing to the gods when he wore the tunic for the first time. Heated by the fire of the altar, the poison seared his body and he suffered excruciating pain, but was unable to remove his clothes. Finally, he asked his son to burn his body on a pyre and so put an end to his torment. Similarly, in the stories of the undead, it is the infected blood that spreads the vampiric plague, and those attacked by a vampire would become one themselves. Even the meat of animals whose blood had been consumed by such a monster would be deadly for the humans who ate it.

War is another expression of duality. Blood shed in battle is sacred, but the image of victory is shadowed by death, and for every winner there is a loser. The blood-drenched battlefields are places of doom, haunted by the restless spirits of the dead and by the creatures of darkness. Here is how the three weird sisters in *Macbeth* make their prophecy: "When the hurly-burly's done, When the battle's lost and won."[19] Evil spirits gather around these places which are marked in blood, and Count Dracula even expresses his disgust at the thought of peaceful times: "The warlike days are over. Blood is too precious a thing in these days of dishonourable peace; and the glories of the great races are a tale that is told."[20] Glory and blood are thus connected and, for centuries, dying in battle meant life after death. This is another element of duality in many vampire stories, such as *Dracula*, which fascinates even today: we do not really know how the prince became a vampire, but this doomed soul brought into the modern age an obsession with glory associated with blood.

In Coppola's film, *Bram Stoker's Dracula*, Vlad the Impaler comes back from battle still wearing his armor. But this is not the shining armor of the medieval hero. It resembles a skinned body, as if it were an indirect prophecy of doom. The prince who kills in the name of God will rise up against his own faith. As a result, he will never find peace in death. There is one particularly powerful scene in the film when Vlad, in his anger against God, thrusts his sword into a stone cross, from which blood gushes profusely, flooding the floors of the chapel.

Blood is also associated with murder. This vital fluid preserves its qualities even after the death of the body. This explains legends where a sacrificial victim becomes the protective spirit of a place or a building and the belief that the blood of Christ gathered in the Holy Grail has magical properties. The blood of the innocent victim marks the life and the spirit of the murderer—the phrase "to have somebody's blood on one's hands" appears in many languages (for example, *manos manchados de sangre* in Spanish, or *a avea mainile patate de sange* in Romanian). Lady Macbeth is the classic image of the woman who has given herself to the evil spirits in order to achieve greatness and power. Seeing the blood on her husband's hands, she tells him: "Go get some water, And wash this filthy witness from your hand."[21] The shadow of the murder of King Duncan hangs over she who has inspired his death. The woman who instigated the "murder of sleep" is cursed to lose hers. Her world is in chaos, and her life and senses are lost, maybe as a token to those dark forces to which she owed her power. In her madness, she senses the bloodstains on her hands: "Here is the smell of blood still: all the perfumes of Arabia will not sweeten this little hand."[22]

Another literary example of blood staining the hands of the murderer can be found in Oscar Wilde's *The Picture of Dorian Gray*. The portrait shows all the signs of Dorian's maleficence, which appear on the canvas rather than on the real person. When Dorian murders Basil, his friend and metaphorical conscience, a stain appeared on the hands of the portrait, "loathsome red dew that gleamed, wet and glistening, on one of the hands, as though the canvas had sweated blood."[23]

Sometimes blood is a motivation for real-life murder. A famous medieval case concerned Gilles de Rais, Marshal of France and hugely influential personality. He was a contemporary of Joan of Arc and helped drive the English from France. Yet, in an astonishing turn of events, he was charged with the murder of 800 children. It was claimed that he stabbed children in the jugular vein and went into ecstasies as the blood spurted over him. In some cases, it was said, he drank their blood.

The stories probably lost nothing in the telling. A conviction of de Rais meant that his lands would be forfeit, and he had many enemies. After attacking a priest, de Rais was charged with heresy, a crime that carried with it the most terrible penalty possible. His servants were tortured until they revealed his crimes. He himself made a confession, admitting responsibility for the murders of the children. He was condemned to be burned at the stake. After appropriate public apologies and asking for forgiveness from his victims' families, he was shown an element of mercy and garroted before his body was burned on October 26, 1440.

Over a century later, another French mass murderer was accused of vampirism. This was Gilles Garnier. His victims were young women: he ate them and drank their blood. The most famous of all murderers who were driven by their thirst for blood was the seventeenth-century countess, Elisabeth Bathory, who will be considered in more detail at a later stage.[24] In modern times, there is a large number of accounts that relate how particularly depraved murderers have been driven literally by a bloodlust (such as the French killer, Antoine Leger, guillotined in 1824). Two particularly shocking cases occurred in Germany during the twentieth century. The so-called "Vampire of Düsseldorf," Peter Kurten, had a lifelong obsession with blood. He started by killing animals, and ended his criminal career by attacking and murdering 29 people. His victims were usually young women. He sexually assaulted and killed them, and then drank their blood. He reputedly said, on the eve of his execution by guillotine in 1932, that his greatest thrill would be that "after my head has been chopped off I will still be able to hear, at least for a moment, the sound of my own blood gushing from the stump of my neck."

The case of the "Hanover Vampire," Fritz Haarmann (executed in 1924), is equally disturbing. His preferred method of killing was to bite the throats of his victims. They were normally young men and boys from the margins of society, who would therefore not be missed. In a particularly macabre twist, parts of their bodies were cooked in pies and sold. Both these cases exhibit a perverted fascination with blood and its association with the life force of the victims. In Britain, too, the "acid bath murderer," John Haigh (hanged in 1949), exhibited vampiric tendencies (though the evidence of these came from Haigh himself and could have been an attempt to convince psychiatric experts that he was insane, which would have saved his life). He first noticed these when he sucked a wound made when his mother beat him across the hands. Later, he had vivid nightmares in which he dreamed he saw a forest of crucifixes. As he approached them, he saw that they were trees dripping blood. A man collected the blood and offered it to Haigh to drink. He later cut the veins of his victims and drank their blood. The Christian symbolism, the forest, and the obsession with blood are all found in vampire lore and literature.

It is an uncomfortable fact that blood continues to act as a catalyst for the crimes of certain particularly unbalanced individuals. In one act of violence disturbingly close to our own times, a 17-year-old youth was found guilty of murdering a 90-year-old widow in north Wales in November 2001. The prosecution claimed that he had drunk her blood in a "macabre ritual." Vampire books and magazines were found in the murderer's bedroom, and it was known that he had visited vampire Web sites. The killer admitted to an interest in immortality and said that he would not have minded being a vampire if that was the price to be paid.

Such stories can be found all round the world. A news report on December 23, 2002 stated that villagers in southern Malawi were fleeing from remote areas because of attacks from those in search of blood. The accounts were somewhat bizarre, as they claimed that international aid organizations were offering food in exchange for the substance, and that the government of the country was implicated. In response, President Muluzi of Malawi said that "no government can go about sucking the blood of its people—that's thuggery." Yet the terror inspired was real enough; one of those suspected of working with the 'vampires' was killed in reprisals by villagers.[25]

Blood also signifies something less violent—family relationship and the characteristics that go from one generation to another. Count Dracula claims to have inherited the blood of Attila, and as he speaks of his ancestors, we see he is one in whom the values of old have been perverted, a return to the core of evil found among the Huns in whose veins it was said that there "ran the blood of those old witches, who, expelled from Scythia, had mated with the devils in the desert."[26] So, in the novel, blood is seen as the vehicle that brought the Spirit of Evil across the centuries into the modern world. The novel *Carmilla* is based on a similar idea, that the blood of young women brings life to the long-dead members of an ancient noble family, and Carmilla needs to return to the home of her ancestors.

From ancient myths to the world of the Bible, children will pay for the sins of their parents, right down to the seventh generation. There is a pattern to this behavior, and sin is thought to propagate itself through the offspring of the sinner. Folk legends say that the seventh son of a seventh son will become a vampire, as will a witch's child, or an illegitimate child whose parents were themselves born out of wedlock. In some traditions, it is possible for a vampire to marry and have children, though these are doomed to become vampires themselves when they die.[27] This is an expression of the immutable, unbreakable link that blood creates between people. There are certain rules to be followed, conventions that society creates for its members, and if these are broken then the abomination of a vampire is the result.

Vampire stories are centered on the power that the creature has over its victims, the supernatural ability to read their thoughts and to order them from a distance. The link of blood is so powerful that the vampire and his victim are connected forever. Vampire legends often state that the undead come to haunt, first of all, their kin. Old beliefs have survived into the modern world. One example is the case of an old woman who died in the Putzic canton, in Prussia in 1913. Soon afterwards, her relatives started to pass away, seven dying in a short space of time. When another of her sons started to feel ill, the rumor spread that she could not find peace in the other world, and was calling her family to join her. Afraid that he might share the fate of the others, the son exhumed his mother, cut off her head, and put it in the coffin at the feet of the corpse. Shortly afterwards he regained his health. [28]

This image of family doom is used by Lord Byron as the basis of his poem, "The Giaour," [29] written in 1813. The full horror of vampirism is described in complete Gothic splendor:

> But first, on earth as Vampire sent,
> Thy corpse shall from its tomb be rent:
> Then ghastly haunt thy native place,
> And suck the blood of all thy race:
> There from thy daughter, sister, wife,
> At midnight drain the stream of life;
> Yet loathe the banquet which perforce
>
> Must feed thy livid living corpse...
> Wet with thine own best blood shall drip
> Thy gnashing tooth and haggard lip;
> Then stalking to thy sullen grave
> Go—and with the Ghouls and Afrits rave;
> Till these in horror shrink away
> From spectre more accursed than they![30]

The poem was influenced by Greek traditions, which Byron knew very well. But it is easy to recognize in nineteenth-century superstitions pre-Christian myths, such as that of Cronus who, afraid that his children would rebel against him as he had himself turned on his own father, would devour his sons. Probably this ancient myth of Time devouring its own creation filtered through Christian thought and evolved into the myth of the vampire as a creature of hell, twice doomed to act against nature: to return from the grave and kill, but most abominable of all, to kill their own kin.

This theme is expressed in a real chiller, the short story "Wake Not the Dead!" attributed to Tieck. In this tale, which in a few pages manages to go through a whole catalog of vampire symbols, a rich nobleman, Walter, cannot get over the death of his young wife, Brunhilda. He is so obsessed with her that he asks a necromancer to bring her back to life. The transaction takes place and she returns, but at terrible cost. Brunhilda has become a vampire. She is also, horror of horrors, that stereotypical evil woman, a stepmother, and a very wicked one at that. Needing young blood to live, she eventually kills her stepchildren. She is a pseudomother with the legal status of a mother, but no maternal instincts to match. There is no real blood-link between her and her adopted offspring, and she has no compunction in killing them; instead, she berates her husband when he shows grief for their demise. It is an interesting use of that classic fairy tale motif, when the wicked stepmother goes out of her way to make her stepchildren's life a misery (for example, "Snow White," "Cinderella," "Hansel and Gretel").

In Polidori's story, the vampire takes his revenge against Aubrey by marrying his sister and killing her. The powerless brother, who had seen his innocent Greek beloved falling victim to the Vampyre, then became a helpless bystander to the doom of his own sister. The revenge was the more terrible, as it struck the innocent and the pure who, unable to read Ruthven's real nature, were incapable of protecting themselves—a motif which strongly marks vampire literature.

The link of blood was sacred and, in older times, it would seal the brotherhood of men. "Blood brothers" would carve a cross in their arms and mix the blood from their wounds. This was a symbol of faith and courage, but in folk tales, it created a bond which could defeat time and space. Often, in Romanian stories, two young men who sealed such a pact would thrust the two knives into the earth before taking different roads, each taking with them a handkerchief. If one of them noticed that the silk was torn or, if coming back, found one of the knives rusty, he knew that great misfortune had befallen his brother.

Sometimes this brotherhood could be one of opposites. In Norse mythology, Odin had sealed such a pact with Loki, who would later bring about Ragnarok or *Gütterdmmerung*, "the Twilight of the Gods." This is an image of duality, paradoxically uniting the principles of Creation and Destruction. The first is personified by Odin, the god who ordered Chaos and created the world, and the second by Loki, whose hatred and cunning brought disaster, and who killed Odin and nearly cast the world back into chaos.

Because blood creates such powerful links, pacts with the forces of the supernatural would be signed in it. We shall see how, at the core of the vampire legend, there is the ancient myth of the Pact, which appeared throughout history in connection with the image of the Magus, of witchcraft, and other recurrent themes. The symbolism of blood strengthened the communication between the human and the supernatural level: runes were colored in red as if painted in blood, which made them magically more powerful.

An interesting development of this theme in vampire literature is that, although they live on blood, the vampires (and their victims) are pale, as if they had none in their veins to color their features. However, their "waxen pallor" is an antithesis to their red lips and eyes, as if all their strength and life is concentrated into their eyes (the doors between the inner and the outside world) and their mouths (not only for the teeth that bite the victim, but also for the lips whose kisses bring both pleasure and death).

One of the ways of destroying a vampire is to cut off its head—symbol of the volition and the power of mind that hypnotizes the victim into total obedience—and to destroy its heart—not only because it pumps blood around the body, but also because it is associated with love and mercy. Bram Stoker emphasizes these symbols, perverted by the touch of evil, on the transformation that the count's victims, such as Lucy, have undergone, in a positive torrent of bloody symbolism and associated motifs: "The sweetness was turned to adamantine, heartless cruelty, and the purity to voluptuous wantonness ... the lips were crimson with fresh blood and the stream had trickled over her chin and stained the purity of her lawn death-robe .... Lucy's eyes unclean and full of hell-fire, instead of the pure orbs we knew."[31] This fragment of the novel has been quoted to emphasize how linguistic and symbolic allusions to blood have been employed by some of the leading writers of vampire literature to conjure up mental images that are positively soaked in it. Blood, punishing fire, devils, wantonness—the entire scenery of hell is used in this description of Lucy, the fallen angel.

The vampire story evolves around the symbolic connection between blood and life. But this is the reverse of the immortality of the soul that is achieved during Holy Communion, where Christ's blood represents eternal life and salvation. Polidori's "Vampyre," as well as Count Dracula and Carmilla, are our guides into a hellish, upside-down world, where virtues and values are twisted and reinterpreted in a dark and sinister key. Renfield in *Dracula,* with his statement that "the blood is the life," is considering this at the physical, not the spiritual, level, thereby shifting the accent from the soul to the body. He offers the key to the mystery, as his madness is a representation of the belief that life can be transmitted from one being to another through their blood. He is Count Dracula's crooked image (as in the novel he is also his servant), submissive and at the same time antagonistic: he calls him Master, but he is the one who, Judas-like, reveals his identity to his pursuers.

In vampire lore, blood is not simply the way to achieve eternal youth and strength, it is also a venom that brings not death, but perdition. Blood is associated with violence and sexuality, as opposed to life and love, in a game of illusions. The count looks younger, and when Lucy dies, she has a new, seductive beauty, unnatural for the dead. The women in the count's castle have "voluptuous lips" and their breath "sweet it was in one sense, honey-sweet, and sent the same tingling through the nerves as her voice, but with a bitter underlying the sweet, a bitter offensiveness, as one smells in blood."[32]

Blood is at the heart of vampirism. The uncontrollable desire experienced by the vampire to take the life force from another, and by doing so, allow them to continue their penumbral half-life, is the key motivation behind their actions. But just as the concept of vampirism is far too complex to be reduced to an examination of a few basic themes, so too is that of blood and its symbolic significance. Blood features as a symbol in legend, history, and literature in a number of different ways which we have examined in the course of this chapter. It is one of the classic motifs employed in vampire lore and literature, but it is, as we shall see, far from the only one.

NOTES

1. Genesis IV: 11.
2. Genesis XII: 13.
3. Leviticus I: 11.
4. Leviticus XVIII: 14.
5. Hebrews IX: 12–14.
6. John VI: 53–56.
7. Luke XXII: 19–20.
8. For further discussion, see for example, *Quest for the Eternal* by John Matthews.
9. *The Quest of the Holy Grail*, p. 277.
10. Matthews, p. 11.
11. In Mircea Eliade, Istoria ideilor si credintelor religioase, p. 55.
12. Ibid., p. 57.
13. Translation by Dan Dutescu.
14. Summers, p. 18.
15. Report in *Daily Telegraph,* Friday 18 July 2003.
16. Historia Ecclesiastiae, Basle, 1553.
17. Malory, Winchester manuscript.
18. Quoted in Ronay.
19. W. Shakespeare, *Macbeth,* I. 1. 3–4.
20. *Dracula,* p. 54.
21. W. Shakespeare, *Macbeth,* II. ii. 45–46.
22. Ibid., V. i. 50–53.
23. Oscar Wilde, p. 138.
24. See pp. 119–121.
25. BBC News website report, 23 December 2002.
26. *Dracula,* p. 53.
27. Florescu and McNally, p.123.
28. Lecouteux, p. 34.
29. The word *giaour* is a derogatory term for a Christian used by their Turkish enemies.
30. *The Works of Lord Byron*, p. 252.
31. *Dracula,* p. 218.
32. Ibid., p. 61.

CHAPTER 5

Landscapes of Magic

A most noble ruin, of immense size, and full of beautiful and romantic bits:
there is a legend that a white lady is seen in one of the windows.
—Bram Stoker, *Dracula*

There are some landscapes which resonate of things supernatural: the mysterious moor, shrouded in enveloping blankets of fog, or the forests, thick with trees that, as night advances, appear to become almost human, with long fingers waiting to grasp the unwary traveler. Or it could be the towering mountains, so high that they seem to touch the sky itself, and in some traditions, represent the home of the gods. There are also some regions, such as Transylvania, setting for Stoker's *Dracula*, and Styria, where Le Fanu sets *Carmilla*, which seem to have about them a sinister, menacing aura, particularly when the audience only knows of them through the images that others have painted in their minds. Such landscapes of horror play a great part in encouraging the reader to set out on a journey, the ultimate destination of which is terror itself.

The initial setting of the earliest folk vampire legends was the village churchyard, where the undead slept unquietly. They needed both their coffin and the nightly "company" of living people to suck their blood. The vampire myth is the more powerful as it is closely linked to the community which it threatens. Later developments enlarged the landscape of the undead, which came to include wild places such as the mountains, the forests, and the heath on a vampire's short list of preferences. At first sight, the reasons for this choice are not clear. Why is Dracula's castle isolated in the mountains? Or why are the ruins of Carmilla's château at the heart of a thick, untrodden forest?

Nature, untamed and unsubdued by man, has always been enthralling. The mystery of the wilderness was associated particularly with the dangers which it concealed, in the form of beasts and monsters. Nature has always had a dual power; threatening and dangerous, on the one hand, and protective for man, beast and spirit, on the other. Folklore all over the world populates forests with supernatural beings, from the oldest legends of the ancients, to modern epics such as Tolkien's *The Lord of the Rings* and Rowling's *Harry Potter* series. For centuries, man coexisted with nature, which significantly influenced his existence and his thinking. Civilization has estranged the two, causing man to drift away from his origins. As humans started to lose their roots, the untamed landscape became the enemy, the unknown, but it still continues to exercise an attraction as something man used to "belong" to. The lore preserves the collective memory of times when the human being was strongly linked to it, and songs, spells, and invocations were ways of achieving harmony with the world.

Mountains, for example, had a very special place in all religions: *axis mundi,* the link between the earth and the sky, between man and divinity. The Greek gods lived on Mount Olympus, where they could watch the affairs of the world while staying aloof from them, where the sky met the earth. Different faiths around the world give mountains a huge symbolic significance, particularly connected to the place where the sacred reveals itself to humanity. Moses climbed Mount Sinai where he talked face-to-face with God and received the Ten Commandments. Elijah held his competition with the priests of Baal in which he demonstrated the superiority of Jehovah on top of Mount Carmel.[1] Even Jesus is tempted by Satan on a mountain.

To Buddhists, Everest personifies Chomolungma, the mother of the world. Prayers are offered to her by those aspiring to climb to the top. There are still taboos attached to the mountain; sexual immorality there is deemed to anger the goddess, and she will punish those who sin against her. Anyone climbing to the summits of hills and mountains of Buddhist countries will still find them home to *ovoos,* large cairns, where offerings to the gods are left. The mountains, inaccessible as they are, can also protect the creatures of the supernatural against the curiosity of human beings. They are sources of wealth, too, as they hide gold, silver, and other metals. Legends were born about the mysterious defenders of this wealth, such as the Spriggans in Cornish tradition, thought to be ghosts of giants guarding the treasures hidden under prehistoric stones.

A similar tradition is used by Stoker in order to paint Transylvania as a land of the supernatural. On the way to Dracula's castle, Jonathan notices that the driver of the caleche repeatedly stops to mark the places where he finds "a faint flickering blue flame." Later, the count would explain to his English visitor that, once a year on St. George's night, when evil spirits visited the earth, blue flames would burn where treasures had been hidden. For Stoker, this is only a literary device, meant to create an eerie atmosphere around the castle of the count which would hint at the menaces of that far-off land to the British reader. The blue flame, interestingly enough, is sometimes found in folklore as a representation of the human soul.[2]

Le Fanu sets *Carmilla* in a *schloss* "on a slight eminence in a forest." Stoker goes even further, placing Dracula's castle in the Carpathians, which he represents as a threatening though beautiful place, inspiring awe and fear. The sights have both the majesty and menace of all places where the wilderness has not been reordered by human hand. There

rose the mighty slopes of forest up to the lofty steeps of the Carpathians themselves. Right and left to us they towered, with the afternoon sun falling full upon them and bringing out all the glorious colours of this beautiful range, deep blue and purple in the shadows of the peaks, green and brown where grass and rock mingled, and an endless perspective of jagged rock and pointed crags, till these were themselves lost in the distance, where the snowy peaks rose grandly.[3]

It is a device frequently used. In the story, "Wake Not the Dead!" Walter takes his resurrected bride to his castle in the mountains. Although presaging Stoker's novel by 70 years, the setting— "the castle ... was situated on a rock between other rocks rising up above it" —paints a mental image eerily similar to that created by the later author.[4] Another story, "A Kiss of Judas," virtually contemporary with *Dracula* (the former was republished in 1894, the latter appeared in 1897), was written by Julian Osgood Field, an acquaintance of Stoker. Here the similarities are even more striking, with the setting a mysterious castle in the Moldavian "Karpaks" (Carpathians), on the other side of the Transylvanian Carpathians where Stoker sets his tale.

Forests, too, have also always been regarded as magical places, as the realm of the supernatural which, unbowed by the profane order of the human mind, has preserved its magic. A journey in the forest is full of perils and strangeness: "The pine woods that seemed in the darkness to be closing upon us, great masses of grayness, which here and there bestrewed the trees, produced a peculiarly weird and solemn effect, which carried on the thoughts and grim fancies."[5] They are opposed to the cultivated plots of land representing the triumph of human order. The forest cannot be mapped, therefore it remains a space that mortal man is unable to possess.

Forests appear frequently as borderlands between the world of mortal man and the supernatural. In *The Mabinogion*, Peredur (Perceval) crosses the "great tangled forest where he saw the tracks of neither man nor herds, only thickets and vegetation,"[6] encountering several adventures. The implication is that this is a place of nature in a state of uncontrolled and

uncontrollable abandon, where man and his "herds" —nature tamed—
have no place. It is a space not of this world: in a passage full of hidden
meaning, the flawed Lancelot is unable to drink from the Holy Grail but
can only watch in a state of paralysis while other more holy men do so.
Blinded by his sinful nature, he wanders aimlessly through the woods
on his doomed quest to find the grail, where he "took up his pursuit
through the thick of the forest, keeping to neither track nor path, but following where fortune led. The darkness of the night served him ill, for he
could make out nothing, either near or far, by which to steer his course.
Notwithstanding, he came at last to a stone cross which stood on a lonely
heath at the parting of two ways." Nearby, there is a chapel, which he
finds "abandoned and ruinous." It is a symbolic landscape reminiscent of
those successfully mined as a source of terror in vampire literature.[7]

The forest can be a sinister space of darkness and all that is born from it,
whether real or imagined. Entrance is granted only to the initiated, those
who know the truths of nature in all its forms, visible or not. Here the
druids had their sacred groves, hidden from the eyes of ordinary mortals.
This idea survives in different guises, even today, where in contemporary
illustrations of this belief, such as the *Harry Potter* series, only fully fledged
wizards can enter the forbidden forest. By its very name, the woods forbid
access into the labyrinth. The motif is universal. To the Ashanti of West
Africa, the forest is a place of spirits where it is dangerous for mortals to
venture out alone. Only the priest would go there. The vampire myth uses
the same pattern of thought; this is a realm where life and death escape
human rules.

The Europe of open lands that we see today is very different from old
landscapes covered by thick woods, inhabited both by beasts and by
supernatural entities (and in some beliefs, the two categories were synonymous, e.g., the werewolf), good or evil. Forests were not the farmed
and controlled places they often are in some areas now (and perhaps the
cultivation of forests has led to a loss of symbolism). They were once on
a huge scale. In Arthurian literature, it can take days for knights to cross
them. A hermit warns Lancelot about the forest which was "more treacherous than any [Lancelot] had known, [where] he could lose his way and
wander many days without finding a soul to help him," as it was "vast
and labyrinthine in its depths; a knight can ride a whole day long and
never find a house or refuge."[8]

The symbolic counterpart of the forest is the labyrinth, dwelling of mythological bloodthirsty monsters. Heroes of the ancients, such as Theseus,
had the courage to enter to kill the monster inside and save the entire community from it. Fairy tales follow this pattern of good fighting against evil
in the maze, as many of them make their heroes battle against the fabulous
creatures of the forest. The forest, like the labyrinth, is especially threatening because it creates a fear that, once lost within it, the victim will never
be able to escape. And this fear of perpetual entrapment is at the core

of effective vampire tales. The victims of vampires are normally urbane, "civilized" people, unaware of the dangers they are facing in the forest, where the creatures of a supernatural world hold sway. In Coppola's film, sleepwalking Lucy is lured by the vampire into a maze. Mina, following her, becomes lost, and her struggle to find the path only increases the terror that would culminate in her finding Lucy as she is being seduced by a werewolf-like monster. The labyrinth becomes the place of lost souls, as well as lost paths.

In literature, the forest often becomes the preserve of the vampire, so that in Polidori's "Vampyre," the young lord Aubrey is warned "not to return [from his journey] at night, as he must necessarily pass through a wood where no Greek would ever remain, after the day has closed, on any consideration" for this is the realm of the undead.[9] And it is here that the heroine Ianthe meets her doom. Stoker also used such a backdrop in *Dracula's Guest.* This reaches its conclusion in the midst of "a great mass of trees, chiefly yew and cypress." The "victim," Jonathan Harker, who barely manages to escape with his life, comes across a deserted village and finds himself in the graveyard. His eye is taken by one particular tomb:

I approached the sepulchre to see what it was, and why such a thing stood alone in such a place. I walked around it, and read, over the Doric door, in German –

COUNTESS DOLINGEN OF GRATZ IN STYRIA SOUGHT AND FOUND DEATH, 1801

On top of the tomb, seemingly driven through the solid marble—for the structure was composed of a few vast blocks of stone—was a great iron spike or stake. On going to the back I saw, graven in great Russian letters:

THE DEAD TRAVEL FAST.[10]

These are eerie—even dangerous—places, jealously defending their secrets and trapping the wanderers, like the Old Forest in Tolkien's novel, with trees that moved, hiding the path, and leading the traveler without escape towards the wood's heart of danger: "The Forest is queer. Everything in it is very much more alive, more aware of what is going on, so to speak, than things are in the Shire. And the trees do not like strangers. They watch you."[11]

The trees themselves have legends. The oak was considered sacred by the Celtic druids; the magical mistletoe which grows on its branches was a sacred symbol to the Celts, who would cut it only with a gold knife and then only on special days. Druids ate acorns before making prophecies, and Zeus's temple at Dodona was in an oak wood where the priestesses foretold the future by interpreting the rustle of the leaves. It was also supposed to give protection from lightning, and the Germanic people associated the oak with the god of thunder, Thor, and planted them around their assembly places. For Scandinavians, the oak was a symbol of sacrifice and rebirth, a theme recurrent in vampire stories. The myth tells that the god Balder was slain with a mistletoe arrow by the evil god Loki. Odin tried to bring Balder back from the realm of the dead, and the goddess Hel agreed to release him if all things on earth wept for his death. This could not happen, because Loki, disguised as a Giantess, refused to do so. The myth was preserved in pagan tradition which celebrates Balder, and all beings would lament his death in order for spring to return to the world. Just to carry an acorn in one's pocket helped preserve youth. Oak was used as a protection against evil powers—oak leaves to transfix lions, the ashes of burnt oak wood would protect the crops from disease, and arrows made of it would keep snakes away.

Hazel cut on St. John's Eve was used in the search for treasure. In making divining rods, a special ritual was to be respected. If they were indeed to be magical, they had to be made at so-called magical moments, on St. John's Day, the Epiphany, Good Friday, or Shrove Tuesday. It is interesting to note that this "pagan" rite was associated with sacred days of the Christian calendar, which hints at an older significance of these days. They could also be made on the first night of the new moon. The hazel had to be cut while facing east, from the eastern side of the tree, and then presented to the rising sun. For the making of magical wands, it was obligatory (in Hebrew traditions) to cut a "virgin" branch, a young one with no other branches grown on it. We have already discussed the importance of purity in much that is connected to the occult, and the importance that it has in the vampire myth.

The willow was the symbol of grief and lost love. But in ancient Greece, it had an erotic symbolism: "There are contradictory reports about the role of the willow in the cult of Asclepius, the ancient god of healing. It was the custom in Athens, during the fertility festival of the Thesmophoriae to place willow branches in women's beds, supposedly to ward off snakes (but perhaps in truth to attract serpentine fertility demons)."[12] The image of the demon crawling into a woman's bed is not very dissimilar to that of the vampire, especially in literature and movies. Willow is also connected to the realm of death, as a symbol of Persephone, the Greek goddess kidnapped by Hades and taken to the Inferno where she would spend half of the year, returning to her mother, Demeter, for the other half—a symbol of the rebirth of nature and of trespassing on the frontiers of death. In Ireland, willow is thought to protect against enchantment. In China, willow branches were laid on top of coffins as a symbol of immortality.

Juniper was particularly useful; the smoke from branches of the tree set ablaze during epidemics was thought to drive away demons. Rowan protected against witchcraft, and in Wales it is thought that the cross on which Christ was crucified was made of rowan. So it was planted in cemeteries, mostly to keep the restless dead inside their graves. Most resonant of all was the yew, a symbol of life; it could live for a thousand years or more and is, therefore, frequently found around cemeteries. Its branches were used to line the graves of the dead. The ash is particularly connected to vampirism, as from its wood the stake that destroys a vampire is often made—hawthorn and maple wood are also used for this purpose.

But what is more interesting in the context of this book is the way vampires became associated with the woods, where they take shelter and gather strength before they appear in the civilized world. The deserted castle of Le Fanu's heroine, Carmilla, is hidden in the depths of a thick forest, a place hardly ever visited by any living soul. Most impressive of all is the ostentatious description in *Dracula*, where all the elements that could induce terror are used to a maximum: the black pinewoods foretelling disaster with every breath of wind, the strange noises, the blue flames, the tunnel-like paths which lead through the maze of the forest toward its dark heart, where lies the doomed castle. Once again, the forest becomes the labyrinth, where the heroes have to fight their way through to destroy the monster hiding at its heart. Jonathan's description of the road to the castle has all the elements of a nightmare. The strange reaction of the people hearing about his destination is a hint of what is to follow, and is meant to create a sum of dreadful expectations for the reader.

Other literary devices add to the effect. The caleche that meets Jonathan has a fairy tale quality, reminding the reader of the age-old fight between good and evil. The black horses increase the oppressive atmosphere, already shaped by the landscape and the dark allusions to the master of the castle. They follow a side road, deep into the woods, into the great Unknown. The forest sends all its menacing messengers to meet them: snow, howling winds, fierce wolves, and even the strange "flickering blue flames" that are thought to be signs of hidden treasures, but are also evil devices to make unwary travelers lose their way. Jonathan notices that they are going in circles—the whirlpool becomes a fantastic maelstrom,[13] and the character, together with the reader, plunges into the realm of nightmare—a descent into our own deepest fears. There are also images of tunnel-like tree arches like a bleak entrance into another world, and hellish precipices that make their way a road to perdition for the soul and the mind.

Jonathan's first journey is almost a disaster, as he is unaware of the dangers that hide in the depths of the forest. But at the end of the novel, the heroes again follow the count into the symbolic maze. But now they are armed with the knowledge of how to defeat their enemy, and they win the final victory. The Victorian melodrama follows an essential pattern of human thought.

The heath and the moor are also places of mystery, where nature rules and man's presence is at the sufferance of a stronger power. Macbeth meets the three witches on the heath. And the star of *The Hound of the Baskervilles* is really Dartmoor, the brooding presence which is never far away, as for example when Dr. Watson looks at it: "I... looked out from my window. It opened upon the grassy space which lay in front of the hall door. Beyond, two copses of trees moaned and swung in a rising wind.

A half moon broke through the rifts of racing clouds. In its cold light I saw beyond the trees a broken fringe of rocks, and the long, low curve of the melancholy moor."[14]

This is a wild, untamed place, where the apparent gentle nature of the terrain might hide bottomless mires which suck the unwary to their doom. The gentle calm of a summer's day can turn into the blast of a blizzard with little warning. It is a place that both attracts by its semi-tamed wildness and horrifies by the barely hidden dangers that lurk there—a good geographical analogy for vampire literature and lore.

The vampire story feels at home in such desolate, large, untamed places, which became wastelands as the undead haunt them. The villages are as deserted as the large open space around them in these realms suspended between a remembrance of life and the overwhelming presence of the dead. Alexis Tolstoy's description of a vampire epidemic in a village in Serbia resembles one of a wasteland: the place was "deserted. No lights shone through the windows, no songs were being sung. I rode past many houses that I knew, all as silent as the grave."[15]

In "Wake Not the Dead!" the deadly presence of Brunhilda transforms the entire human and spiritual geography of a place into a desert of dread, an apocalyptic realm of wasted life:

Thus did the castle assume a more desolate appearance; daily did its environs become more deserted; none but a few aged decrepit old women and grey-headed menials were to be seen remaining of the once numerous retinue. Such will in the latter days of the earth, be the last generation of mortals, when childbearing shall have ceased, when youth shall no more be seen, nor any arise to replace those who shall await their fate in silence.[16]

These powerful images haunt our imagination and our souls. Such deserted places inspire tales of fear, and they grow from legend into some of the masterpieces of literature. They are symbolic as well as physical wastelands, where evil spirits predominate and the atmosphere is one of decay, desolation, and death—metaphors for vampirism. These upside down realms spread their shadows into other forms of literature. In *The Lord of the Rings*, the Dead Marshes are visited by no one, elves, orcs, or humans. The only inhabitants are the bodies of the dead. But these bodies do not decay and they still have a residual spiritual force, allowing them to exercise an almost fatal hypnotic influence over Frodo. They are evil beings who entrance him into the water where he nearly loses his life and his soul. This wasteland is the home of creatures not that different from vampires—although physically dead, their bodies show no signs of decay, and they have the ability to control the minds of the living and lure them into a terrible half-life for eternity.

Dark, too, are the tones in which J.R.R. Tolkien describes the realm of Sauron and the lands around it, like images of supreme doom:

Dreadful as the Dead Marshes had been, and the arid moors of the Noman-lands, more loathsome far was the country that the crawling day now slowly unveiled…here no spring nor summer would ever come again. Here nothing lived, not even the leprous growth that fed on rottenness. …a land defiled, dis-eased beyond all healing—unless the Great Sea should enter in and wash it into oblivion. [17]

The image of death and corruption of life is so acute that it influences not only the people and the other living beings, but also the landscape and the atmosphere. This is in the same spirit as the vampire story. Sauron is a vampire-like being—he corrupts elves into orcs, changing them into foul creatures under his evil control. In his land there is no sun, no warmth, no vegetation, only a permanent winter of death.

In classic English fairy tales, such as *Childe Rowland*, moorland is associated with the realm of the spirits who kidnap humans and hold them prisoners in a state which is neither alive nor dead, much like the vam-pires who lure their victims into their world of doom. Childe Rowland's sister, Burd Helen, tries to retrieve a ball thrown into the churchyard: "So, as Burd Helen ran the nearest way to get it, she ran contrary to the sun's course, and the light, shining full on her face, sent her shadow behind her. Thus that happened which will happen at times when folk forget and run widdershins, that is against the light, so that their shadows are out of sight and cannot be taken care of properly."[18]

So Burd Helen is kidnapped by the King of Elfland and taken to his Dark Tower. The indirect warning of the storyteller is very interesting, as it derives from the ancient idea that a person's shadow retains some of their spirit, but it can pass over the boundaries between the world of the living and the realm of the dead. Thus, the "shadows of the dead" can find their way back, but a living person, too, can fall under the power of darkness if their shadow is stolen. This reflects Eastern and Central European legends that tell of people whose shadow has been stolen in a sacrifice ritual who will die soon afterwards. In the context of vampirism, this belief is reflected in the way in which the vampire does not have a shadow, because it is not in the true sense of the word alive.

With Merlin's help, Childe Rowland enters the Land of Faery, depicted as a "wide moorland" haunted by ghastly apparitions such as wild horses with eyes "like coals of fire" and cows with "fiery eyes." Finally, Row-land arrives at the Dark Tower, whose gates open only if he goes around it widdershins while he utters a magic formula. There he finds his sister bewitched; when she speaks to him "her voice came like the voice of the dead." To release her from the spell, he decapitates her, much as vampires are decapitated in order to deliver them from damnation and offer them eternal rest. In the story, Burd Helen does not die, because it is only her en-chanted image that is before him. Similarly, destroying a vampire means allowing the soul to obtain everlasting life.

This inspired one of Robert Browning's nightmarish poems, "Childe Roland to the Dark Tower Came," another description of a land of darkness, dominated by images of death and ghostly apparitions, where the hero of the quest finds "failure in its scope." He follows the road indicated by a crippled man of evil appearance, which takes him off the safe path into a grey plain of "starved ignoble nature" and of imprisoned spirits. It is a demonic land, where he finds signs of battle, torture, decay, and death. Before the Dark Tower, he sees all the dead knights who had failed in their quest:

> There they stood, ranged along the hillsides, met
> To view the last of me, a living frame
> For one more picture: in a sheet of flame
> I saw them all and I knew them all.

Just as the wasteland provides a powerful backdrop for vampire tales, so too do crossroads. To reach Dracula's castle, Jonathan Harker travels towards the "extreme east of the country, just on the border of three states, Transylvania, Moldavia and Bukovina, in the midst of the Carpathian mountains; one of the wildest and least known portions of Europe";[19] the crossroads between three countries. There are many superstitions linked to the place where roads meet. They are often thought of as symbolizing points of intersection between the path of the living and that of the dead. It was believed that pursuing spirits (including vampires) halt at crossroads, as they are uncertain which way they should proceed. Suicides and others who cannot be buried in consecrated ground are interred at crossroads, sometimes with stakes through their hearts. They were often places of judgment and death, where gallows were erected. Certain residents of Abruzzi in Italy were believed to have the power to stand at a crossroads and see the spirits passing, though little good it did them as they invariably went mad. And in a story from Dorset, a ghostly coffin is still said to appear in the road at Wimborne. In the coffin is the corpse of a suicide who was buried at a crossroads with a stake through his heart. To add to the ritual significance of the place, it is also at the boundary between two parishes.[20]

Hecate, the goddess of the Underworld, the land of the dead, was also associated with magic and enchantments. She had power over demonic creatures whom she sent to earth to torment mortals. Hecate haunted places like cemeteries, scenes of crimes or, more frequently, crossroads, demonstrating a very old link between death and such places. Her image as a three-faced goddess appeared on columns at crossroads, where offerings were brought on the eve of the full moon. This theme can also be found in vampire literature where, for example, in one of the hunts for the creatures in *Varney the Vampyre*, we find out that "a vampyre is quite as secure buried in a cross-road with a stake through his body, as if you burned it in all the fires in the world."[21]

Crossroads are also referred to in "Wake Not the Dead!" The sorcerer who gives life to the vampiric Brunhilda also offers to help should the young lord ever regret his decision. Walter, horrified by what he has done, seeks his advice again: "Just then the full moon darted from beneath the bustling clouds; and the sight recalled to his remembrance the advice of the sorcerer, when he trembled at the first apparition of Brunhilda rising from her sleep of death; namely, to seek him, at the season of the full moon, in the mountains, where three roads met. Scarcely had this gleam of hope broke in on his bewildered mind, than he flew to the appointed spot."[22] The combination of the haunting presence of the full moon, the untamed wildness of the mountains, and the mystical power of the crossroads paints a backdrop of horror that hints effectively at the presence of the supernatural.

For Jonathan Harker in *Dracula*, the crossroads is the point where his journey into the frightening world of the undead begins. The border he has to cross is not just between two countries or civilizations. It is the frontier between the civilized world and the wilderness, between reason and darkness, and most importantly, between reality and imagination. Stoker chose to locate Dracula's castle at a place where historically none exists. The author may have a special purpose in this: to hint that the book itself is a border that opens our way into a world of our own fears, where appearances are deceiving and imagination opens a way that is both amazing and perilous.

Man-made edifices can also provide the setting for vampire stories. One such example is the ruined, deserted castle. The romantic "Byronic" vampire is of noble blood, descendant of an old, aristocratic family—an image much more appealing to the nouveaux riches of the Victorian age than the simple peasant or the clerk. The castle provides a suitably romantic and aristocratic backdrop, and the fact that it is often decaying is a symbolic connection to the undead state of the vampire. Count Dracula's castle conjures up powerful and atmospheric images, with its great passages and winding stairs: "We saw it in all its grandeur, perched a thousand feet on the summit of a sheer precipice, and with seemingly a great gap between it and the adjacent mountain on any side. There was something uncanny and wild about the place."[23] It seems suspended between the mountain and the sky, an unearthly apparition.

There is one particularly significant literary device that Stoker uses: all the descriptions are made by the characters, so the castle is always seen through a screen of fear and horror. And yet a sense of greatness and beauty is always present, a sign that there is more than darkness and hopelessness in the story of Count Dracula. The castle is not described in thorough detail which makes it fit the general pattern of a medieval castle in the imagination of the reader. It is located high on a mountain, on the margin of a precipice (and of reality), which makes it difficult to conquer. Its thick stone walls offer protection to those living there against invaders' attacks, although in the novel, this place of refuge turns into a dangerous trap.

The description of the interior swings between images of richness and of decrepitude. "The table service is of gold, and so beautifully wrought that it must be of immense value."[24] The priceless tapestries and upholstery, though centuries old, are in "excellent order," unlike the "frayed and moth-rotten" ones in museums. Time seems to stand still in Dracula's castle—the first in a series of illusions on which the whole book is constructed, a novel built on a skeleton of phantasms. These lavish areas only increase the sensation of decay and death in the rooms where Jonathan discovers Dracula's coffins. The sense of oppression is emphasized by the multitude of doors that hint at freedom yet are locked. The whole place appears to be full of almost obsessive menacing secrets: "Doors, doors, doors everywhere, and all locked and bolted!"[25] – another image of the labyrinth, which offers no key to its mystery and allows no escape.

The castle seems to be alive, it "is old, and it has many memories,"[26] says the count. It is not just a witness to history, it is a concentrated representation of the country itself, a mirror image of its violent past. Dracula says that his ancestor was Attila, and speaks of the blood his forefathers shed in terrible battles. The element of duality is present on several levels. There is an antithesis between the violent but proud past of a conquering race and the present. The apparent peacefulness of the wing that Jonathan recklessly visits hides unexpected perils. Within the castle walls, contradictory emotions exist. They inspire fantasies of domesticity in Jonathan, of women of a long-forgotten past that he imagines, when "old ladies had sat and sung and lived sweet lives while their gentle breasts were sad for their menfolk away in the midst of the remorseless war,"[27] while also protecting the three voluptuous women-vampires that are ready to kill him to drink his blood.

All these authorial devices take the book beyond a game of illusion and reality, forcing its limits to the frontier between sanity and madness, between life and death, all in an ingeniously built nightmarish atmosphere, somewhere in a strange, exotic, and frightening land. It is important to understand that what Stoker is doing here is to create a totally convincing setting for his story, imbued with layer upon layer of detail, which accumulates to create a menacing backdrop that inspires fear in the reader. The old castle, unique and solitary, separate from all that is common and ordinary, witness to the secrets of generations which are kept alive in its memories of traditions otherwise dead, is a powerful motif. And when all human life becomes extinct, it is only the dead and their existence imprinted in the ruined walls and in the decrepit furniture who survive. The isolation of the castle makes it impossible for the victims of the undead to ask for help, a strong psychological device in vampire stories. The idea proved to function well, and it was borrowed in much more recent versions of the vampire myth. In *Interview with the Vampire*, for example, the story begins in a sumptuous mansion in the American South, a space of dark magic and frightening practices, set on a plantation where the slaves use voodoo and black magic.

Another man-made setting is perhaps an even more powerful stimulant of fear: the decaying church. This is a favorite of vampire writers. We have referred elsewhere to the deserted churchyard in "Dracula's Guest," for example. If a church is still being used for the glory of God, then it is as powerful a protection in many works of vampire literature as it is possible to get. In the "Family of the Vourdalak," for example, the main character is implicitly safe when he is at the Monastery of Our Lady of the Oak, but is in danger as soon as he leaves. But if a church is ruined and in decay, then it is as if it has been abandoned even by God, and the forces of evil are therefore supremely powerful there.

The description of the environs in *Carmilla* is full of romantic elements foretelling disaster. "A ruined village, with its quaint little church, now roofless, in the aisle of which are the mouldering tombs of the proud family of Karnstein, now extinct, who once owned the equally desolate château which, in the thick of the forest, overlooks the silent ruins of the town."[28] The image of this deserted place of God is enough to send shivers down the spine of any Christian. The conclusion of *Carmilla* takes place in this church, a place once holy, now profaned, once alive and vibrant, now decaying, as it ekes out its remaining days towards an inevitable death. The language is evocative of decline, gloom, and mortality; in short, a perfect setting for a vampire story:

In this solitude, having just listened to so strange a story, connected, as it was, with the great and titled dead, whose monuments were mouldering among the dust and ivy around us, and every incident of which bore so awfully upon my own mysterious case—in this haunted spot, darkened by the towering foliage that rose on every side, dense and high above its noiseless walls—a horror began to steal over me, and my heart sank as I thought that my friends were, after all, now about to enter and disturb this triste and ominous scene.[29]

It was another masterstroke to set part of *Dracula* in Whitby, a place dominated by a ruined abbey, the same symbol of (Christian) decline and decay. Such places exercised a great fascination among nineteenth-century romanticists, evidenced perhaps most powerfully by the paintings of Turner, who fully appreciated the symbolic resonances of sites such as the Cistercian abbey at Tintern. Writers such as Sir Walter Scott, too, saw the power to thrill their readers by references to such places. In *Marmion*, he refers to a legend in which a nun is bricked up alive in the walls of an abbey when she tries to flee with her lover. The abbey in question is Whitby, and Stoker is quick to refer his readers to the legend in *Dracula*. This story of forbidden love and divine punishment adds to the atmosphere of fear and melancholy of the place, something that Stoker mines well in his novel.

We have referred many times to the fact that vampire mythology continues to evolve. Dracula is the more threatening as he leaves his castle for the glamour and elegance of Victorian London. In *Interview with the Vampire*, the search for fellow vampires proves useless as long as Louis and Claudia follow the classical itinerary of vampirism, visiting places such as Transylvania. Instead, the vampires turn out at the very heart of the civilized world: Paris, the City of Light. The climax of the storyline takes place in Los Angeles, ironically, when we consider the significance of the name of the place. The city of angels becomes a vampires' favorite landscape in *Buffy*, too. Here, Angel, the demon with a story of doom and resurrection, tries to fight off vampires.

In *Buffy the Vampire Slayer*, the world of the vampires is threateningly close to the world of the audience, as the action is much more likely to take place in a dark urban alley or a building site at night than in an old castle or church. The technique is highly efficient; it is one thing to believe that some region at the end of the world may be the home of monsters, and quite another to discover that your high school is infested with vampires who are extremely likely to attack you in your campus dormitory.

These are images and mechanisms frequently used to create a fictional landscape of fear. The themes of death and decay, of love and passion, of the quest against the darkness, have the same power over the mind in all their manifestations. The vampire feeds on the blood of our own fears and frustrations. He exists where there is a place for him, a mental realm of darkness and wilderness, places where men metaphorically, as well as physically, fear to tread.

NOTES

1. I Kings, 17.
2. See Barber, p. 70.
3. *Dracula*, p. 33.
4. The story is reprinted in full in *Vampyres;* quote is from p. 172 of this book.
5. *Dracula*, p. 34.
6. *The Mabinogion*, p. 228.
7. *The Quest of the Holy Grail*, pp. 81–82.
8. Ibid., pp. 160–161.
9. *Great Vampire Stories*, p. 28.
10. In Frayling, p. 358.
11. J.R.R. Tolkien, *The Fellowship of the Ring*, pp. 145–146.
12. *Wordsworth Dictionary of Symbolism* under "Willow."
13. In Edgar Allan Poe's "A Descent into the Maelstrom," the hero miraculously escapes from the terrifying whirlpool and, just like Jonathan Harker, his black hair turns completely white.
14. Doyle, p. 51.

15. In Frayling, p. 273.
16. Ibid., p. 178.
17. Tolkien, *The Two Towers*, p. 293.
18. In *English Fairy Tales*, p. 197.
19. *Dracula*, p. 27.
20. *Mysterious Dorset*, p. 23.
21. In Frayling, p. 158.
22. Ibid., p. 183.
23. *Dracula*, p. 363.
24. Ibid., p. 44.
25. Ibid., p. 51.
26. Ibid., p. 57.
27. Ibid., p. 60.
28. *Carmilla*, p. 3.
29. Ibid., p. 84.

CHAPTER 6

Times of Magic

Midnight till one belongs to the dead: Good Lord, deliver us!
> —John Carpenter, *The Fog*

Human life is trapped inside a strange paradox created around the concept of Time as an essential dimension of existence. There are two aspects of temporality closely connected to the vampire myth. One is the destructive power of passing time, which is mirrored in the obsession with youth and strength. The other is the sacred value of certain moments which make contact between our world and that of the supernatural possible.

The first is most fascinatingly illustrated by the Greek myth of Cronus, the embodiment of Time, devouring his own children, his own creation. Although the individual cannot exist outside it, Time is perceived as a force of universal destruction, crushing everything that comes within its power. The unstoppable flow of time is one of the most oppressive images to haunt human imagination, like the temporal wastelands that feature so heavily in Salvador Dali's pictures. Regulated by the planetary movements, by the succession of day and night, by the hours and minutes slowly filtered by the clock, time is a reminder of our mortality and ephemeral existence. Time is a final frontier. The black figure of death imposes its rule and its boundaries over human life.

Time destroys and disfigures, bringing not only death, but also decrepitude, illness, weakness. "For there is such a little time that your youth will last—such little time…. But we never get back our youth. The pulse of joy that beats in us at twenty, becomes sluggish. Our limbs fail, our senses rot. We degenerate into hideous puppets, haunted by the memory of the passions of which we were too much afraid, and the exquisite temptations that we had not the courage to yield to. Youth! Youth! There is absolutely nothing in the world but youth!"[1] More than an artistic statement, this is one idea to which man, frightened by his own mortality, has always tried to find a solution.

Wilde's *The Picture of Dorian Gray* has, as its central theme, the halting of the inexorable march of time. But this theme is also a core part of the vampire myth. The unnatural state of vampires means that they not only deny death, they also contradict the normal rules of aging. Their diet of blood enables them to retain youth and vigor. Carmilla, despite the fact that she "died" and was buried several hundred years previously, still looks like a beautiful young woman. It is the blood of young victims that enables her to defy the laws of nature. Such beliefs were the key motivation of the real-life vampire, Countess Bathory, who used to kill young girls and bathe in their blood[2] because she believed that doing so would preserve her once famous beauty.

The halting of time, the reversal of its normal rules, is a core part of the vampire legend, in which death and physical decline is arrested. Stereotypical literary vampires are handsome or beautiful, virile, full of strength and, apparently, at the peak of their physical powers. When Dracula drinks blood, he visibly gets younger while his victims decline, because their life force has been transferred to him, something forcefully brought out by Coppola in *Bram Stoker's Dracula*. There is a gruesome parallel of this belief found in the cases we have already discussed when frightened villagers dug up the corpses of possible vampires in their local cemeteries. What they were looking for was evidence that the process of decline in death as opposed to life had been arrested. Many of the legends related to the vampire epidemics describe the preservation of the dead body as a clear sign of being undead. In some, such as that of Paole referred to earlier, some corpses actually look healthier dead than they did when they were alive. The lack of deterioration is a clear signal to the onlooker that the normal rules of nature (as they perceive them) and the passage of time, in death as well as in life, have been reversed, and that what they are looking at is therefore unnatural, that is, a vampire.

Some of the oldest known systems of thought from all over the world, from Sumerian myths to Egyptian religious beliefs, from early China to ancient Greece, attached a deep significance to the concept of time, which became manifested primarily in the establishing of fixed dates for religious celebrations and festivities. Symbolically connected to the rhythms of nature, which yields to death every winter and is restored every spring, some moments had magical significance and then the flow of time could be suspended. This periodic revival of the vegetation hinted at the possibility that death was not the end, but merely a passage to another level of existence. "Time is neither homogenous, nor continuous for the religious man. There are intervals of sacred Time, as for example during celebrations (most of them periodical ones), and, on the other hand, profane Time, the usual periodical duration, which includes all those acts which lack religious significance. Between these two types, there is of course a breach, but, through rites, religious man can "pass" easily from the profane dimension into sacred Time."[3]

This is why certain moments represent a breach of the flow of time, when the laws of everyday life are abolished, or at least suspended. Even today, these are usually connected to religious celebrations: Christmas, Easter, Hanukkah, Ramadan come to mind. There are others, too, with less obvious religious meaning, but still essentially a "special time": the New Year, the solstices, the equinoxes. These latter have represented, ever since man became conscious of the regularity of the movement of the planets and stars, moments full of significance. And they still continue to play a part in our world.

Different forms of ritual have grown around these "moments of sacredness," as they became the center of varied beliefs in each culture. What they had in common was the fact that they marked a dissolution of the borders between man and deities, between the physical world and the realm of the spirits. One of the most important aspects of religious celebrations all over the world is represented by the "Days of the Dead," periods when rituals had to be performed in order to ensure that the departed would find peace in their graves and would not return to haunt the living. In ancient Greece, for example, there were days when the dead would come and mingle with the living, asking for food and drink. In other beliefs, the humans had to keep these dark spirits at bay. Many so-called pagan rituals have been preserved right up to the present day, sometimes borrowing "Christian apparel" and often including features that can be traced in the vampire myth, too.

For westerners, the best-known moment when the boundaries between two worlds are annulled, when spirits good and evil roam abroad, is the night of Halloween, representing an ancient tradition inherited from the Celts, the festival of Samhain. As in other old religions, this was a celebration during which men must protect themselves against the spirits of the dead. Samhain was a time to mark the cycle of death and life. Surplus livestock was slaughtered in preparation for the winter. But sheep were also mated so that, in the spring, lambs would be born and the circle of life would restart. Fires would be lit, a symbolic assertion that the sun would return with its life-giving powers in the following year. This was a watershed time, when the old year died and the new was born. Between the two, there was a short period of limbo when the spirits of the dead and the forces of evil held sway. When the Christian Church arrived, it was not strong enough to completely obliterate the old pagan influences, instead assimilating them into its own framework. So, in the year 835, All Saints' Day was introduced, and its eve, Halloween, replaced Samhain.

"Days of the Dead" are a feature of many cultures worldwide. On such days, it was important to follow certain rituals to prevent the dead from creating havoc in the world of the living. On one such day in Abruzzi, Italy, for example, on November 1, candles were placed on the graves of the departed, and houses were kept well lit so that the dead could easily find their way back to them. A meal would be laid out on the kitchen table for them. The dead would march back in procession, with the righteous at their head and the wicked at the rear. In Romania, the tradition still exists of offering food to the spirits of the dead several times during the year. Some of these occasions are days when the dead in general are remembered, others are related specifically to the anniversary of the demise of an individual.

These traditions are rooted in ancient history. In Athens, the dead were deemed to return from Hades during the festival of Anthestria, an occasion related to Dionysus. The dead were believed to mingle with the living, sharing food and drink. The Athenians also used ritual magic to keep away any evil spirits who might return during the festival. They chewed the leaves of whitethorn and daubed their doors with tar. The tradition continued in the Roman festival of Lemuria, which lasted for four days in May. The dead were again supposed to return to the land of the living. Many rituals were indulged in to appease the spirits who were, significantly, of those who had not received a proper burial. In contrast to the Greek tradition, which was something of a celebration of the dead, this was a time of great fear. The spirits often took the form of horrible monsters that would haunt the homes of those who had formerly been their friends or family. The traditions so enshrined continue into the Christian world in the existence of All Souls' Day and Halloween.

Summers quotes a particularly telling example of how these legends live on in Christian lands, with a description of how the dead return on the eve of All Souls when, after Vespers, the living return home to

gather round the fire and talk in hushed tones of those who have gone before, while the good housewife covers the table with a spotless white cloth, sets cheese and cider and pancakes hot from the oven thereon, which done the family retire to rest. All night long the dead warm themselves at the hearth and feed upon the viands that have been prepared. There are those who will tell you that on that haunted night they have heard the benches creak and stealthy footsteps crossing the floor like the rustling of dry leaves.[4]

Old legends about Halloween and Samhain live on. This is unmistakably a Night of the Dead. One story concerns a Bronze Age barrow at Fortingall in Glen Lyon, Scotland—still a place of remote, brooding intensity. In this case, rituals took place, not on Halloween, but on 11 November 11—the same as the Christian saint's day of Martinmas and with the same roots dating back to Samhain. On this date, piles of gorse would be gathered on the hillside and built into a pyre on the mound, which was believed to be a place of burial for plague victims (it was known as The Mound of the Dead). When the fire was lit, the villagers danced around it in a circle, and the young men of the village ran through the fields with torches of furze ignited from the pyre. A similar tradition is found in Romania on St. Andrew's night, when the spirits of the dead are believed to wander the earth. All kinds of pots should be kept covered, as vampires (locally, *moroi*) might hide in them. One of the best ways to protect a house and its inhabitants (in addition to holy water or incense) is to rub garlic on the chimney and window- and door-frames, a method that Professor van Helsing successfully borrowed.

There was a corresponding day of celebration to mark the return of summer, known during Celtic times as Beltane, when fires would be lit to welcome the new season. This became a night of great occult activity, known as May Eve or Walpurgis night. In Germany, especially, this night saw the power of the witch at its height. The following day, May Day, would be marked by a ceremony known as "Burning out the witches," when villagers would process around their communities with burning torches to frighten away the witches in the area.[5] The occult power of Walpurgis night forms the basis of Stoker's posthumously published story, "Dracula's Guest." The plot revolves around the fact that Jonathan Harker chooses to journey abroad in Bavaria on this dangerously charged night. In true melodramatic tradition, the story begins when, as Jonathan leaves for a drive in the forest, his hotelier warns his driver: "Remember you are back by nightfall. The sky looks bright but there is a shiver in the north wind that says there may be a sudden storm. But I am sure you will not be late ... for you know what night it is."[6]

The night, it turns out, is Walpurgisnacht. Jonathan's driver becomes ever more frantic as he heads deeper into the forest, terrified because he knows that at its heart there is a vampire-infested village whose undead inhabitants haunt the area on this very night. Jonathan gets progressively more irritated with his nervous coachman, eventually saying with classic national stereotyping that "Walpurgisnacht doesn't concern Englishmen." But it transpires that the weak "foreign" coachman has far more sense than Jonathan does, for the latter is indeed attacked and barely escapes with his life.

St. George's Eve was another "occult night": significantly, it is the night when Jonathan arrives at Dracula's castle. Summers notes that this is the time of year—along with St. Andrew's Eve—that vampires were at their most active.[7] George is perhaps the most prominent of all saints, and adopting him as a patron was widespread across Europe. His fight with and defeat of the dragon is emblematic for the fight with evil spirits in all forms. He was also the patron saint of wolves, which is not without its importance in the context of treating the eve of his feast day as a special time for occult activity. In Romania, for example, certain types of occult creatures (*strigoi*) are closely linked to lycanthropy and werewolves. There were believed to be two kinds of *strigoi:* "the living' ones who, during daytime, took up human form, but at night would turn into wolves, killing and preying on the unwary; and "the dead" ones, who are a form of vampire. There were, and are, widespread rituals concerning both of these saints' days. So in Swabia, church bells would ring throughout St. George's Eve to keep evil spirits at bay. St. George celebrations take place on the same day as the Roman festival of Parilia, a shepherds' festival, connected to fertility rites. Here we have another example of the duality that so often surrounds the mysteries of life and death: in one guise, this is a day of the dead, in another, a day of new life, a reflection of the cycle of life—death and rebirth that underlies much of the vampire myth.

Midsummer's Day was also a magical moment. The summer solstice marks the time when the sun is at its most powerful, but it has also been "borrowed" by Christianity as St. John's Day. The design of Stonehenge (and many other megalithic monuments) proves the significance of this time for our ancestors. Standing stones were aligned so that the exact arrival of Midsummer's Day (and also midwinter and the equinoxes) could be identified and celebrated by the people. Midsummer is one of those moments when evil spirits haunt the earth, trying to harm men and cattle. All over Europe, bonfires were lit either as a symbol of the sun whose power must be enhanced or as protection against witchcraft.

In Norway, they were lit to keep away the witches who are flying towards Blocksberg, the home of the Great Witch. In Norrland, fires at crossroads were meant to frighten away the trolls who came out of the cavernous depths of the mountains during that night. It was not a good time for goats to roam about in those parts, as everybody would be convinced that the Evil One had taken on the form of this animal. In Bohemia, people who gathered around the bonfires wore mugwort crowns or garlands as protection against ghosts, witches, and sickness, especially sore eyes. As cattle were prime targets for witchcraft, in Bohemia, Russia, and Lithuania, the herds were driven through the fire so that the animals would be protected against sorcery.

The epiphany was an important day in fighting against vampires in Wallachia, now a part of modern Romania. Some vampires (*moroi*) are stillborn children, or children who have died unbaptized, which can also hint at other terrible taboos: children born out of wedlock who are killed by their mothers and buried outside cemeteries. Seven years after death, the spirit of the deceased will cry out, and if the call is not heard, they will return in different forms—from flames to dogs or cats—and kill the people they meet, and they do not fear in any way the sign of the cross. Traditionally, January 6 is the day when Jesus was baptized, so the graves of these children have to be sprinkled with holy water on this day for seven years in a row, a symbolic baptism which would cleanse the sins which had turned the baby into a *moroi.*

In some instances, specific days of the week have significance. In many south European countries, including Greece, Saturday is a day on which vampires must remain in their graves, as a result of which they are in great danger from enthusiastic vampire hunters. In parts of Serbia and Croatia, the theme is extended so that those born on a Saturday can also see and kill vampires on this day.[8] It is tempting to see a Christian element in this. Christ died and was buried on a Friday and rose again on a Sunday; only on Saturday was He in the grave throughout the day.

Just as there are special anniversaries throughout the year that are of significance in occult terms, so does every day have its important symbolic moments. Both sun and moon have great ritualistic meaning, and have long been the subject of veneration and awe. In the past, an eclipse had a cosmic symbolism, as it was often interpreted as an interruption of the essential rhythms of the universe. People were terrified that the sun or the moon were being devoured by some demonic being and would be lost forever, with catastrophic results for the world. Tribes from Africa and South America would shoot blazing arrows at the sun in an attempt to relight it. Tribes in Mexico averred that the god of the sun was "He by whom men live."[9] In Christian theology, the sun was synonymous with the forces of good. Medieval Christian kings, such as Edward IV of England, would adopt it as their banner. The moon, on the other hand, was associated with the forces of evil—it was sinister, menacing, the symbol of Diana, goddess of the witches. Men were thought to lose their senses when the moon was full, the werewolf walked the earth, and the powers of evil in general were exulted.

The sun's movements were carefully studied, as it was perceived as the source of life. Special moments in the solar calendar were scrupulously observed. But the sun also serves another purpose; it lights up the day and drives away the darkness, which is the time when the powers of evil are preeminent. Daybreak has a special significance. In folklore, the first crow of the cockerel at dawn is the signal for the spirits of darkness to return to their resting place. For the dead, it is the tomb that awaits. For witches returning from their sabbats, it is the moment to return to their homes and the disguise of everyday existence.

Daybreak and sundown play a strong part in vampire literature, and cinematography, of course. The arrival of the sun is the kiss of death for Nosferatu in the film of that name, and frequently kills off Dracula in movies (though not, as noted previously, in the novel). And one of the most powerful scenes in the film *Interview with the Vampire* is when the terrifying child-creature Claudia is destroyed by the sun's rays. In the same film, there is a moving scene, when Louis looks upon his last dawn. It is the moment when he has to choose between his life as a human being or the bloodthirsty immortality of the vampire. The theme is further developed when Lestat is frightened by the lights of the search helicopter, which turn out to be harmless for him, as the electric light has not the same power to destroy evil as sunlight.

Sometimes the vampire myth has become distorted in this respect. So, contrary to popular belief, Dracula can come out in the daylight (Jonathan and Mina see him in the park in London), though he tends to sleep during the day and his activity is heavily focused on nighttime. Other vampires, in both literature and folklore, appear during the day. That said, it is a recurrent motif that vampires tend to become active during the night, the moment when they are most powerful. Dracula meets his end at sundown, at the very moment that he issues forth from his coffin, his body reinvigorated by the growing power of darkness. In this scene in the novel, it is clear that his would-be destroyers face a battle against time, for as the sun's rays fade away and the power of night grows stronger, so too does the count. The nighttime is his time.

The night is a time of fear. In Christian homes, it was customary to say prayers to protect oneself during the hours of darkness. Many a simple child's prayer thinly disguises the terror of the sunless hours:

And now I lay me down to sleep
I pray the Lord my soul to keep
If I should die before I wake
I pray the Lord my soul to take.

The real terror here was not that someone might die but that they might lose their soul to the Satanic legions of the night. To protect against this, charms were used. They might take the form of Christian totems, but they were charms nevertheless. The seventeenth-century writer Guazzo wrote in his *Compendium Maleficarum* that, to keep yourself safe, you should say psalms and appropriate prayers. However, to make doubly sure, then "let them have by them a waxen Agnus Dei blessed by the pope, or some holy relics. For such devotions are the safest protection against all the wiles of the prince of darkness." The night was the time when witches plied their evil trade, when nightmares took a terrifying grip of the soul, and when carnal visitations from incubi and succubi took place. To wake alive and untroubled to the first rays of a new dawn was blessing indeed.

In *Dracula*, more than half of the novel, especially the more significant moments, takes place at night, when the world seems to be redefined and reshaped under a lunar influence. "The waxing and waning of the moon, and the inevitable return of the same lunar form, make a striking symbol for all philosophies combining death and rebirth.... It was always believed that the phases of the moon influenced events on earth: not only the ebb and flow of the tides, but also the rising and falling of sap in plants; haircuts and blood-letting were scheduled with reference to the lunar cycle."[10]

The influence of the moon is complex, much depends on its phases. A new moon was believed to bring good luck, unless seen through glass, for this distorts its powers and reverses its effects—something to be avoided at all costs. A moon that was waxing was thought to bring power—as it grew, so too did the vitality and strength of life. Farmers would plant their crops so that new plants would grow with the moon, and marriages were arranged to coincide with the waxing moon. Biodynamic farming, quite popular in Europe, still practices the former, making the moon, in this instance, a good influence. *Varney the Vampyre* uses this link with vitality as a core part of the plot. Varney cannot be killed because each time he is exposed to moonlight, his body is miraculously revived from whatever measures have been taken to destroy him. It is an interesting technique, previously employed by Polidori. Not only does the latter make the symbolic link between the moon and life, but by his connection of it with Ruthven (aka Lord Byron), he tells his readers that the real-life lord was a creature of the night, with all the sinister connotations that entails.

In *Dracula*, Lucy is a sleepwalker, and she is influenced by the phases of the moon. Mina finds her in the cemetery on a night when "there was a bright full moon, with heavy, black driving clouds, which threw the whole scene into a fleeting diorama of light and shade."[11] So for Mina, the presence of the vampire over Lucy's body seems only a momentary illusion. It was a moonlit night when Mina herself became Dracula's victim: "All was dark and silent, the black shadows thrown by the moonlight seeming full of a silent mystery of their own." Lucy dies during a night when the moon is full (the fact that one full moon occurs on August 11 and the other on September 20 does not seem to be a problem for the writer!).

The moon is associated with women and sexuality, as in the case of the ancient Greek goddess of the night, Nyx, with magic and witchcraft. It is also connected to madness, and European languages preserve this thought pattern in words such as "lunatic." This has even been given legal effect. The 1842 United Kingdom Lunacy Act describes a lunatic as one "afflicted with a period of fatuity in the period following the full moon."[12] The night is a realm of distorted logic, as the moonlight casts shadows that seem to transform the world, like a game of reality and deceit, where reason can no longer fight against phantasms. Mina writes in her diary that it is strange to be "kept in the dark," as the light of the sun is associated with reasonable, logical explanations and with direct knowledge, while moonlight is the symbol of indirect, occult knowledge.

Symbolically, too, the moon is linked with water, an element associated with life and fertility, on the one hand, and with submersion and destruction, on the other. As the moon influences the tides, the superstition goes that the undead cannot cross water except at the turn of the tide. The Romanian sailor on the ship that brings Dracula to England throws himself into the sea to escape the evil. During his journey to Transylvania, Jonathan complains of thirst, which keeps him awake and gives him nightmares. Water is also associated with memory, and we should note the characters' obsessive need to remember each and every detail of their adventures, hence the construction of the novel around a series of diaries and letters. A similar approach is used in *Carmilla*, where the written account helps to validate the events described.

Ancient mythologies associated the moon with goddesses and placed femininity under its sign. In Greek myths, the night was portrayed as the winged goddess Nyx, dressed in a black starry robe, and traversing the sky in a chariot pulled by black horses. She has several different images, as she is the mother of Hypnos, the god of dreams, but also of the Moros (doom), of Nemesis, the revenge goddess, and of the Moirae, the weavers of fate. At the same time, Nyx symbolically reigns over sleep, sexual pleasure, and death—the double image of Eros and Thanatos. Nyx was born from Chaos, and together with her brother Erebos (darkness), she conceived Ether and Hemera (day). The myth of the day as an offspring of the night allowed psychoanalysts to associate night with the protection of the womb and with motherhood. In Egyptian myths, it is associated with Thoth, the supreme magician, also responsible for regulating the months and seasons, symbolically placing the rhythms of nature and secret, occult knowledge under the sign of the moon.

Horror writers have a vast array of tools available with which to paint their literary canvas. Because of its connotations, moonlight is often used as an accessory to the machinery of fear. It is the perfect backdrop, given its associations with the black arts. One writer who used it splendidly was the twentieth-century author, F. Marion Crawford, who put together the whole assemblage of classic vampiric devices in "For the Blood is the Life." The story has many of the standard ingredients; the vampire is a beautiful, seductive gypsy girl, Cristina, who is murdered. Three classic horror elements are used—the seductress, the Other as represented by her gypsy background, and her violent death. She returns to the man she loved in life and slowly drains him of his blood.

But even after she is destroyed by a priest armed with holy water, a stake, and his prayer book, her shade can still be seen. And there is one ingredient above all others that the observer notices—the effect of moonlight on her grave: "It makes no difference whether the moon is rising or setting, or waxing or waning. If there's any moonlight at all, from east or west or overhead, so long as it shines on the grave you can see the outline of the body on top."[13] It is as if it is the moon that now gives her spirit life of a sort—a menacing, evil form of half-life. Most of the "great" vampire stories of the nineteenth century—*Dracula, Carmilla,* "The Vampyre," for example—utilize the moon to great effect. Sinister, mysterious, powerful— all these are poetic qualities owned by it.

The human mind has always swung between the fear and the fascination of the unknown, in all its representations: the future, a faraway civilization, the Other that we find in the person next to us, and, more than anything, the great mysteries of death and afterlife. The vampire became, in a strange way, the embodiment of all these, an entity whose existence links two worlds that seem never to communicate, even though they meet incessantly: the world of the living and the dark realm of the dead. It has acquired everlasting life, and yet it is dead. The night is its realm, "when the moon shone with a light so intense it was well known that it indicated a special spiritual activity. The effect of the full moon in such a state of brilliancy was manifold. It acted on dreams, it acted on lunacy, it acted on nervous people; it had marvellous physical influences connected with life." [14]

But, after all, our perception of the world is constructed on the models that Nature and its elements offer to us. At the same time, all the symbols that we attach to natural phenomena place the plethora of shapes and forms into strict frames of mind. Fear of night and darkness is enhanced by other elements in the same key. Among these are the "creatures of the night," animals such as bats, owls, rats, and wolves, which are inextricably associated in human consciousness with the powers of darkness. The fear and repulsion that they can spread by their mere presence, the atmosphere of pestilence, and the omens of death that they bring as messengers of the other world, all build up into the perfect background for the vampire story.

NOTES

1. Oscar Wilde, *The Picture of Dorian Gray*, p. 22.
2. See Chapter 8.
3. Mircea Eliade, *Sacrul si profanul*, p. 48.
4. *The Vampire in Lore and Legend*, p. 12.
5. See Fraser, p. 559.
6. Quoted in Frayling, p. 353.
7. Summers, p. 311.
8. See Barber, p. 67.
9. Fraser, p. 79.
10. Hans Biedermann, *Dictionary of Symbolism*.
11. *Dracula*, p. 110.
12. See *Folklore, Myths and Legends of Britain*, p. 20.
13. *Great Vampire Stories*, p. 10.
14. *Carmilla*, p. 11.

Whitby Abbey, a haunting presence in Bram Stoker's Dracula. (Author's collection).

The church adjacent to Whitby Abbey: another brooding atmospheric setting utilized in Dracula. (Author's collection).

The loss of control over one's mind is an ancient motif used in vampire lore, as suggested by this mosaic of Medusa from Rhodes. (Author's collection).

A landscape of mystery and fear: the hills and forests of Transylvania. (Author's collection).

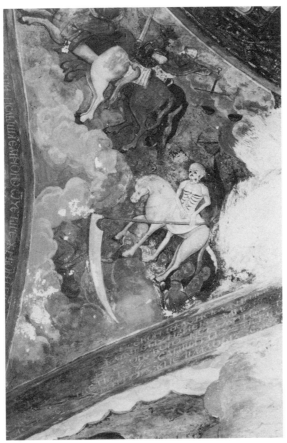

Death stalks humanity: a sixteenth-century wall painting
from the exterior of a Romanian monastery. (Author's
collection).

The fear of being buried alive led to this mausoleum in
Christchurch, Dorset, being constructed with the ability
to be opened from the inside. (Author's collection).

Countess Elisabeth Bathory, one of the most famous devotees of the cult of blood. (Mary Evans Picture Library).

The end of a vampire in a Bohemian village, from a book of
1864. (Mary Evans Picture Library).

The cover of the book, *Varney the Vampire*, one of the earliest Victorian vampire horror tales. (Mary Evans Picture Library).

Burial at a crossroads from a print circa 1840: such places were places of occult significance even in Antiquity. (Mary Evans Picture Library).

The North Berwick witches dance widdershins around a church. (Mary Evans Picture Library).

CHAPTER 7

Mother Nature and the World of the Vampire

Monstrous and abominable eyes they were, bestial and yet filled with purpose and with hideous delight, gloating over their prey trapped beyond all hope of escape.

—J.R.R. Tolkien, *The Two Towers*

The effectiveness of the vampire tale is increased by the way it uses the ambivalence of our views of nature, as the fascination it exercises on us is often hedged around with fear. Animals play an important role in the vampire story, and explanations for this phenomenon range from traditional rituals connected to the passing of the soul into the other world to symbolic features of different animals and their evolution in the human imagination. One example is the belief that animals have a so-called sixth sense, which makes them aware of the presence of ghosts or other evil spirits, such as revenants. The late twelfth-century writer, William of Newburgh, describes how the dogs of Berwick were uncontrollable when a vampire was in the vicinity. This belief was incorporated into vampire stories and became a common device, very efficiently hinting at the supernatural dimension of the events described. It is used very early on in *Dracula* when, even before he meets the count, Jonathan's sleep is disturbed by the persistent barking of a dog outside his bedroom window. The dog knows what is coming.[1] So too do the pet poodles of an aristocrat who is about to become a victim of Louis in *Interview with the Vampire*.

There are indeed many facets to consider when reviewing the role of animals in vampirism. For example, animals are particularly perilous to the newly dead. Different traditions considered it highly dangerous to let an animal cross over a corpse because of the risk that the soul of the dead human would pass into the animal and possess it (a particularly wide-spread belief, found as far apart as Europe and China). This could some-times be bad news for an animal. In parts of Europe, a dead cat would be laid across the threshold of the house of the newly dead as a protec-tion against vampirism. And the eighteenth-century collector of Highland folklore, Pennant, tells his readers that if a dog or cat should happen to pass over a body, then the animal would be killed immediately because of the harmful effect that this might have on the soul of the departed.[2]

The association of animals with vampirism, and the danger that the vampire could take the form of almost any creature, is also widespread. In Russia, when a vampire was incinerated on a funeral pyre, it was critical that any life form that tried to escape from the flames was destroyed. This included anything as insignificant as a flea, as there was no creature that could not be taken over by the vampire. In regions of Yugoslavia, virtually any animal can become a vampire, but snakes—predictably, given their Satanic connections—are particularly perilous.

There are two types of animal commonly associated with vampires. One is the predator: the wolf, the cat, the owl, for example, who patrol the night hours looking for their prey in the same way that vampires search out their victims and then suddenly pounce on them. The other type of ani-mal, such as the rat, is a pest, a bringer of disease—a classic vampiric motif in both folklore and literature. In a lesser-known work called "And No Bird Sings" (1928) by E. F. Benson, the vampire is in the form of a slug!

The roles played by animals can be quite complex. In some stories, the animal is the vampire, on other occasions, it falls under the influence of one, and in yet others, it is an enemy of the undead. The links have become accentuated because, in popular literature, the image of the fanged vam-pire plays on the unnatural appearance of a human with animal features. In legend, though, the image of a vampire as a creature with fang-like teeth rarely appears, and bizarrely, in some cultures, the tongue was a more commonplace weapon. But the bestial qualities of the vampire are especially emphasized because, often in folklore, there are connections between the vampire and its supernatural cousin, the werewolf.

The beastly appearance of the undead is milked for all it is worth in lit-erature. Varney the vampire is described as having teeth "projecting like those of some wild animal. Hideously, glaringly white, and fang-like."[3] And Dracula is said to have uncommonly hairy palms. In *Dracula*, the atmosphere of fear is carefully constructed through linguistic devices as well as images hinting at the unnatural features of the vampire, and cumu-latively they create a powerful animal-like image of the count, undoubtedly shocking for the Victorian English reader. For example, when Dracula's unfortunate victim, Lucy Westenra, is attacked, she writes in her diary that she first of all heard "a howl like a dog's," then that she saw "a big bat, which had evidently been buffeting its wings against the window."

When her bedroom window is broken just before the final, fatal assault on her, "there was the head of a great, gaunt grey wolf."[4] It is certainly suggestive that van Helsing describes his band of followers as "hunters of wild beast."[5] In these suggestions of animal-like qualities, the reader is given the impression that there is in nature something sinister, menacing, other-worldly, something, in short, to be afraid of.

Fear and awe have been entwined in the way man perceived animals ever since prehistoric times (evidenced, for example, by the prominence of animals in cave paintings that have survived). Elaborate myths grew around the figure of the hunter, and the encounter between man and beast took on epic dimensions in many cultures. The hunter became the hero of the community, and in many religions—and Christianity is no exception—the beast became the embodiment of evil. So at the very beginning of Genesis, we find Satan appearing to Eve as a serpent. And the image of St. George slaying the dragon, a metaphor for victory over the Devil, was a symbolic representation of the triumph of the Church over evil.

Another striking image is that of a creature that is half-man and half-beast. Again, this is one of the images that form the base of the vampire story, yet there is nothing original about this particular creation. It is one more borrowed element. The Minotaur of ancient Cretan fame, half-man and half-beast, born from the union between Pasiphae, the wife of King Minos, and a bull, claimed a tribute of blood: seven young women and seven young men, which he devoured every year. The centaurs, mythical beings, half-men and half-horses, often appear in Greek legends as lustful creatures, trying to kidnap women and rape them. The god Pan was represented as half-goat and half-man and would chase women, nymphs, and goats with the same lascivious thoughts. He appears in Roman mythology as Lupercus.

The image of the vampire is often associated with another great legendary phenomenon. The werewolf, like the vampire, played a prominent role in the pantheon of creatures of horror and grew into a historical phenomenon, with ample echoes in folklore and, later, in literature. Just as the eighteenth century was the era of the vampire epidemic, so the sixteenth was that of the werewolf—it has been claimed that there were 30,000 cases reported between 1520 and 1630.[6] Stories of werewolves were largely delimited by geographical region, hinting at a basis, however slight, in fact, for many of the stories. Often nature and folklore appeared to get mixed up, so it is little surprise, for example, that there is no real tradition of werewolves in Britain, where wolves were obliterated long ago. Instead, there are myriad accounts of ghostly dogs from the British Isles—the dreaded Black Shuck (of East Anglia), for example—reflecting the fact that the hound was common in everyday life, whereas the wolf was not.

A number of the accounts of werewolf activity share common features with tales of vampires. In Wallachia, werewolves were synonymous with so-called living vampires (*strigoi*), or vampires which had not died but who, in the daytime, lived a normal life, undergoing a horrific transformation at night. Sometimes they could be the seventh or the ninth child of a couple or, alternatively, they would bear the punishment for the breaking of a taboo. In Ukraine it was believed that when werewolves died, they would become vampires. In several Slavic countries, the word for werewolf—for example, the Greek *vrykolakas* – is the same as that for a vampire. In other versions of the werewolf legend, the creature was believed to dig up corpses and eat them—something that vampires were also capable of doing. And in Greece, anybody who ate a sheep killed by a wolf would, on their death, become a vampire. In Western Europe, the legends of werewolves go back to Teutonic beliefs that the human spirit could leave the body and "borrow" the appearance of an animal. The metamorphosis had several explanations here. The werewolf could be the victim of an evil spell, but others were thought to be sorcerers who could change their shape at will. The legends were so powerful that they grew into historical accounts that claimed to be factual.

In 1521, a trial took place at Poligny, France, conducted by the infamous Inquisition. In the witness box were three men accused of being werewolves, Pierre Bourgot, Philibert Mentot, and Michel Verdung. A traveler passing through the region was attacked by a wolf; Verdung's wife was later found nursing wounds which had been caused when the attacker had been driven off (a recurrent theme in tales of witchcraft, as we shall see later in this chapter).

At the trial, Bourgot told how he had become a werewolf when, in 1502, a terrible storm had scattered his flocks (storms are often closely connected with a vampire attack, certainly in literature). While he was trying to find his sheep, he met three horsemen clad in black. One offered to help him recover the animals if he would serve him. The bargain was struck and the sheep returned. The man in black was none other than a servant of Satan, a good example of the occult pact we will consider later. At their next meeting, the demon disclosed his identity, and Pierre swore fealty to Satan by kissing his hand, which he described as being icy cold. He and his two accomplices became werewolves; they killed young children and ate them. They could turn into werewolves by the application of some magic ointment, and could turn back again by a repetition of the same treatment. At the conclusion of the trial, all three men were found guilty and duly burned.[7]

In another outbreak (1598) in St-Claude (in the Jura region of France), the lycanthropes did not transform completely, but retained human hands. This allowed one of the supposed werewolves to stab a 16-year-old youth. A girl, Perrenette Gandillon, was assumed to be the killer and was lynched by an angry crowd. Her sister was alleged to have the power to raise hailstorms (as Count Dracula, too, is able to control the weather), and had also attended sabbats. Again, they were able to transform themselves into wolves by the use of a salve. She and two other members of the family, Pierre and Georges, were convicted and burned at the stake.[8]

As in many cases of the vampire epidemics, these, too, probably started from actual events, which were easier to explain through the filter of old beliefs rather than natural explanations. In these stories, we find trends consistent with those of certain aspects of the vampire legend: the meta-morphosis, the pact with Satan, the ability to control the elements, the need to destroy the werewolf by means of fire. It is also easy to see how, in coun-tries where the wolf lived, it became associated with vampire activity. It is likely that in regions such as these, bodies would be exhumed and eaten by the animal, especially if the corpses had been buried in shallow graves.

This was particularly likely to happen in times of plague. Burial was hasty—nobody wanted plague-ridden corpses lying around and, given the cause of death, few gravediggers wanted to spend hours digging a deep grave. This would make it relatively easy for a wolf (or other ani-mal) to dig away the earth over a body and help itself to a meal from the cadaver. But, rather than seeing a natural explanation in this, folklore and superstition saw the presence of animals in cemeteries as evidence of vampire activity. Normally, creatures haunting cemeteries, whether real or imagined, became associated with the powers of darkness, as disturbing the rest of the dead was seen as a supreme sacrilege.

The wolf has strong negative symbolism in many beliefs, being associ-ated with the ferocious side of nature as, unlike dogs, it is not domes-ticated. In many superstitions, it is thought to be able to hypnotize its victims (like Dracula) or leave them speechless. The Romans associated it with the god of war, Mars, and it also appeared on Dacian[9] banners. Genghis Khan claimed to be the descendant of a "chosen great grey wolf," and on the Turkish steppes it was a national totem—probably Western crusaders associated the wolf with the infidel and the Orient, especially since, in religious iconology, it was a representation of the Satanic enemy attacking the flock of the faithful.

We must not forget that, until relatively recently, Europe was covered by great, dark forests, where wolves roamed free, and for pastoral civiliza-tions in Eastern Europe, they were a fearsome enemy. Together with the werewolf, this is one of the reference points in negative European imag-ery in *Dracula*. On his way to the castle in this so-called "wolf country", Jonathan is frightened by them as he enters the dark realm of the night: "Just then the moon, sailing through the black clouds, appeared behind the jagged crest of a beetling, pineclad rock, and by its light I saw around us a ring of wolves, with white teeth and lolling red tongues, with long sinewy limbs and shaggy hair. They were a hundred times more terrible in the grim silence which held them than even when they howled. For myself, I felt a sort of paralysis of fear."[10]

The ring is a symbol of a closed, self-sufficient, enchanted space, and the wolves make it impossible for Jonathan to escape, so much so that he is made to think that the count's caleche is a place of safety. The count calls them "children of the night" and thinks that their howling is like a song—a dreadful, but not unexpected coalition between these dark, violent, and bloodthirsty creatures, whether they belong to reality or imagination. The wolf connection with the count is brought out particularly strongly in Coppola's *Dracula,* and in the scene when he first "seduces" Lucy (if that is the right word for an action which looks horribly bestial), it is interesting that he appears to take the form of a werewolf rather than a traditional vampire.

Cats, too, play a big role in occult beliefs. The association of cats, vampires, and death is illustrated powerfully in European folklore in the story of the Pentsch Vampire, related by Henry More in 1653. A prominent local citizen of Pentsch, Silesia, one Johannes Cuntius died after being kicked by a horse. Before his death, he confessed that he had lived an evil life and that he believed his soul was therefore in mortal danger. As he lay dying, a black cat attacked him. During his burial, a terrible storm blew up. Soon after, rumors that he had returned from the grave swept the town. It was decided that he should be exhumed. When this was done, his body was in a state of perfect preservation. Subsequent attempts to burn his cadaver failed. It was only when his body was cut into pieces that it could be incinerated. The ashes were thrown into the nearby river and the appearances ceased.

Cats are often linked with vampires across the world, perhaps reflecting the belief that the animal was a regular familiar of the witch. In Malaysia, a male vampire known as the *bajang* often appeared as a polecat. The victims of another variant of the Malaysian vampire, the *pelesit,* frequently scream that they are being attacked by a cat. The feline connection is found in another interesting story from Japan. A demon in the form of a cat took the life of a concubine of the prince of Hizen. It then appeared as the dead concubine and, in this guise, carried on sleeping with the prince. Inexorably, the demon took the power of the prince, who grew progressively weaker, an allusion to the combination of male energy and power often referred to in eastern philosophy. Much like Dr. Seward and van Helsing in *Dracula,* the royal doctors were perplexed, but noticed that he invariably worsened at night.

To protect the prince, a guard was placed over his quarters as he slept. One of the sentinels, Soda, was particularly vigilant. Owing to his presence, the demon was unable to enter the room and therefore began to lose its influence over the prince, who started to recover. One night, Soda noticed a beautiful woman in the prince's apartment. Soda suspected who she was and attacked her. The woman turned into a cat and escaped to the mountains. Determined to stamp out the threat once and for all, a great hunt was launched, and the cat was slain, though this did not appear to end all stories of the feline vampire, last reported as being seen in 1929.

Another creature regularly linked with vampires was the owl, inevitable given its nocturnal habits and its stealthy predatory instincts, so reminiscent of the shadowy threat of the vampire. The association between the owl and the powers of darkness is one of the oldest known to man. A Sumerian tablet dating back to 2000 B.C. has on it two owls flanking a goddess. The deity is believed to be the goddess of death. Roman writers such as Ovid and Pliny described the bird as a harbinger of doom, and when an owl appeared on Capitol Hill in Rome, so great was the alarm that the whole area had to be fumigated with holy incense. The ancient Roman *strix* was a spectral screech owl, which had the nasty habit of feeding off the blood of children. This creature later evolved into the *striges,* a witch-vampire that was believed to have the power to transform itself into an owl. In Persia, too, the bird is regarded as the angel of death. The owl is also associated with witchcraft in many African countries, and in North America many tribes regarded it as an evil spirit. In Eastern Europe, it was greatly feared, and direct reference to its name was often avoided.

An animal which plays a bigger role in vampire literature than in folklore is the bat. This does not mean that it was the vampire story which created the connection with the powers of darkness. An ancient Dionysian legend is one example of the way bats were perceived as odious beings. Dionysus was an "imported" foreign god, who was not universally accepted in Greece. Not everyone joined in the Dionysian celebrations, and there were some who would not accept his divine nature. One legend speaks about the three daughters of Minyas, the king of Boeotia, who did not respond to the call of the god's priest and failed to join in the festivities taking place in the forests and mountains. All the other women had formed a cortège for the god. They were covered in ivy and holding thyrsi (short staffs) in their hands, singing, dancing, and bringing sacrifices to the god of wine.

Only the king's three daughters stayed at home, weaving, and refusing to stop work, even at dusk. Suddenly, the palace miraculously changed. The threads of wool turned into long trails of vine, heavy under the burden of grapes, ivy grew around the weaving looms, the sound of flutes and mirth invaded the halls. The young girls, amazed at this miracle, suddenly heard the frightening roars of wild beasts, lions, and panthers that appeared all over the castle. The three girls tried to hide, but they could not find any place of safety in their father's palace. But the revenge of the god did not stop here. He transformed them into bats, small winged animals with mouse-like skin, creatures that flee from the light of day and hide in dark caves and ruins.

The bat, with its dual symbolism, as a winged mammal (mammals don't normally fly!), was associated with witches' sabbats, and the devil was portrayed as a fallen angel with a bat's wings that hides away from the light.

English language preserves the link between bats and madness: to have "bats in the belfry," "to be batty." Quincey Morris speaks about the bloodsucking vampire bats in South America, and the ability of Count

Dracula to transform himself into one is a well-known facet of the myth. (Incidentally, it was the vampire bat that was named after the vampire and not the other way round. And the bat certainly does attack animals and suck blood from them, as no less a naturalist than Darwin found out on an expedition to South America in the early nineteenth century).

The unusual nature of the bat, that is, a mammal that flies, is connected to an especially dangerous ritualistic belief. The creature is "abnormal" in that it is capable of doing things that creatures of its type cannot normally do. It has therefore crossed a boundary, the normal rules of nature have been reversed, and so the animal is, in a symbolic sense, threatening. Thus, it is quite natural to connect such a beast with an abomination of nature like the vampire.

Beliefs that a vampire could "shape-shift" into the form of an animal were particularly prominent in Slavic tradition; here, the vampire was believed to be able to turn itself into a cat, dog, rat, bird, frog, flea, or other insect. The vampire may also appear in the form of a horse, normally black—significantly, the color of the horses that draw Count Dracula's carriage in the novel. It was a feature of tradition in Dalmatia that there was often a struggle between an evil wizard-vampire, the *kudlak,* and a "good" magus, the *kresnik,* who did all that he could to defend those at risk. In this confrontation, both protagonists would assume the shape of an animal, and in the case of the *kudlak,* inevitably one of a black color. These beliefs have very close connections with witchcraft, where shape-shifting is a common feature.

We have argued in this book that the vampire myth uses legends and images found in other areas of occult tradition. It is a common characteristic of witches that they can assume the shape of an animal. A complete chapter could be written of such tales from witchcraft, but in the interests of brevity, one illustrative example concerns a witch from Dorset called Jinny Gould. She was a well-known local figure who lived in a cottage by a toll gate. After her death, her spirit was supposed to have continued to open the gate for travelers. One night shortly before she died, a passing traveler noticed a large cat staring at him from the gate. He had sampled rather too much of the local beer and, in his inebriated state, he struck out at the animal, which had something sinister about it, cutting its back with his whip. The cat ran off in the direction of the nearby cottage. Next day, Jinny Gould was ill in bed and died soon afterwards. When she was being prepared for burial, a livid fresh scar was found on her back.[11]

So the ability to change into an animal appears to be one characteristic that witches and vampires share. And the ability of the latter to do so is not just a literary invention. The metamorphosis of the vampire in literature is a device lifted straight from folklore. When the writer, Charles de Schertz, wrote an account in 1706 of a series of attacks, he told of a woman who had been buried without receiving the last rites (emphasizing once again the importance of observing the proper religious ceremonials if the souls of the dead are to find rest). Four days later, there was a terrible storm (another sure sign of activity from beyond the grave) and the woman reappeared, sometimes in the form of a dog, and at other times in the shape of a giant man. In these shapes, she attacked not only humans, but also animals, who were victims of the undead more often than might be thought. As well as evidencing some of the mass hysteria that might explain why accounts of vampires were so common (how after all could the local population know it was the woman if she appeared in a different form than she had when alive?), this account also demonstrates how widespread a belief in vampires' shape-shifting skills actually was.

According to Summers, "In Russia (at least until lately), in Poland, in Serbia, and among the Slavonic peoples generally, an epidemic among the cattle is generally ascribed to a vampire who is draining them of their vitality."[12] Reports of vampire activity in history often coincide with the "dark side of nature": disease. In the all too frequent epidemics of the past, as those who had seen both their loved ones and their livelihood wiped out searched around for explanations, they sought scapegoats to blame for their troubles. The newly dead, often perhaps the first victims of plague themselves, are the most convenient candidates. The image is strengthened as the families of those perceived to be the cause of the infestation are the first to die. This is hardly surprising in the case of a virulent, contagious disease, but it is easy to see how, in a world that did not have the medical knowledge base of that in which we live, and that had a different framework for explaining events than we do, such epidemics could be seen as the work of evil forces. The links between plague and vampirism may have been further strengthened, because in the pneumonic version of plague that attacks the lungs, bleeding from the mouth was one of the symptoms.[13]

Inevitably, given the paradigms of the times, there was a strong belief that the powers of evil and disease were intertwined. Sometimes, demons were believed physically to stalk the earth, spreading plague and pestilence in their wake. This has been employed as a literary device in "The Masque of the Red Death," and more recently by Peter Ackroyd in *Hawksmoor*: "It was said (and I recall my Parents saying) that before the Pestilence there were seen publicly Daemons in Humane shape, which struck those they met, and those struck were presently seiz'd with the Desease; even those who saw such Apparitions (call'd Hollow Men), grew much altered."[14]

Connections between disease and vampirism are very old. In 1343, the Black Death was imminent, about to stalk across Europe like an angel of doom. In that year, there were reports of a number of vampire cases, including one at Marienburg Abbey. Several monks were believed to have died as a result of vampire attacks. In a situation where many of the population died, to blame the forces of evil was an obvious explanation.

And the belief lived on, with reports that, as late as 1855 in Danzig, an outbreak of cholera was attributed to the activities of vampires. The link between plague and vampirism is an immutable one; so, for example, Saint Roch is often prayed to for protection against the former, but in Poland is also deemed to be an effective guard against the latter.[15]

A well-known protection against such attacks was the use of the so-called need fire found across Europe. In times of epidemic, huge bonfires were constructed and set alight. References to the use of these can be found as far back as the year 750, but we may be sure that it dates back much further than that. As in all such ceremonials, it is necessary to follow the script to the letter if the remedy is to be successful. All fires in the village must be put out before the need fire is lit. When the fire is ignited, it must be done by "natural" means, by the use of friction rather than a match. In times of epidemic, it was common to find such fires ablaze. Often, the bodies of those thought to be vampires were exhumed and burned to stop them from walking the earth.

Plague attacks were associated with rodents such as rats. Both rats and mice have a very sinister place in the history of occult ideas (and continue to do so—in the *Harry Potter* series, the villainous Peter Pettigrew takes the form of a rat). In times gone by, mice were associated with the human soul, which could take this form to escape from the sleeping body. The Pied Piper is considered an allegory of the devil leading innocent souls towards the pits of Hell. A German legend speaks of a Bishop Hatto from Bingen, who was eaten by mice in his "mouse tower." Known as a mean and selfish man, people believed that the mice which devoured him were the souls of all the people who died of starvation because of his greed and cruelty.

Stoker himself uses this theme in one of his stories, "The Judge's House" (1891). A young mathematician chooses to spend his summer in an old house which had once belonged to a particularly bloodthirsty judge. For years the house had been inhabited solely by rats, and the young man's nights are disturbed by their ghastly noises. One of them, "an enormous rat, steadily glaring at him with baleful eyes" preferred an old armchair near the fireplace, over which hangs a bell-rope—nothing less than the hangman's noose used for the judge's victims. When hit by a Bible thrown at him, the rat disappears near an old painting, in which the young man recognizes, to his horror, the figure of the old judge, sitting in the armchair. He is struck by a very strange resemblance: "His face was strong and merciless, evil, crafty, and vindictive, with a sensual mouth and a hooked nose of ruddy colour, shaped like the beak of a bird of prey. The rest of the face was of a cadaverous colour. The eyes were of peculiar brilliance and had a terribly malignant expression ... the very counterpart of the eyes of the great rat."[16] As the story draws to an end, the young man falls under the malign power which resides in the house. The figure in the painting comes out of its frame,[17] and he is found one morning hanged by the very rope which had been the instrument of death for many victims of the judge's malice.

One film that brings out the connection between the rat and vampirism is *Nosferatu*. Not only does Max Shreck cut a rodent-like figure, but in a scene where his coffin is opened on board a ship, a swarm of rats issue forth, one of whom bites a seaman on the foot. In *Interview with the Vampire*, Lestat—who is one of the most loathsome of vampire figures—excites our disgust when, in the absence of humans to feed on, he kills a rat and drains its blood into a glass. But Louis, who struggles to retain his fading links with his humanity, drinks the blood of rats rather than attack humans: a powerful piece of symbolism by Rice, who portrays the initially "decent" victim of Lestat as preferring to sink to the depths of existing off rats than taking the life of a human. The idea appears elsewhere. In *Buffy*, the re-ensouled Angel, no longer able to kill human beings, but still reliant on blood to live, tries to catch rats and mice in the back alleys of twentieth-century America.

Often the cause of the destruction of grain, mice, and rats represented a great danger for agricultural communities, dependent on the crops they could gather. Thus they were associated with witches and sorcerers, servants of the devil who would raise storms and bring disease to animals, and could employ the rodents to help them spread starvation and harm. Medieval English language preserved this fear of mice and rats, in the word "to mouse", which meant "to pillage".

In the distant past, long before the Black Death, mice were associated with the plague. Myths speak of Apollo Smintheus, protector of the crops by destroying the mice, who also shot arrows bearing the plague. We have already shown the folkloric connection between plagues and the apparition of vampires, so it is no surprise to see Dracula surrounded by these messengers of pestilence: "The whole place was becoming alive with rats…. They seemed to swarm over the place all at once, till the lamplight, shining on their moving dark bodies and glittering, baleful eyes, made the place look like a bank of earth set with fireflies…. The rats were multiplying in thousands…"[18]

The vampire also has the power to command animals. So Count Azzo, in the story of *The Mysterious Stranger*, can control the wolves, as Count Dracula does. When Dracula's caleche is surrounded by the ring of wolves, he descends from the carriage and confronts them: "I heard his voice raised in a tone of imperious command, and looking towards the sound, saw him standing in the roadway. As he swept his long arms, as though brushing aside some impalpable obstacle, the wolves fell back and back further still. Just then a heavy cloud passed across the face of the moon, so that we were again in darkness."[19]

This is a very powerful scene, an excellent example of Stoker's ability to bring together symbols of magic and the Other, and in the process, to paint a picture of the count which demonstrates all the terrible abilities that he has. He controls nature itself; even the wolf fears and obeys him. His magus-like qualities are so powerful that the light of the moon is obscured from the view of Man by the clouds of night. For his is the Power of Darkness.

The role of animals in vampire lore is often ambivalent. Some animals are ferocious vampire hunters. Black dogs are deemed to be particularly effective, more surprisingly so are black cows. According to gypsies in Romania, white wolves in cemeteries will keep away vampires. And in Albania, a vampire known as the *lugat* was in trouble if it was confronted by a wolf, as the latter would often bite off its legs. These beliefs possibly exist because of the carrion-loving qualities of the wolf, something that is also in keeping with crows, themselves sometimes considered to be enemies of the vampire. It is a sympathetic connection: an animal that consumes dead bodies must be an enemy of the undead as they negate the vampire's ability to walk the earth by destroying them in their graves.

It is not just in terms of fauna that there are connections with vampires; the same applies to flora. Plant life has many associations with the Other. An understanding of the power of plants, and their dual nature (some plants kill, others heal, and some can do both depending on the quantities administered), was at the heart of many stories of witchcraft. The best-known connection between vampires and plant life is, of course, garlic, long considered to be an antidote to the undead, both in literature and folklore. Traditionally, those deceased who were deemed to be at special risk of becoming vampires would have their mouths stuffed with cloves of garlic.

Superstitions surrounding the plant go as far back as ancient Egypt, where garlic was believed to have healing powers. Even in recent times in Eastern Europe, during outbreaks of an epidemic, children wore little bags of garlic and camphor around their necks. Garlic is the best-known and most powerful deterrent to a vampire, perhaps because its pungent aroma is a counterbalance to the awful smell of putrefying flesh so often associated with vampires and, of course, an unavoidable part of death and decay (such aromatic qualities are also, when combined with religious symbolism, perhaps the reason that incense is a strong shield against creatures of evil).

When Lucy Westenra is in peril because of the count's attentions, van Helsing immediately prescribes large numbers of garlic plants as a protection. They are literally everywhere; a garland is made for her and placed round her neck, while the door frame and the windows are liberally smeared with the plant so that "every whiff of air that might get in would be laden with the garlic smell."

Although she is incredulous at first, Lucy finds that "I never liked garlic before, but tonight it is delightful! There is peace in its smell; I feel sleep coming already."[20] The count is only able to approach Lucy when her mother tears the garland off her in a dying fit.

Beliefs concerning garlic lasted well into modern times. Summers[21] quotes a report from the *Daily Telegraph* on February 15, 1912. It refers to the death of a 14-year-old boy in Hungary. He had worked for a farmer who, after his death, swore that the boy continued to visit him. To put a stop to this disconcerting occurrence, the farmer and a group of friends made their way to the cemetery where the boy was buried. They dug up his body, placed three stones and three pieces of garlic in his mouth, and drove a stake through his body.

The dog rose is another plant deemed to be effective against the unwelcome return of the dead. In Eastern Europe, it was customary to place sprigs of the plant in coffins, the thorns that attached themselves to the shrouds of the dead being particularly effective in keeping the dead in their place. Roses were sprinkled around the grave as a protection against the Bulgarian vampire, the *krvoijac*, while in Romania, it was customary to tie garlands of roses around the coffin to prevent outbreaks of vampirism. And on St. George's Eve, a night of great occult activity, branches of wild rose bushes would be tied to the gates of Transylvanian farms as a deterrent to witches.

Another plant often linked with vampirism was the hawthorn, the wood of which was sometimes used as stakes to kill a vampire. In Bosnia, visitors to the houses of the recently deceased would take a sprig of hawthorn with them and throw it behind them as they walked down the road on their return homewards. It was believed that this would stop the spirit of the dead from following them, as it would be unable to resist the urge to pick up the sprig. This reflects very old traditions; in ancient times, hawthorn was considered a protection against witchcraft. The thorns were again placed in the shrouds of the dead to ensure the dead stayed in their coffins. In a famous case from real life (1728), involving vampire activity around Belgrade and a revenant named Peter Plogojowitz, many bodies were exhumed from graves. Those who showed no traces of vampirism were reburied with due reverence, both garlic and whitethorn being placed in their coffins.

This device is exploited by horror writers, as an added illustration of how all the weapons that nature provides will be employed to defeat the undead. So, when Dracula flees from London back to his castle in Transylvania, van Helsing tells his entourage that "we shall at first board the ship; then, when we have identified the box, we shall place a branch of the wild rose on it. This we shall fasten, for when it is there none can emerge; so at least says the superstition."[22] This is one of many examples when "real" folklore is used as an integral part of the author's literary armory.

Nature therefore plays a part in the vampire myth in many forms. This all adds to the sense of horror engendered by the creature. Its bestial characteristics reinforce the vampire's link with nature and enhance the feeling of fear that the myth inspires. Its ability to control and manipulate nature reinforces the image of the vampire's power. Although the creature is an unnatural freak, its multifarious connections with the natural world are a powerful part of the vampire storyteller's toolbox.

NOTES

1. In some cases, however, the reverse is true. In some gypsy folklore, if the dogs are quiet, then there are vampires around. See Barber, p. 69.
2. Quoted in *Folklore of the Scottish Highlands,* p. 108.
3. Quoted in Summers, p. 109.
4. *Dracula,* p. 157. This is a good example, as the three images appear on one page. There are also allusions elsewhere in the book to other animals, for example, panthers, vipers, and foxes.
5. *Dracula, p.* 305.
6. See "Werewolf," in *The Vampire Encyclopaedia.*
7. For further information, see under "Werewolves of Poligny," in *Encyclopaedia of Witchcraft and Demonology.*
8. Ibid., under "Werewolves of St. Claude."
9. The Dacians were Indo-European tribes partly conquered by the Romans, who lived in the territories where Romania is now.
10. *Dracula,* p. 38.
11. *Witches of Dorset,* p. 55.
12. Summers, p. 162.
13. Barber, p. 42.
14. Hawksmoor, p. 16.
15. Summers, p. 163.
16. Bram Stoker, "The Judge's House," in David Stuart Davies, p. 163.
17. Strangely reminding the reader of the more famous *The Picture of Dorian Gray* (1890), by Stoker's friend, Oscar Wilde.
18. *Dracula,* p. 255.
19. Ibid., p. 39.
20. Ibid., p. 147.
21. Summers, p. 173.
22. *Dracula,* p. 323.

CHAPTER 8

A Complementary Figure of Blood—the Witch

They either beheld their children sink one after the other into the grave, or their youthful forms, withered by the unholy, vampire embrace of Brunhilda, assume the decrepitude of sudden age.
—Johann Ludwig Tieck, "Wake Not the Dead!"

Vampires attract humans into their topsy-turvy world, where all the laws of nature are reversed: life is confused with death, the night is dedicated to action and the day to sleep, youth is won at the price of eternal doom. This grotesque existence is a contorted image of the universe, a perilous deviation from normality. This is one of the most fascinating aspects of vampire mythology, and yet it is in no way innovative or original. Witches and vampires are closely connected. They both own powers far above those of mortal men, powers which in addition are unnatural and used for evil. According to Montague Summers, "certain aspects of witchcraft have much in common with the vampire tradition, especially the exercise of that malign power whereby the witch caused her enemies to dwindle, peak and pine, draining them dry as hay."[1] The association goes back to Classical times. The Greek goddess Hecate later came to be regarded as the goddess of witches. She was also the Queen of the Phantom World. In this guise, she was responsible for many supernatural entities, including the vampiric *empusas* and the sinister *mormos*, as well as the *lamia*.

Carmilla, Lucy, the women in Dracula's castle, the little girl Claudia in *Interview with the Vampire*, are literary granddaughters of the medieval witches and owe them a lot. Superficially, there is little resemblance between Coppola's Lucy in her sexy red silk nightdress and the dozens of women who were drowned or burned at the stake across Europe a few centuries ago. And yet, there is a close connection between them.[2]

The woman vampire is made up of two images. One of them is the seductive temptress who lures unsuspecting young men to their doom. A detailed consideration of this will be the subject of a later chapter. But a more grotesque image is of the witch-like vampire who feeds on the lifeblood of innocents, especially children. We will now consider just what makes this image so powerful. In the process, we will see that it has been created as a result of a number of different influences, not just that of the vampire. In medieval times, those who were witches were a threat to the established order of the Church; they were also deemed to be at risk of returning as vampires when they died, and their rituals were abhorrent as a result.[3]

The second-century writer Lucius Apuleius made an explicit link between witches and vampire-like activity when he wrote *The Golden Ass*. One story tells of Aristomenes and Socrates, two young friends, who meet after a long separation. Aristomenes is shocked at how disheveled his friend is. Socrates explains that he has come under the influence of a woman who has forced him to work as her servant. When Aristomenes angrily tells him to quit, Socrates replies that he cannot because this woman is a witch. Aristomenes laughs and tells him to come away with him. Socrates, against his better judgment, agrees to do so, and they resolve to escape as quickly as possible next morning.

As they sleep, however, Aristomenes is aware of a noise in the room. In a horrified trance, he sees two women, the witch and a friend, enter the room, cut Socrates's throat, and collect the blood in a goblet. They then leave. Aristomenes tries to attract attention, but the door is locked and he cannot. In the morning, to his intense relief Aristomenes sees that Socrates is still very much alive. It had been nothing save a terrible nightmare. There were no injuries anywhere on Socrates's body, though he clearly had not slept well as he was extremely pale. The two men proceed on their journey. After a while, hot and tired, they stop at a river to drink. As soon as the running water touches Socrates's lips, he drops down dead, a wound in his throat, and his corpse already emaciated and gaunt. The running water, a totem of power in many supernatural stories, has shown Socrates as he really is—very much dead as a result of the vampire-witches' activities.

Apuleius, initiated in several religions and mysteries, used in his works elements of folklore, as well as his inside knowledge of secret ceremonies, some of which in one way or another "traveled" over time and evolved under the influence of new religions and ways of thinking. One example of such evolution concerned the celebrations of the Greek god Dionysus. He was the son of Zeus and a mortal woman, Semele. Hera hated this baby, and she asked the Titans to kill him and cut his body into pieces, boil them inside a cauldron, and eat them. But a goddess found his heart and saved it, and Rhea gave life to Dionysus again.

The myth associates Dionysus with life and death, with the cycles and rebirth of nature, with wine and its powers over the mind, with music and song (his ceremonies were wild and memorable), and with fertility and eroticism. The spring public ceremonies celebrating him were one of the most important moments of the year. Symbolically, Dionysus himself appeared from the sea, holding a branch of vine. A cortège processed to the temple called *Limnaion,* where the god was joined by the queen: their sacred union brought fertility and wealth to the entire community.

This union between the supernatural and the mortal was a common theme in Greek myths. Eroticism and fertility represented the basis of many traditions, and rituals and divine intervention could only enhance the symbolism. The gods would appear in human or animal form and make love to mortals. Later, Christianity saw the ancient myths as blasphemy and heresy, and what was once the celebrated union between gods and mortals now took on a demonic dimension. The clash between the new religion and the pagan myths, together with old images of blood-sucking demons, turned out to be fertile soil for the vampire myth. Under the influence of Christianity, the old fertility rituals were read in a negative key, and the vampire borrows the sexual attributes of the ancient deities and spirits in an inverted form. Thus, reinterpreted, the vampire is seen as a demonic harbinger of death for the community, no longer the guarantor of the richness of lands and fertile wombs. More than that, the embrace of the vampire brings not new life but death.

The celebrations of Dionysus included an element of the malefic, too, as at the time of his festivals the spirits of the dead returned from the Inferno, especially the *Kere,* carriers of evil influences from the world of darkness. The third day of the celebrations was dedicated to them, and a special broth was made which had to be consumed before nightfall. When night came, the spirits returned to Hades, but during this festival the dead brought to the earth the promise of good crops and riches. Dionysus, revealed as a god of the dead and of fertility at the same time, governs over both life and death. It is no coincidence that the cult of Dionysus has been shown to be connected with human sacrifice, for example, on Chios and Lesbos.

From these public celebrations, a different cult was born, more violent and frenetic, where women had a very strange part. These rites were celebrated at nighttime, in forests and in the mountains, far away from the cities and their order. Dressed in animal skins and wearing ivy in their hair and snakes around their waists, they went into the forest, where they sang and danced in circles, like whirlwinds, and waited for the god to reveal himself to them. They were said to have miraculous powers, and could make milk or wine spring from rocks and honey drip from their staffs. They carried and breastfed small does or wolf cubs, flames burned in their hair. The climax was the violent sacrifice of animals (and maybe even humans) whose meat they ate raw. It was the symbolic killing of the god himself, who was afterwards resurrected. This total freedom from all norms, conventions, and interdictions was also an initiation into the mysteries of nature and of the three-times-born god. It was the triumph of life over death, in the divine being, in nature and in man, and gave them magic powers, such as the ability to see the future. The sacred ecstasy revealed the body as a vessel for the immortal soul.

What is striking is how many similarities exist between the descriptions of these rituals and the accounts of witches' sabbats in medieval treatises. The concept had appeared by the fourteenth century. The figure of the medieval witch is another example of ancient mythology reread in a Christian key. The old prophetesses, the nymphs, and the fertility goddesses with their power over nature and man did not fit well in what was largely a man's world. The Middle Ages could be a hard time to be a woman. Having few rights, they were often placed at the mercy of their fathers, brothers, and husbands. With the exception of those women who devoted themselves to God in a nunnery, a woman's rightful place was in the house, working; elsewhere, a woman was seen as a temptress, a devilish trick to lure men to perdition.

The Fathers of the Church sometimes described woman as impure in body and in spirit, and therefore dangerous and even demonic. Mankind had, after all, been brought low by a woman, Eve. Women had become a threat for the Church, and the most grotesque representations of them emanated from the monasteries. These representations reached their peak in the demonology tracts written for the Inquisitors. From *Malleus Maleficarum,* first published in 1486, to Francesco Maria Guazzo's *Compendium Maleficarum,* published with pictures of the sabbat in 1608, the image of the witch was "embellished" by these men of the Church in the most striking ways.

The very structure of the sabbat respects the stages of so-called pagan rites. Just like the ancient descriptions of Apuleius, for example, the witches would gather in forests, where they waited for the Devil to appear to them, often in the shape of a goat or a dog (*Compendium Maleficarum*). The newcomers were initiated in these dark rituals, and they would swear allegiance to Satan, who would then officiate over a Black Mass. Reading the Holy Mass from back to front was one of the accusations brought against witches by the Inquisition tribunals. This "Black Mass" is sometimes linked with vampirism; it has, for example, appeared on several occasions as a method of reviving a vampire in films.[4] Symbolically, the Mass was a devilish inversion of the word of God. And as the Bible describes the *Logos* as the source of divine Creation, reading the Mass from back to front was more than a sacrilege, it was a symbolic way of bringing the world back into chaos and recreating it as the realm of the Devil, who becomes the creator and the destroyer at the same time. The Black Mass was followed by a banquet where witches danced in a circle and ate human flesh, especially unbaptized babies. Intercourse with the

Devil (among others) was also part of the sabbat, and a regular accusation in witchcraft trials. These are three themes which went straight from the Inquisition halls into the vampire legends.

The dance of the witches includes one element which represents a terrifying threat to all that is good: the women danced widdershins. Seen as a reversal of natural harmony, the anticlockwise movement is a way to destroy the essential order of the world and to recreate it under the sign of evil. From this point of view, a predecessor of the vampire and a complementary figure of blood is the witch. At the witches' sabbat, the participants danced widdershins, replacing the life-bringing movement of the sun with a hellish ritual symbolizing the destruction of the world.

In this symbol which belongs to the *mundus inversus* of the witch and the vampire, we can recognize a similar deconstruction of the world like the one mirrored in much older, Celtic superstitions concerning widdershins movements, which reverse the laws of nature as they are dictated by the movement of the sun. Going against the established laws of the universe means jeopardizing the order which ensures its very existence. The movement of the sun, one of the first natural elements to be integrated into religious thought all over the world, dictated the rules of life and the evolution of the natural world to which man was sacredly integrated. The reversed movement, anticlockwise, invited disaster, because it defied the laws of life itself. During the Middle Ages, before attacking a castle, an army would march round its walls anticlockwise as a way of invoking supernatural assistance. Such thinking can be found even at the heart of Christmas traditions: stirring the ingredients of the Christmas pudding clockwise would certainly make a wish come true.

The disturbance of these universal structures is a threat to all forms of life, because order and coherence keep the world from disintegration. The vampire threatens an entire community, as its touch contaminates all that is pure and orderly with the unholy and un-whole patterns of the dark and the abnormal existence of the undead. Just like the witches, the vampires destroy the normality of the universal laws, and the latest developments of the myth take this to the level where the spirits of darkness want to destroy the world—Buffy the Vampire Slayer is not fighting against isolated cases of vampirism, but she has to stop "organized" demons from taking over the world. As Buffy repeatedly averts the end of the world, her friend Riley confesses: "I suddenly feel myself needing to know the plural of 'apocalypse'" ("A New Man," season four). Buffy's epitaph is a reminder of this: "She saved the world. A lot" ("The Gift," season five).

Another element which makes the transition between the witches' sabbat and the vampire story is the banquet and the killing of children and eating their flesh, not only as a heresy—although it was undoubtedly a symbol of a profane and perverted mirror image of the Eucharist—but also due to the curative and magical powers which blood (especially innocent blood) was supposed to have.

Babies were symbols of purity and the link between the present and the future. They were a sign that the gods favored a home, and the expression "to be blessed with children" exists in many languages. Children were also seen as a way of achieving immortality, of ensuring the survival of a family, and they were representations of future life for the community. Killing babies means jeopardizing the very future of the community. Destroying innocence means pushing the world out of joint, undermining its foundations. In witches' trials, the witnesses spoke of babies being eaten at a devilish banquet: "The meat they ordinarily eat is the flesh of young children, which they cook and make ready in the synagogue, sometimes bringing them thither alive by stealing them from the houses where they have opportunity to come."[5]

Consequently, those who threaten the lives of children horrify society in a way that few others do. Those who eat their flesh are regarded as the most evil of all monsters. The terror of the image is at the heart of the blacker children's fairy tales: Hansel and Gretel wandering through the forest and being fattened for the witch's dinner is one good example, Little Red Riding Hood and the Big Bad Wolf, another.

The position of the woman inside the home and the community was a very special one, and its importance was mirrored in the fear that this position could be converted to serve evil. She took care of the hearth, a very special role,[6] as fire is associated with life, purification, and power, on the one hand, and with destruction and the flames of hell, on the other. Women also made food for the family, and often knew traditional cures for disease and even evil spells. In some ways, the image of the witch whispering incantations over her bubbling cauldron is an inverted image of the housewife busy with her pots.

Women were also knowledgeable about the rituals connected to the essential moments of life: birth, marriage, pregnancy, death. They knew what was allowable and what was strictly forbidden, and made sure that these conventions were followed in order to ensure that these important events respected the ancient traditions that protected mankind from evil in a mixture of pagan and Christian ritual.

There were two figures in particular linked to the idea of life, death, and magic. One of the most respected and feared figures in the community was the midwife. She attended the pregnant woman before, during, and after childbirth. She delivered the baby and knew all the relevant traditional remedies and customs. Generally regarded as "white witches," legends grew around them, such as the East Anglian belief that they had supernatural powers which helped them to arrive in time to deliver a baby. In those times, when life was very fragile and often the mother, the child, or even both could die in childbirth, the midwife was regarded with fear, as one who had power over life and death.

The other figure was also connected to small babies and mothers. For various reasons, such as the mother's weakness or unfortunate death, or the custom which said that rich women should not breastfeed their babies, small children were given to the care of a woman to feed and even raise them. Because of the poor conditions of the age and the lack of skill and medicine, not many children survived their first year. The nanny was often blamed for this, especially if the child was a boy. The nanny was treated with caution; she could turn out to be a witch and harm the baby or sell it to the Devil.

This idea, again, has its roots deep in pre-Christian thought. In Greek mythology, the goddess Demeter, heartbroken after her daughter Persephone was kidnapped by Hades, the god of the Inferno, went to work as a servant for Celeus, the king of Eleusis. She took care of his son, Demophošn, and she decided to give immortality to the little boy. She anointed him with ambrosia and at nighttime, when everybody was asleep, she put him into a heated oven. One night, his mother woke up and went to his room. There she saw the stranger to whom she had entrusted her child putting the baby into the flames. Frightened, she tried to save him, when the stranger revealed herself in her divine aura. She scolded the frightened mother for her foolishness and told her that she only wanted to offer to her son the godly gift of immortality: "Had it not been for your impudence, I should have put this child forever beyond the reach of old age and death; but now it is no longer possible for me to shelter him from death." Having interrupted the ritual, it was impossible to complete it.[7] The goddess left and asked the king to build a temple for her in Eleusis, but as a sign of gratitude, she gave to Triptolemus, Celeus' oldest son, the first grain of corn and showed him how to cultivate it. Archaeological research shows that the temple in Eleusis was probably built in the fifteenth century B.C. and ceremonies, public and secret, went on there for 2,000 years. In this story we see how the mother involved is faced with a huge dilemma. On the one hand, she is terrified of dealing with a witch-like figure, but on the other, her child is offered the prospect of eternal life. This is analogous with the basic concept underlying vampirism, that in return for accessing so-called unnatural powers, with all their attendant risks, a person can achieve a kind of immortality.

The image of a woman killing small children is so contrary to nature and so grotesque that it represented a gold mine for authors of vampire stories. Carmilla first appears in her victim's vision when the girl was about 10, and the series of killings in the neighborhood start with young girls, which also refers to the symbolism of blood as a source of youth and beauty. The vampire ladies of the castle in Transylvania and Lucy, in *Dracula*, are the more monstrous as their victims are small children. These creatures of hell feed on innocence. Their voluptuous beauty becomes horrible when they attack such pure victims:

When Lucy—I call the thing that was before us Lucy because it bore her shape—saw us she drew back with an angry snarl, such as a cat gives when taken

unawares.... As she looked, her eyes blazed with unholy light, and the face became wreathed with a voluptuous smile. With a careless motion she flung to the
ground, callous as a devil, the child that up to now she had clutched strenuously
at her breast, growling over it as a dog growls over a bone. The child gave a sharp
cry, and lay there moaning. There was a coldbloodedness in the act....[8]

More horrible even than this is the episode where Jonathan Harker nar-
rowly escapes a curse that will last for eternity when he is pulled from the
clutches of three female vampires by the count. However, what happens
as a result is perhaps one of the more shocking episodes in the book:

"Are we to have nothing tonight?'" said one of them, with a low laugh, as she
pointed to the bag which he had thrown upon the floor, and which moved as
though there were some living thing within it. For answer he nodded his head.
One of the women jumped forward and opened it. If my ears did not deceive
me there was a gasp and a low wail, as of a half-smothered child. The women
closed round, while I was aghast with horror; but as I looked they disappeared,
and with them the dreadful bag. There was no door near them, and they could not
have passed me without my noticing. They simply seemed to fade into the rays of
the moonlight and pass out through the window, for I could see outside the dim,
shadowy forms for a moment before they entirely faded away.
     Then the horror faded away, and I sank down unconscious.[9]

     Little wonder.
     One of the more graphic and gruesome descriptions of the vampires'
love for the blood of innocents is to be found in "Wake Not the Dead!"
Brunhilda needs young blood to restore vitality to her dead body and

whenever she beheld some innocent child, whose lovely face denoted the exuber-
ance of infantine health and vigour, she would entice it by soothing words and
fond caresses into her most secret apartment, where, lulling it to sleep in her arms,
she would then in a similar manner drain his veins of the vital juice. Thus children, youths and maidens quickly faded away, as flowers gnawn by the cankering
worm: the fullness of their limbs disappeared; a sallow line succeeded to the rosy
freshness of their cheeks, the liquid lustre of the eye was deadened, even as the
sparkling stream when arrested by the touch of frost; and their locks became thick
and grey, as if already ravaged by the storm of life.

It is the betrayal of innocence that is the most shocking of all. The
vampire is an enchantress, luring the unwary to destruction. As their life
force weakens, so hers gets stronger, as they lose their vigor and vitality,
so she assumes it. Some women who preyed on young children were condemned to a half-life beyond the grave in folklore, too. One of these was
the White Lady, a woman who committed infanticide. The first known
mention of her dates back to 1552, and relates the story of the widow of the
count of Orlamunde who murdered two children in the hope of endear-
ing herself to a rich and powerful nobleman. This developed into a later

tale of a woman who was seduced by a knight. She gave birth to a child but, being rejected by her lover, she threw the child under his horse and murdered the knight. While she was in jail, she hanged herself. She later returned as a wraith at the scene of the murders she committed. Those that saw her were doomed to die soon afterwards as a result of her awful curse.

A Greek legend speaks about Lamia, a beautiful mortal loved by Zeus, who gave him many children. Hera, the jealous supreme goddess, killed all Lamia's offspring. Grief-stricken, Lamia lost her mind and started to attack and devour any child that she met. As punishment, she was transformed into a dog. Later, the legend was modified, and *lamiae* became vampire-like creatures which sucked the blood of men.

This image is found elsewhere in the vampire myth, too. The undead come to haunt their families. At the beginning of the twentieth century, the folklorist A. Murgoci heard the following story from Romanian peasants:

Some fifteen years ago, the old mother of a peasant called Dinu Gheorghita died in Amarasti village, in the northern part of Dolj county. After a few months, her eldest son's children started to die one after the other, and they were followed by the children of her younger son. The old woman's sons were frightened, so they opened the tomb, cut the body in two and put it back. In spite of all this, the deaths did not stop. They opened the tomb for a second time and what did they see? The corpse was untouched, with no sign of any wound! It was a very strange thing. They took her body into a forest and placed it under a tree, in an untrodden corner of the woods. There, they opened the body, took out the heart, which bled profusely, cut it in four, which they threw into the fire and burnt. They gathered the ashes, mixed them with water and gave this drink to the children. They threw the body into flames, burnt it and buried the ashes. The deaths stopped.[10]

The third element we mentioned is yet another link that goes from the orgiastic celebrations of Dionysus to the witches' sabbat, and then was assimilated into the vampire myth. The witches were accused of having intercourse with Satan. Even the image of the Devil resembles mythological figures, such as the inoffensive half-god Pan, with his he-goat's horns, beard, tail, and cloven feet. The vampire, half-human, half-demon, has the power of attraction and the immortality of old pagan figures. Women-vampires, especially, resemble the medieval descriptions of the witches at their sabbat, who were also reminiscent of their ancestors who joined the secret initiation of Dionysus and Bacchus.

Symbols have a powerful part to play in all this. Although witches were, in the eyes of the Church, reversing the symbolic values implicit in Christianity when they conducted their ceremonies, they would be powerless when confronted by "true" Christian symbols. This was, for example, why they were unable to recite the Lord's Prayer, as the forces of righteousness will always outwit and defeat those of evil. So it was with the undead. Vampire literature and cinematography often depict the forces of evil as being powerless when faced with a crucifix, symbol of Christ's sacrifice and might. The image was well known to the medieval world, and the undead, who were unnatural in the sight of God, could not resist its power. And, even in the contemporary *Buffy the Vampire Slayer,* the power of the cross is still used as an antidote to vampires, although this is somewhat ambiguous as the crucifix is still an effective deterrent even though the *Buffy* series seems to have little other regard for the power of Christianity.[11]

This is an old motif, as shown in a story told by the medieval chronicler, Walter Map, of a man who had died an atheist but could not find peace (a classic vampire story element, this—the earth will not receive the body of the unjust). His animate corpse wandered the region, but was eventually trapped in an orchard. When he tried to return to his grave, he found that Roger, the Bishop of Worcester, had erected a cross over his resting place. The symbol was too powerful for him to confront, and he could not bypass it to get to his tomb, so he retreated. The crowd that had assembled removed the cross and the "corpse" rushed back to the grave, covering himself with earth. Once he was safely covered up, the cross was raised in the soil over his grave and his spirit wandered no more.

In later times, when the modus operandi of the Church started to change, placing greater focus on confession, cases of witchcraft turned into cases of possession.[12] Those possessed were no longer women at the margin of society, in small villages, but people in the towns, often nuns (the classic example being the case of the Loudun nuns in 1630). There is no longer the aspect of the pact; rather, the victim tries to resist evil, but has not enough power—a classic attribute of female victims in vampire literature. This strengthened element of duality is more powerful in the consciousness of the seventeenth and eighteenth centuries, and would come to represent an important part of the imaginative mixture that forms the basis of the corpus of texts that have the vampire as a central figure.

Woman's weakness made it easy for the Devil to transform her into his instrument, by possessing her body and spirit. The idea of devilish possession was borrowed by the vampire myth. The victims of the undead are entirely under their power, unable to defend themselves and to fight. Mina, without realizing what is going on, describes in her diary her first encounter with Dracula: "I was powerless to act; my feet, and my hands, and my brain were weighted, so that nothing could proceed at the usual pace...some leaden lethargy seemed to chain my limbs and even my will."[13]

In some vampire traditions, the link between women and sin is very explicitly made. One example is the *eretica,* a Russian vampire. This was a woman who had, during life, offered her soul to Satan in return for magical powers. After death, she returned to the earth, disguised as an old woman during the daytime. She was only active during spring and autumn. At other times, she slept in the coffins of those who had led unchristian lives. If someone were unlucky enough to fall into her grave, then they would slowly fade away. In common with other vampires, this one could be destroyed by use of a stake or by burning.

The image of an aged woman is found elsewhere in vampire lore, as well as in witchcraft. There was, for example, the *vetala,* an Indian vampire. This creature was traditionally seen mounted on a green horse. She appeared as an old woman and sucked blood from females. The stories surrounding her were later adapted by Richard Burton in "Vikram and the Vampire," and may have had an influence on Bram Stoker. The figure is also part of East European vampire lore and has been used in literature, albeit in lesser-known works, such as "Good Lady Ducayne" by Mary Braddon (1896) and "The Room in the Tower" by E. F. Benson (1912).

The power of blood is a common feature of the witch's power, just as it is for vampire literature and lore. Blood could be used to seal a pact with the Devil,[14] but drawing it can drain the life force of a witch if it is not offered freely. This is a common focus for English legends. One such was of two old women living in Morvah, Cornwall. One was convinced that the other was bewitching her. In order to destroy the power of the enchantment, she attacked the supposed witch with a nail, drawing her blood in an attempt to drain the life force from her, and so removing the spell.[15] In 1884, in Sherborne, Dorset, a trial took place where the accused, Tamar Humphries, was charged with attacking her neighbor, Sarah Smith. The latter, described as "on the shady side of eighty," was suddenly approached by the defendant who accused her of bewitching her child. She attacked her with a knitting needle, saying that "you're a witch, and I'll draw the blood of thee." In this particular case, the defendant was found guilty.[16]

The most famous so-called real vampire of all is probably Countess Elisabeth Bathory, who achieved notoriety at the beginning of the seventeenth century. The tale brings witchcraft, vampirism and an obsession with the power of blood together: all played a significant part in the events of the time (1611). The countess was an illustrious Hungarian noblewoman. She was rich and powerful. But she was also an aging widow. And this, it seemed, was what led her to commit acts of unspeakable sadism and cruelty, leading ultimately to murder: nothing less than a literal thirst for blood.

The countess had married young and, to all intents and purposes, enjoyed a normal relationship with her husband. They had several children and the countess appeared to be a good mother. But over time, there were rumors that she was an enthusiastic participant in the lesbian orgies for which her aunt, Klara Bathory, was renowned. The countess also started to exhibit cruel tendencies. Servant girls who made the smallest of mistakes were beaten remorselessly. In one case, a girl was stripped naked, tied to a tree, and smeared with honey so that the insects would be irresistibly attracted to her.

When the count died in 1604, her excesses got progressively worse. One day, an incident occurred which was to have terrible consequences. In a frenzied rage, the countess beat one of her serving girls until she was awash with blood. Some of the blood splashed on to the countess's skin. The countess noticed when she next looked in the mirror that the skin where the blood had been splashed appeared younger than the rest of her body. Convinced this meant that blood had restorative powers, the countess now had a raison d' être for her hitherto pointless sadism.

From this point on, the countess had an unquenchable lust for blood. She had been struggling to cope with the physical and psychological effects of the aging process for some time. At the height of her physical powers she had been a society beauty, but age had taken its toll. She had already turned to sorcery to try to counteract the process. She had a number of female servants who assisted her, of whom the most notorious was Dorottya "Dorka" Szentes. The countess tried to destroy her enemies by burning wax effigies of them. She beat cockerels to death, thinking that their spilled blood would be a protection against her foes. But, as she sat in front of her looking glass for several hours a day, her invocations to prevent the aging process from taking effect were in vain (a classic fairy tale motif that most children would recognize from the story of Snow White).

She quickly began to decimate the local population of its virgin girls. Servants were taken on at a rapid rate, in many cases never to be seen again. The accusations made at the later trial concerning the fate of these young women were almost beyond belief. It was said that, at four o'clock in the morning, a magical hour, as it was the transition point from night to day, the countess would take a bath, not in water scented with oils, but in the blood of young virgins. The torture she inflicted on them was horrific: one account from an accomplice during the trial speaks of her having "stark-naked girls laid flat on the floor of her bedroom, and she tortured them so much that they had to scoop up the blood by the pailful afterwards and bring up cinders to cover the pools."

She constructed a version of the iron maiden in which the victim would be forced into a box shaped like a human body with sharp nails pointing inwards. As the lid was slammed shut, the nails would pierce the body, causing immense pain and suffering, as well as huge bloodshed. The maiden would then be pulled up into the air on pulleys, and one of the countess's servants would burn the victim with a torch, causing her to writhe in agony and impale herself on the spikes. The countess would sit underneath the cage, as the blood showered down. The sadoerotic significance of these actions was evidenced by the fact that the instrument of torture had pubic hair and red nipples painted on it. The blood would run down specially constructed channels, where it could be filtered into a container, collected and used later for the countess's bath of blood.

Practical problems were to lead to the undoing of the countess. She initially sated her lust with the blood of young peasant girls whose disappearance would not be noted. But then she started to turn to girls of the minor nobility, "blue blood," so to speak—a variation on the superior powers of noble blood as espoused in Arthurian literature.[17] The disappearance of these girls was much harder to cover up. She was also faced with the problem of what to do with the bodies. The local clergy were becoming increasingly uncomfortable at the large number of girls they were burying who had previously served at Csejthe Castle, the countess's home. And the countess herself was making the classic mistake of the overconfident criminal, thinking that she was indestructible and not taking due care over how she disposed of the bodies.

Soon, rumors were flying around the countryside. The King of Hungary set up a commission to investigate the accuracy of the allegations. It was headed by the Palatine, one of his highest-ranking officials. He arrived at the castle of Csejthe just after Christmas, 1610. He questioned the countess and ordered that the castle be searched. There were a number of subterranean passages where the torture normally took place, but his men managed to find their way around with the help of some local people who knew something of their design. What those searching the castle found shocked them to the core. In one of the chambers, they found a buxom, fair-haired, naked girl lying dead on the floor. Her hair had been torn out, her thighs and genitals burned, her skin ripped to pieces. One of those who found her said that "her own mother wouldn't recognise her."

Two other naked girls, close to death, were found nearby. Other girls were found locked in cages, deprived of food, soon to be the victim of the countess's pleasure. Her accomplices soon admitted to their part in the crimes committed in the castle. Individually, they confessed to taking part in dozens of killings. But the most chilling statement of all was from Jakab Szilvassy from Csejthe. He told of the existence of a book "which put the number of girls killed at 650, and that number [was written] in her Ladyship's own hand."

When the evidence was provided to the king, he was outraged. "On seeing the signs of her terrible and beastly cruelties, his highness became most indignant. At one with the counsel of his retinue, he ordered the widow of Count Nadasdy, as befitting a bloodthirsty and blood-sucking Godless woman caught in the act, should be arrested, and he sentenced her to lifelong imprisonment in Csejthe Castle."

Her accomplices were "unimportant" compared to the countess, and four of them were subjected to the full humiliation of a trial. The charges included sorcery, vampirism, ritual murder, and blood magic. Attempts to also put the countess on trial failed. Indeed, everything possible was done to avoid embarrassing her more than she already had been. All references to bloodbaths were quashed, although the prosecutor attempted to table the subject. The sentence on the countess was confirmed, but for the others, there would be no mercy (except for one, where a lack of evidence saved her).

The trial documents testify with graphic clarity to the horror of the fate awaiting them:

First of all Ilona [one of the maidservants], secondly Dorottya [Dorka], as the foremost perpetrators of this great blood crime, and in accordance with the lawful punishment of murderers, to have all the fingers on their hands, which they used as instruments in so much torture and butcherings and which they dipped in the blood of Christians, torn out by the public executioner with a pair of red-hot pincers; thereafter they shall be thrown alive on the fire. As to Ficzko [the manservant], because of his youthful age and complicity in fewer crimes, him we sentence to decapitation. His body, drained of blood, should then be reunited with his two fellow accomplices where we wish that he be burned.

The guilty parties were all executed on January 7, 1611. Subsequent attempts by the countess's relatives to have her sentence overturned failed. The king confirmed the findings and ordered that the countess be bricked up in a small room in her castle, with only a small opening through which food could be passed to her. To the end, the countess showed no remorse. She berated those who had accused her, and called on her supporters to rise up in rebellion against the injustice of her sentence. But it was in vain. Her sentence was carried out, and she was bricked up in her own castle, deprived of light, of company, of hope. She died on "August 14th, 1614, suddenly and without a crucifix and without light."[18] It was a fitting end to a depraved life.

The story of the countess seems incredible, yet it is derived from the trial records and a flow of correspondence between the King of Hungary and his officials—in other words, on historical documents rather than some literary yarn. Unless those testifying were deliberately lying (and there is no evidence of this), then there is no doubt that the events described actually took place, or were genuinely believed to have taken place. These extraordinary happenings were later recorded by the Revd. Sabine Baring-Gould (writer of the words to the famous hymn "Onward Christian Soldiers") in his book, *The Book of Were-wolves: Being an Account of a Terrible Superstition* (1865). This was to be one of the source research documents used by an Irish civil servant turned theater manager and author of a book called *Dracula*.

The countess is a rare example of someone obsessed with the rejuvenative power of blood. It also neatly links the two worlds of witchcraft and vampirism, although really, they are both inhabitants of the same demonic land. There are strong thematic similarities between the two, for example, vampires and witches are sometimes supposed to be able to make themselves invisible in folklore. In vampire legend, however, the link occasionally becomes explicit. So in Russia, for example, where the vampire was known as *myertovets, vurdulak,* or *upierzh,* a person became a vampire if they were the offspring of a werewolf or a witch, or as a result of witchcraft. In Portugal, where the vampire was known as a *bruxsa*, witchcraft was again the cause of vampirism.

The two brands of demonic activity were part of the same closely linked world. Both were inversions of the normal rules of Christian goodness. The female vampire, in the guise of the seductive temptress or the evil being thirsting for the flesh and blood of children, closely resembles the enchantress. The mass hysteria which characterized the witch hunts was also present in the reactions of the populace when faced with the outbreak of a supposed vampire epidemic. Witchcraft threatened the immortal soul of man in a similar way to vampirism. Even the remedies used to dispose of the bodies of witches sometimes resembled those used to deal with a vampire.[19] At the heart of vampire lore were witch-like beings who sold their souls to the Devil in return for the promise of a twisted, perverted immortality which sentenced them to eternal damnation as they searched in vain for peace.

NOTES

1. *The Vampire in Lore and Legend,* p. xv.

2. It has been suggested that one possible root of the word "vampire" is the Turkish *uber* meaning "witch". See *Encyclopaedia of Witchcraft and Demonology* under "Vampire."

3. See "Black Mass," in *The Vampire Encyclopaedia.*

4. See for example, *Taste the Blood of Dracula,* a 1969 Hammer film. The finale takes place, *Carmilla*-like, in an abandoned church.

5. The 1611 testimony of Sister Madeleine de Demandolx, in *The Encyclopedia of Witchcraft and Demonology,* under "Sabbath."

6. A similar role at community level was held by the blacksmith, who had power over fire and metals, like the Greek god Hephaistos. Not only did they have a strong ascendancy over all the craftsmen of the community, who literally depended on them for their tools and instruments, but they were also thought to have the power to cure the sick. It is interesting that in the novel, *Varney the Vampyre,* the man who kills the vampire Clare is a blacksmith, who, as a result of his actions, removes the plague of vampirism from his community.

7. The same theme also appears in Egyptian mythology, where Isis, during her quest to find the dead body of her husband and brother, Osiris, arrived at the court of the King of Byblos. She was entrusted with the care of the king's newly born son. The sacred ritual of fire was interrupted by Astarte, the baby's mother, and thus it became impossible for the goddess to confer immortality to their son.

8. *Dracula,* p. 219.

9. Ibid., p. 63.

10. In Claude Lecouteux, *Vampiri si vampirism,* p. 103.

11. For further consideration of the relatively minor role given to religion in *Buffy,* see *Buffy the Vampire Slayer and Philosophy,* chap. 16.

12. See Michel Foucault, *Anormalii,* pp. 224–252.

13. *Dracula,* p. 309.

14. See Chapter 10.

15. *The Folklore of Cornwall,* p. 117.

16. *Witches of Dorset,* p. 29.

17. See Chapter 4.

18. For a more detailed discussion of the countess's case, see *The Dracula Myth,* chap. 9–14.

19. See Barber, p. 20, footnote.

CHAPTER 9

The Magus

The vampire…is of cunning more than mortal, for his cunning be the growth of ages; he have still the aids of necromancy, which is, as his etymology imply, the divination of the dead, and all the dead that he can come nigh to are for him at command…

—Bram Stoker, *Dracula*

Strip the vampire of his long fangs and his preference for sleeping in a coffin and you will find beneath his black cape a figure that has long fascinated the human mind and given rise to numerous speculations and controversies. Just like the vampire, this figure was known under many different names: the sorcerer, the alchemist, the necromancer, the magus. He is an image of duality, seen both as the fool who has wasted his days chasing the impossible and the wise man who discovers the deepest secrets of life; as one with power over the elements and the charlatan who feeds on the fears and illusions of the simple; as the sorcerer who sells his soul to the Devil and finds the secret of wealth and immortality.

From the medicine man to the priest in the temple, from the priest-king to the magician of the palace, the figure of the man who mastered occult knowledge and sciences was a dominant one across many millennia and many cultures. In the Christian world, he was often a member of the clergy with the power to summon dark spirits as well as exorcise them. He knew the necessary rituals, as the invocation of the demons was only a reversed invocation of the divinity.

The figure of the magus was borrowed by vampire tales in two different ways. The first is that of the opponent of the vampire, the man with the wisdom of the ancients and of the arts of magic as well, able to face up to and even defeat the powers of the undead. The second instance is that of the vampire itself who, like a magus, has power over the dead and over death. He also has control over the minds and bodies of the human beings that fall under his influence, and even over nature (which we will consider in the next chapter, as it is a fundamental feature of the pact).

Homo magus is a complex figure in all ancient cultures, a man of great wisdom and cunning, with power over nature, the ability to bring the dead back to life, and to halt the aging process. In Indian tradition, Kavya Usanas was a magus involved in a conflict between gods and demons. He would let nobody, from either side, have access to his secret science, until finally he accepted one of the gods as his disciple. Iranian legends speak of a priest-king, Kavi-Usan, who had the power to rejuvenate people. His powers made him vain, and the demons ensnared him in a war meant to provoke the fall of the gods. His unique knowledge strengthens his position between two clashing forces, the demons and the gods. As teacher of the demons, he strengthens one of the poles of power to the detriment of the other. Kavi-Usan, the destroyer of order, is the only one who can restore it. By accepting one of the gods as his disciple, he allows the balance of power to regain its equilibrium.

Improper use of magic can destroy the equilibrium of the world as magical knowledge can be good or evil, depending on how it is used. In this way, in vampirism, we have vampire-like figures that use magic, such as Dracula. Glory in *Buffy* wants to destroy the world as we know it and to open the gates to the demonic realm. On the other hand, there is the healer like van Helsing. Giles—the magus-like librarian—is a commander figure because he uses the ancient knowledge which offers him more power than the methods of the Initiative, a government body that uses only modern weaponry.

An association between science and magic was to play a significant role in ancient mythology in the role of the magus, and is also obvious in the methods that van Helsing uses in *Dracula.* "Tradition and superstition are everything,"[1] he says, but he uses the knowledge of books as well as the wisdom of lore. What we often find in vampire tales is a tension between the forces of conventional science and that of old traditions, symbolizing difficulties that have been present in much more mundane spheres than vampirology. This may refer to the fact that there is often a thin dividing line between superstition and science. In the past, men who dared to cross that line and challenge accepted norms, such as Copernicus or Galileo, found themselves at serious odds with the forces of conservatism, in their case, the Church.

The magi that we find in vampire literature often seem to reverse this trend, effectively stating that "old" superstitions are more powerful than "new" science. Science is limited by what can be explained by man, but the vampire defies logical explanation and can therefore only be destroyed by seemingly illogical means. Van Helsing is not afraid to use the forces of science—he experiments with blood transfusions, for example—but ultimately reverts to the use of crosses, garlic, stakes through the heart, and magic circles, among other seemingly superstitious remedies, to fight against his enemy. In *Buffy*, both superstition and science are used to fight against the forces of darkness. Giles has his esoteric knowledge, but the Initiative use modern technology in the battle. The former method is noticeably more effective than the latter.

The tensions between superstition and science are brought together in the short story "Mrs. Amworth" (1923), written by the English writer E. F. Benson. The story is not a particularly innovative one, but successfully brings together a number of typical vampire motifs. The storyline is straightforward enough. A widow comes to live in an English village, having arrived from India where her husband has died. Soon, people in the village fall ill. When one of the villagers realizes that Mrs. Amworth is a vampire and takes preventive measures, the illness stops. The widow is killed in an accident, but returns from beyond the grave to prey on the village. Only when her body is exhumed and a stake driven through the heart are the attacks halted.

The particular relevance of the story to the magus motif is that the vampire is uncovered by Francis Urcombe. Urcombe has an impressive academic pedigree, having once been a lecturer at Cambridge. However, he resigned his position at the university because his interests in the occult increasingly put him at odds with the scientific community. He has some exotic ideas, one of which is that all doctors should be made to study mesmerism. His thoughts on the scientific establishment were expressed explicitly when he says that "there is nothing that these seats of learning are so frightened of as knowledge, and the road to knowledge lies in the study of occult sciences." To Urcombe, the world as explained by science has tight restrictions: outside them lie "huge tracts of undiscovered country, which certainly exist, and the real pioneers of knowledge are those who, at the cost of being derided as credulous and superstitious, want to push on into these misty and probably perilous places."[2]

Urcombe becomes a classic magus figure in the fight against the vampire. An avid student of relevant lore, he knows exactly what to do when confronted with his enemy. And as he studies, his powers increase. He recognizes Mrs. Amworth instinctively as a vampire. And in his final confrontation with her, when her identity has been confirmed, merely tracing the sign of the cross with his fingers is enough to repulse her.

This link, sometimes complementary, sometimes contradictory, between science and superstition, reflects old beliefs, where the worlds of science and magic were linked. It can be found in Egyptian mythology, for example, in the figure of the god Thoth. He was a moon god (signifying occult knowledge), portrayed as a man with the head of an ibis. He was endowed with supreme wisdom, and was the creator of all sciences and arts: geometry, arithmetic, astronomy, medicine, surgery, soothsaying, music, drawing, and magic.

He was also connected with the rituals of death and rebirth. With his magic incantations and practices, he purified the dismembered body of Osiris and assisted in his resurrection. This burial ritual made it possible for the soul to be resurrected instead of returning to the world as a haunting shadow. At the final judgment, it is he who decides if the soul of the dead will be received by Osiris or is sentenced to wander endlessly across the earth instead. He also invented hieroglyphs, and was the scribe of the gods, keeper of archives concerning deities, the land of Egypt, and the life of every human being. He was the speaker of truth and recorder of history. The many images of Thoth as master of secret burial rituals that view death as a passage from one level of existence to another, as supreme magician and inventor of writing, and as a god of science, is highly significant to the evolution of the magus figure, as they, too, normally exhibit possession of some or all of these attributes to some degree.

The meaning of "Thoth" (three times great) was borrowed in Greek tradition for the god Hermes. Later, the legendary figure of Hermes Trismegistus, the archetypal magician, alchemist, and astrologer, was important not only for classical Greece, but also because he influenced the thinking of the fifteenth century when he reemerged among the alchemists of the Middle Ages. Numerous magicians and alchemists claimed they had inherited the wisdom of Thoth, that his occult knowledge was preserved in a corpus of texts that revealed the ancient magic and gave to the magus power over secret forces. There is indeed a group of texts which form the early practices and traditions of what was called, after the Greek transcription of Thoth's name, Hermetism. There are two initial types of texts, some of them of popular origin (referring to astrology, alchemy, magic, occult sciences), going back to the third century B.C. and early Hermetic literature, the most important being *Corpus Hermeticum*, particularly popular during the second century a.d. They contain a synthesis of Jewish, Egyptian, Greek, and even Iranian elements of thought.

Around 1460, Cosimo de Medici bought a manuscript of *Corpus Hermeticum* and asked the great Florentine humanist Marsilio Ficino (1433–1499) to translate it from Greek into Latin. In 1480, the image of Hermes Trismegistus appeared in a mosaic in the Cathedral of Siena, an interesting connection between Christian religion and magical thinking. The translation of his works into Latin influenced European philosophy through its most eminent thinkers and scientists (including Copernicus, Roger Bacon, and Isaac Newton [3]) for a long time. But most important for our study is the development that this corpus of Hermetic texts brought to the science of astrology and alchemy.

Alchemy was a complex science known to many ancient civilizations in Asia and Europe. At its center, there are two concepts which present a special interest in our particular quest: the philosopher's stone and the elixir of life. These two have been interpreted in many ways, as the language of the Hermetic texts is deliberately obscure. They have been read in a symbolic or religious key or with a very literal meaning, which sometimes distinguished the thinker and philosopher on the one side from the charlatan on the other. At the literal level (which influenced popular thinking far more than complex philosophical, religious, and esoteric interpretations), the philosopher's stone and the elixir of life have the magical properties of offering the owner eternal life and the power to transform inferior metals into gold. The fascination with wealth and immortality found in the "universal science" another of its countless avatars. It is these paths and not that of the esoteric interpretations that we are to follow here, as they will lead us closer to the heart of the vampire myth.[4]

Alchemy presents two elements that are core to many aspects of the vampire myth. The first and most important is the idea of obtaining eternal life, of defying death through magic; thus van Helsing describes Dracula as an alchemist. The elixir of life in vampire lore is, of course, blood. In "Wake Not the Dead!" for Brunhilda "it was necessary that a magic draught should animate the dark current in her veins, and awaken her to the glow of life and the flame of love—a potion of abomination—one not even to be named without a curse—human blood, imbibed while yet warm, from the veins of youth."[5]

The second aspect, turning base metals into gold, has more subtle resonances in many works of vampire literature. In a deviation from the figure of the vampire in folklore, literature often paints vampires as rich aristocrats: again, Dracula, but also Lord Ruthven in Polidori's "Vampyre," Varney the vampire, Louis (and many others) in *Interview with the Vampire*, and certainly, in a female representation, Carmilla for example. There is usually no obvious explanation for their wealth and the implication is that it comes from occult sources.

Ask any 12-year-old who Nicholas Flamel was and they will answer without too much hesitation: the owner of the philosopher's stone that Harry Potter kept from Voldemort. J. K. Rowling knows her history of the occult well, and it is interesting to find a famous fourteenth-century French alchemist as the friend of Albus Dumbledore. The story goes that, in the year 1357, Flamel bought an old booklet, written in Latin, and containing strange drawings, in which he thought he had found a sacred Judaic book that had been saved from the Temple of Jerusalem and contained the secret of the philosopher's stone. He dedicated his entire life to the deciphering of the secret drawings in the book.

Books with symbols and narrative that can only be deciphered by the initiated are connected in many instances to the magus in vampire tales. Van Helsing has access to a vast store of knowledge in such tomes which, because he has the skills required to interpret it, is his main, indeed his only, weapon against his archenemy Dracula. Giles in *Buffy* has a library which he accesses in order to help the Slayer in her battle against evil forces. Texts in coded symbols appear in the series. In *Nosferatu*, "Dracula" and Renfield communicate through letters written in magic signs that only they are able to understand.

In Flamel's book, one page in particular strikes us as being connected to the rituals of blood in which the sacrifice of the innocent can lead to the discovery of eternal life: "There was a king, with a sword in his hand, superintending a number of soldiers, who, in execution of his orders, were killing a great multitude of young children, spurning the prayers and fears of their mothers, who tried to save them from destruction. The blood of the children was carefully collected by another party of soldiers and put into a large vessel, in which two allegorical figures of the sun and moon were bathing themselves."[6]

In search of the key to this mystery, Flamel traveled for years in Spain, a land where Arab, Jewish, and Christian traditions mixed in a unique way. There he met a converted Jew, Cauches, who, hearing about the book, set out for Paris immediately. Unfortunately, he died en route and Nicholas Flamel returned alone to his study. But his trip was not wasted. On January 13, 1382, he is supposed to have obtained silver from mercury and on April 25 he finally obtained gold. He was an old man by that time, and it seems that the philosopher's stone only prolonged his life until the age of 116, one year after the death of his wife Petronella.

The ability to interpret esoteric texts is one aspect of the magus figure that is relevant to vampirology. Another aspect to consider is that of the necromancer. A wizard or magus was seen as somebody who could reverse the rites of passage and call the dead to wander the land of the living. He had the power to call spirits from beyond the grave. They would obey his summons and reveal to him the secrets of the future. Originally, the word necromancy meant the foretelling of the future with the aid of the dead. Later, in the Middle Ages, the word experienced a change of form into nigromancy, from the Latin niger, meaning black. This metamorphosis mirrored a change of significance. Necromancy (or nigromancy) was identified with black magic, and the spirits summoned were deemed to be demons who came under the power of the magician.

Because summoning the dead had become the preserve of witches and sorcerers, the magus became a figure of darkness. The idea of an archvampire who has the help of the hosts of the undead is even more terrifying. Van Helsing describes Dracula as a necromancer who would make use of the hosts of demons that he can summon through black magic.[7] In *Buffy*, Glory has the aid of spirits of the inferno, and in one episode ("Graduation Day," part 2, season 3), the mayor uses an army of vampires to take over the world. This power to summon such otherworldly forces is also found in nonvampiric literature. Shakespeare gives the power to summon the spirits of the dead and of those as yet unborn to the three Weird Sisters in *Macbeth*. Hecate, an important occult figure connected to witchcraft, death, and vampirism, opens the gates of the Inferno in order to let ghosts and evil apparitions appear before Macbeth and his wife, allowing their bloodstained past to haunt their present and predict their dark future.

In the context of resurrecting the dead, the story of Isis and Osiris is very significant as it became the foundation of burial rituals and passage beliefs in Egyptian thought and emerged in Christian Europe, thousands of years later, in the form of necromancy and black magic. Osiris, grandson of Ra, the sun god, married his sister Isis. But his evil brother Seth killed him and hid the body in a coffer which he threw in the Nile. When Isis heard this, she searched for his body. But Seth found it first and cut it into pieces which he spread all over the world. Isis, undeterred, located all the pieces, except for the phallus, which had been devoured by a Nile crab, and put them together. She was helped by Thoth, the master of magic, to bring Osiris back to life. By using magical formulas and incantations, they revived the murdered god. Isis, by the power of magic, conceived a son with him, Horus, who later avenged the murder of his father. After his resurrection, Osiris did not return to the earth but became a divinity of the dead, welcoming the souls of the just into the realm of eternal life.

The symbolic meaning of the myth which is built around Osiris as a divinity who dies and comes back to life is, of course, not unique. But there is something interesting about its ending. Although revived, Osiris chooses to give up the throne and retires to the underworld, which signifies that death, although defeated by magic, etches upon the soul a mark that cannot be removed.

In Christianity, the resurrected Christ assumes a different form than he had before his death and ascends to heaven shortly after his resurrection. Even if life is apparently restored, it has a different, darker dimension, which projects the spirit outside the world of the living. Through death, the soul can achieve immortality, but on a different level of existence.

The idea of bringing the dead back to life by means of magic survived, often in a literal sense. Those initiated in the mysteries of the occult, holders of the secrets of ancient gods and magicians, had the power to raise the dead from their graves, but at the same time, they knew that the life so offered was one of doom and eternal death. The figure of the vampire, and the magus who normally opposes him, is connected to both passage rituals and the use of magic, supernatural powers.[8]

Very occasionally, the role of the magus in the vampire story is explicitly linked to necromancy. For example, the necromancer plays a prominent role in "Wake Not the Dead!" when Walter meets a sorcerer, capable of bringing Brunhilda back from beyond the grave. Despite the warnings of the tragic consequences of doing so, the lord begs the wizard to restore life to his bride. He does so, drawing a circle round the grave, muttering magic words. The grave opens, exposing the coffin. He then scatters herbs of "magic power" into the gaping earth, and completes his ritual by pouring blood from a human skull over the coffin. The exercise is a complete success until it transpires that the reborn bride is in fact a vampire who requires human blood to live. The result is a catastrophe, inevitable because the laws of nature have been interfered with. This story reflects folklore. As well as being in grave danger of becoming revenants, some traditions (such as Romanian) assert that sorcerers can cause a corpse to become one.[9]

In *Buffy,* there are several instances when the dead are brought from their graves through magic. The effects are terrible. Even Buffy is resurrected ("The Gift," season 5) but this is done through a dark ritual performed by other members of the Scooby Gang. But her return is shadowed by her longing for the lost paradise. This is when Buffy herself is transformed, her darker side later revealed in the sadistic relationship she has with a vampire named Spike, the only one who understands that she is no longer purely human.

In the example from "Wake Not the Dead!" the magus is an inverted image of a priest who officiates over a burial ritual. His knowledge of the occult gives him the power to open the gates between the two worlds, and this places him in an omnipotent position. This theme appears in the works of more modern writers, and it proves to be a very powerful and effective literary device. One of the darkest scenes in J. K. Rowling's series is at the end of the fourth volume, *Harry Potter and the Goblet of Fire,* where Harry assists at the resurrection of Lord Voldemort. In the darkness of the cemetery where his father was buried, Voldemort sees the end of his years of waiting approaching. Reduced to a powerless, shapeless creature, he needs the help of his servant, Wormtail, to have his powers restored. Wormtail plays the role of the magus here, although he is only the servant of Voldemort. But by taking the part of evil, rather than good, he reinforces the point that the magus has powers which must be used with caution. Wormtail uses a huge cauldron for his magic in which he places the strange creature to which Voldemort had been reduced. But inside he adds three elements, each with a deep significance. As Wormtail pronounces the magic formulas, Voldemort's powers increase again: bone of the father, flesh of the servant, blood of the enemy.

Resurrection of the body in this case is closely linked to human sacrifice and requires the three essential elements of the body: bones and flesh as symbols of power and, most important, blood as the supreme symbol of life. The significance is deepened by the source of the three. Bone of the father, a necessary return to origins, to the creation of life; flesh of the servant, the acceptable sacrifice to the master; the blood of the enemy, who has brought about his doom, but also has the power to reverse the process of destruction, while at the same time a gesture of the final defeat of the foe. Ritual sacrifice has often been linked to revival of a divine being, of nature or renewal of time. This particular scene in *Harry Potter and the Goblet of Fire* adds the element of black magic to the bloody sacrifice, as the ritual is dedicated to a being of darkness, a demonic magus.

The importance of Wormtail in the scene is not to be underestimated, although he is more shadowy than the stronger personalities of Voldemort and Harry. He becomes the link between the two poles of the story, an intermediary between the principles of good and evil. The secret knowledge of the magus places him in a preferential position, as it is a source of power. His neutrality is essential for the equilibrium between the two, and his assistance to one of them destroys the harmony of the world, just as in the Indian myth of Kavya Usanas, the magus who could bring the dead back to life and magically alter age.

But overt statements in literature to necromancers bringing someone back from the dead and creating a vampire are comparatively rare. Rather, it is the vampire who normally opens the gates from this world to the next from the other side. The necromancer image in many vampire tales is significant, particularly in the context of the magus, as they use their knowledge of the world of the dead to protect the living from the predations of the revenant. This may be just by using the forces of nature to ward off the attack, for example, by the knowledge that using garlic will protect potential victims. But this is a fairly basic level of knowledge, something that most peasants in nineteenth-century Eastern Europe would have known anyway. Far more indicative of the magus-like qualities they possess is the use of magic to fight off the enemy, such as by the drawing of magic circles and symbols. These qualities are overtly demonstrated by van Helsing when he protects Mina from the vampires who would entrap her by drawing magic symbols around her which they cannot cross. The necromancer who brings Walter's bride back from the grave in "Wake Not the Dead!" subsequently protects him by housing him in a cave and drawing a magic circle around the threshold so that his vampire wife cannot pass through.

The use of such symbols is a frequent reference point in the history of magic. The magus in "history" "often began by drawing circles on the ground or on the floor, and inside or outside them they marked characters meant to attract the summoned spirits. Then they recited their incantations, imploring the demons to appear in a peaceful form and to obey their wish through the power of sacred persons, objects and events."[10] A famous illustration of the Elizabethan necromancers, John Dee and Edward Kelly, raising the dead in a moonlit churchyard, has them safely protected within the impenetrable boundaries of such a circle. References in vampire literature have a direct connection, through their use of magic symbols and the knowledge to control the power of the vampire, two features found elsewhere in occultism and the history of magic.

Sometimes in this literature, the undead does not play a central role, as the vampire remains shrouded in shadow and mystery. It is rather a report of the "hunt" that characterizes the key feature of the work. This echoes the motif of the sacred quest for redemption found in so many legends and myths where good fights the forces of evil. In *Dracula* and *Carmilla*, as well as in *Buffy,* the characters gather around the magus figure, like a group of disciples around a teacher. In many mythical battles against evil there is a magus who guides the heroes: King Arthur had the help of Merlin, Gandalf led the Fellowship of the Ring, Albus Dumbledore is the headmaster and mentor of Harry Potter and his friends. And so, too, with vampire literature, where the magus offers them the knowledge without which they are helpless in the face of the enemy, unable even to recognize him. Guided by him, following his teaching, they obtain new powers which equip them to fight the demon. The description of Arthur, Lucy's fiancé, as "a figure of Thor" may well seem farfetched, but it fits within an ancient pattern of thinking, where the hero can defeat evil only if he attains supernatural, god-like powers.

The crucial role of the magus to the success of the battle against evil is evidenced by what happens when he is not there. In *Dracula*, Lucy dies when van Helsing is away. There is simply no one with the requisite knowledge to take command when the moment of crisis arrives. The position of Aubrey in Polidori's "Vampyre" is even more hopeless. With no one to guide him, he is forced to rely largely on his own inadequate devices to fight off Lord Ruthven. It is a futile battle of desperately unequal odds; the "uninitiated" Aubrey against the experienced and powerful vampire. The final catastrophic defeat of Aubrey may be delayed until the eleventh hour but it is an inevitability.

The position of the magus is a dual one. His knowledge grants him access to the secrets of the world of the living and to the darkness of the realm of the dead. He is an intermediary between the two, and he is able to help the passage from one to the other. The figure of the magician in the Middle Ages had two faces, the scholar and the sorcerer, and we find echoes of these in vampire literature. He had access to the wisdom of books and lore, he knew the secrets of nature and could control the elements, he could heal and kill, enter the world of shadows, or summon the spirits to his aid. His occult knowledge put him in opposition both to official dogma and to popular superstition and lore. He was the Other, and his intellect, more than anything, made him both revered and feared.

This characteristic of "Otherness" is emphasized by the fact that the magus in vampire stories usually comes from a different country, like van Helsing (an anagram of "English") or his friend, the Hungarian scholar Arminius. In *Carmilla*, there is a Moravian nobleman who delivers the village from a vampire. In *Buffy*, Giles is an Englishman whose accent, as well as his knowledge, differentiates him from the other characters. More than that, he takes Willow abroad to England to teach her how to master her magical powers as a witch.

The Stranger is another figure of duality, as he inspires fear and fascination at the same time. He is a representative of worlds we have not seen, and what we do not fully understand often inspires our fear. In most novels, the victims of the vampire find it difficult to believe that the magus and his knowledge is taken as superstition. The stranger is a carrier of news and of strange traditions; he belongs to another world and represents the unknown, the "huge tracts of undiscovered country," as Francis Urcombe calls them, a world with a different perspective. It is no coincidence that in the story of Nicholas Flamel, it was a Spanish Jewish scholar who helped him to understand the mysterious pictures that revealed the secret of the philosopher's stone. And in the account of vampire activity on Mykonos, it is an Albanian visitor to the Greek island who gives good advice on how to deal with the disturbing visitations.

In *Carmilla,* there is also an old physician from Gratz, the odd-looking man who was able to reveal the evil powers of Carmilla-Millarca-Mircalla and to find her grave: "He was tall, narrow-chested, stooping, with high shoulders, and dressed in black. His face was brown and dried in with deep furrows; he wore an oddly-shaped hat with a broad leaf. His hair, long and grizzled, hung on his shoulders. He wore a pair of gold spectacles, and walked slowly, with an odd shambling gait, with his face sometimes turned up to the sky and sometimes bowed down toward the ground."[11] The oddity of his appearance and his manner is doubled by his strange books: *Magia Posthuma, Phlegon de Mirabilibus, Philosophicae et Christianae Cogitationes de Vampiris.* The reference to a man in black is particularly striking; it is an image associated with Satan in the history of magic.

The "man in black" in *Carmilla* hints at a crucial quality of the magus—he has great powers, but he has the choice to exercise them for good or evil. If he chooses the latter, then the effect is terrifying. The magus is usually a powerful force for good in vampire tales, but in a more negative tone, he can also be the vampire himself. Bram Stoker clad his most famous character with the cloak of a lord of dark magic. "The Draculas were … a great and noble race, though now and again were scions who were held by their coevals to have dealings with the Evil One. They learned his secrets in the Scholomance, among the mountains over Lake Hermanstadt, where the devil claims the tenth scholar as his due."[12] There is, therefore, a strong implicit link between Stoker's vampire and the magus. In this particular guise, he is a multifaceted character, capable of adapting himself to the needs of the moment: "The power of the vampire is very great and many-sided, even in his lifetime. He can kill people and even eat them alive; can bring into being, or remove, various sicknesses and epidemics, storms, rain, hail, and such; he casts spells on the cows and their milk, the crops and the husbandry generally; he knows all secrets and the future, etc. Besides this he can make himself invisible or transform himself into various objects, especially into animal forms."[13]

In *Harry Potter,* Voldemort is an evil magus and also a vampire-like figure. He commits the greatest of all sins, that of taking the blood of the purest of all creatures, the unicorn. It is a heinous crime to slay this symbol of purity, and the punishment is eternal damnation. As such, only a desperate man or woman, having already lost their soul, would do it. The blood of the unicorn can heal, but the act of violence turns this blessing into a curse. The killing of this pure and vulnerable creature is the perfect metaphor for the vampire myth: by slaying the innocent, life—after a fashion—is sustained, but it is a grotesque distortion of life as it should be.

So magi are connected to the forces of evil as well as the forces of good. This reflects the ambiguous position they are in. They are the possessors of the knowledge of another world, a dangerous and potentially evil place that can destroy any individual or, in its most awful manifestation, humanity itself. While the victims of vampirism welcome their aid, they are also suspicious of them. This duality is sometimes reflected in the actions of the magi themselves. There is a neat twist on the vampire tale in *The League of Extraordinary Gentlemen*, released in 2003 and starring Sean Connery. This film brings together a number of characters from nineteenth- and early twentieth-century literature, for example, H. G. Wells' *Invisible Man*, Stevenson's *Doctor Jekyll and Mr. Hyde*, in a battle against evil. One member of this extraordinary alliance is Mina Harker (played by Peta Wilson), now a vampire, but still fighting alongside the other members of the League in order to save the world from destruction. It is interesting to see her battle against Dorian Gray, another literary figure linked to immortality and immorality who, in the plot, is a sinister enemy of mankind. She uses her knowledge to fight him, but she also acts like a vampire, attacking and draining the blood from her victims. We swing between admiration and fear of Mina, which makes her role a fascinating one for the audience.

Magi are often forced to reject a normal life as the price for their knowledge. Their role is sometimes not one they choose: Buffy is born to be a vampire slayer but, in her own words, this is a curse as well as a gift. When, in "The Gift," a youth she has rescued wonders how she can show such powers when she is "just a girl," Buffy replies, in a tone of despairing resignation, "That's what I keep saying." For her, the cost of her powers is immense; her sister is lost in the battle against evil, and she herself loses Angel. It is a fitting reminder of the truly exorbitant toll that can be extracted from the magi in return for their attainment of the hidden secrets of nature and the supernatural. Her sacrifice may be an extreme one, but for many magi, the rejection of a so-called normal life in the quest for knowledge that they embark upon is a painful enough reminder of the terrible price of the secrets of immortality.

NOTES

1. *Dracula*, p. 243.

2. From "Mrs Amworth," in *Great Vampire Stories*, p. 39.

3. Professor Betty Teeter Dobbs, in *The Foundations of Newton's Alchemy* (1975), suggests that "Newton's alchemic thinking was so solid that in all his books he never denied its general validity. In a certain way, Newton's entire career after 1675 can be interpreted as a long effort to integrate alchemy and mechanic philosophy" (p. 230).

4. The stone and the elixir are sometimes symbolically linked. Dr John Dee, the famous Elizabethan necromancer, could commune with the dead by means of a "show stone."

5. In Frayling, p. 177.

6. Charles Mackay, *Extraordinary Popular Delusions and the Madness of Crowds,* p. 125.

7. See chapter epigraph.

8. In Norse mythology, Odin is the creator of the runes and the master of magic, another link between words and magic.

9. See Barber, p. 30, quoting Créméné, *La Mythologie du vampire en Roumanie* (Monaco, 1981).

10. Richard Kieckhefer, "Magic and Witchcraft in Medieval Europe," in *Magia si Vrajitoria in Europa,* ed. Robert Muchembled, p. 28 (author's translation).

11. *Carmilla,* p. 86.

12. *Dracula,* p. 245.

13. Barber, p. 87, quoting Juljan Kaworskij (*Galician Folklore*).

CHAPTER 10

The Pact

FAUST: So hell has its own laws and regulations too?
That's very good! So tell me—I daresay
It's possible to make a pact with you?

MEPHISTO: Indeed; if you negotiate with us,
You'll find the offer tempting—and we never cheat.
But these things can't be rushed, so we'll discuss
The matter in more detail the next time we meet.

—Johann Wolfgang von Goethe, *Faust*

In a world of dualities, man was trapped between the two dominating principles that mapped his life, two principles whose boundaries were often blurred. In the perpetual fight between Good and Evil, he was placed in a rather delicate position, which he tried to trade for a better, more secure one. Sacrifices and ritual offerings represent man's part in a contract with the gods. A core theme of vampirism is the pact with the forces of the darkness, yet another concept that has been borrowed from older beliefs and that became a successful ingredient of the vampire story. The pact may take different forms, but essentially it can be reduced to the idea that, in return for giving up something of oneself, a human being may receive special powers. The greater the reward, then the greater the price that must be paid. In the case of vampires, the price for the defiance of death is, paradoxically, one's immortal soul, as the eternal life on offer is far from paradisiacal. It is the terrifying immortality of the corpse that cannot rest in its grave.

Some religious beliefs see good and evil as an amalgam which cannot be split. A significant example is that of the Roman god Janus, guardian of gates and thresholds, always represented with two faces, one looking forward, the other back. The beginning of the year was placed under his influence (the first month of the year was called Januarius, becoming January in English). As a symbol of duality, he came to represent the positive and the negative intermingled in every situation or action. In Chinese symbolism, the sign of the mandala represents the subtle blending between opposites: good/evil, masculine/feminine, light/ darkness, and their complementary roles.

But in many religious beliefs, good and evil are polarized. They became antagonistic figures, representations of "pure" principles in which the opposition is complete and unbreakable. Satan, for example, was a firmly established figure of evil during the medieval period. So, too, were his legions. The demonologies of the time give us a vivid insight into how prevalent the forces of evil were. The result was a period of great upheaval with frequent outbreaks of hysteria. Hell with its demons was not some distant, theoretical concept, it was an everyday reality that was never far away from the inhabitants of a world in which life often hung by a thread. At a time when Church attendance was often compulsory, when thousands of people could take to the streets in the year 1000 convinced that the world was to come to an end, it was as easy to believe in the existence of devils as it was in angels. There were indeed some astonishing calculations performed at the time, which asserted that there were nine orders of angels, each with 6,666 legions and with 6,666 angels in each one (an apparent reference to the Mark of the Beast, 666, in the Book of Revelation). There was a difference of opinion about those available to Satan, with some asserting that he had 133,306,668 demons available and others a mere 44,435,566.[1] In this atmosphere of terror, when gods and demons were fighting for supremacy over the human soul, the contract with the gods was suddenly open to renegotiation.

Satan was a tempter. He was, after all, ambitious. He had tried to trick Christ himself into accepting his claims on His soul, though Jesus had been too righteous to fall for the trap. Holy men could see through the ruses of Satan. St. Dunstan, for example, was approached by a beautiful damsel. However, he saw through her charms and perceived that she was in fact the Devil incarnate. He picked up a red-hot set of pincers and grabbed the damsel by the nose. Screaming, she changed into the shape of the Devil and ran away howling. But not all men were saints, and they were duped by the attractive offers that Satan made when in disguise. Just as it was difficult to see that the Devil, who often appeared, superficially, to be attractive, was in reality only interested in trapping the souls of the naïve and innocent, so too was it difficult for the victims of the vampire to perceive the enormous danger they were in.

There are striking resemblances between the pact with the Devil, as described in the treatises on the occult written during the Middle Ages, and the vampire story. Books written by medieval scholars formed the basis for the Inquisition trials. In addition to that, popular beliefs and superstitions came to enhance the idea of the terrifying pact. During the witch hunts, the trials culminated with the hysteria surrounding the sabbat when witches would enter into a pact with the Devil and seal it with acts of gross indecency. This was a group act, when the body of witches as a whole entered into an agreement with Satan, as well as the individuals within it. The idea of a group pact with the Devil, leading to the final destruction of the world of God, gave a great reason to panic, far more so than when a lone individual entered into the pact.

Entire communities who had to deal permanently with epidemics, a high rate of child mortality, bad weather that could destroy the crops, resulting inevitably in months of famine, were quick to find a scapegoat in the margins: beggars, old women, malformed individuals, and so on. Sorcery and witchcraft, just like vampirism, were a threat to the entire community, as the servants of the Devil had the power and the obligation, as a result of demonic pacts, to bring disease to men and animals, to summon haze and storms to ruin the crops, to cast the evil eye, and to steal babies for their feasts. The corruption of the innocent played a major part in the trials, as many witnesses were children who testified against their neighbors or even members of their own family—and such was the febrile atmosphere that many did so willingly.[2]

We recognize a similar type of hysteria in the vampire epidemics, where the community had to face the threat of the demonic attacks from beyond the grave. The idea of a vampiric conspiracy against the order of the world forms the basis of the storyline in *Buffy the Vampire Slayer*, equally infested with vampires, witches, demon motorcycle gangs, and even a teacher who turns out to be a "virgin-eating giant mantis."[3] Hellmouth is the headquarters of a group of vampires, ruled by the Master, an ancient vampire, who repeatedly tries to bring about the end of the world by opening the Hellmouth through a mixture of sacrificial rituals, black magic, incantations, and pure violence. The theme of the pact appears even more clearly in the efforts of the demonized Mayor Richard P. Wilkins III who is trying to take over the world with the aid of vampires. In "Graduation Day" (season four), he plans to eat the class while delivering his speech. The students find out and fight against him and his allies, so the mayor's only victim is Principal Snyder. The Initiative itself could be a modern day counterpart of the Inquisition. This is a government-run unit which combines military skill and advanced research techniques in order to identify and destroy vampires.

The medieval "pact" was clearly described by so-called witnesses of the sabbat and in the books which represented the theological base of the witch trials. It was seen as a total inversion of the holy rites, which meant the undermining of the very mechanisms and images which represented the sacred power of the Church. "The witches promise never to adore the Holy Sacrament, always to abuse the Virgin and the saints, spit on and destroy holy relics as much as possible, not to use holy water and holy candles, never to make full confession of their sins, and finally to maintain the strictest silence about their traffic with the Devil,"[4] wrote Francesco-Maria Guazzo, a seventeenth-century friar and the author of *Compendium Maleficarum.* Heavily illustrated with very descriptive images of the sabbat, this was to become one of the most important treatises on demonology of the age. We can find similar themes in vampirism. In Coppola's *Bram Stoker's Dracula,* the prince becomes a vampire as he rebels against God, thrusts his sword in the cross, and spills holy water on the floor. In literature, vampires often, as already mentioned, seem to be especially attracted to ruined churches, places where the existence of God is denied and forgotten.

The other figure associated with the demonic pact, even late into the Renaissance, was the magus, who would sell his soul to the Devil in return for secret, occult knowledge and eternal life. Both were seen as unnatural and against the law of God. Pietro d'Apone, astrologer, alchemist, and eminent physician, born at Apone, near Padua, was brought before the tribunal of the Inquisition and accused of sorcery and heresy. It was said that he had in his service seven evil spirits which he had summoned from hell and kept in seven crystal bowls. Each of them possessed ultimate knowledge in one domain of science or art: philosophy, alchemy, astrology, physics, poetry, music, and painting. As a result, Pietro d'Apone had access to the deepest secrets of each of them, as they were revealed to him on request by the seven demons. Another rumor circulated that he had such power over silver and gold that, when he paid somebody, he could, by force of magic, bring the money back to him by dawn the next day, no matter how well guarded or locked it might have been. For these, as well as for comments criticizing the Church, he was tortured to death, then afterwards found guilty, his corpse disinterred and publicly burned, as well as his effigy, in the streets of Padua.

Cornelius Agrippa, a chemist and alchemist born in Cologne in 1486, was also believed to be able to invoke the Devil. Agrippa was secretary to the Emperor Maximilian, and also a professor of Hebrew who delivered lectures on the writings of Hermes Trismegistus, the famous alchemist. While he was in the service of Margaret of Austria, he dedicated a treatise to her called *The Superiority of the Female Sex.* He also wrote *Vanity and Nothingness of Human Knowledge.* Strange tales are connected to his name, such as the way in which the gold that he paid was always bright, but turned into stone within 24 hours. Another tells of a young man who managed to enter his study while Agrippa was away. Curious about the contents of the alchemist's books, the young man started to read from a grimoire (book of spells), but on uttering the first word, he heard a knock on the door.

When he said "Come in," a stranger appeared and asked why he had been called. The young man denied calling him, but the stranger grew terribly angry, saying that "the demons are not to be invoked in vain."

When Agrippa returned home, a host of demons were occupying his chambers. In the middle of the room, he found the dead body of the young man who, because of his curiosity, had met his end. The alchemist ordered the demons to disappear, demanding an explanation from their master. The Devil answered that the reckless youth deserved his death, but Agrippa ordered him to return life to the body and walk with the young man in the marketplace. The demon obeyed and, that afternoon, the young man walked around the market for a long time, accompanied by a stranger that nobody recognized, finally falling dead in what was thought to be a fit of apoplexy. The stranger disappeared, and the doctor found strangulation marks on the neck of the dead man. Not long afterwards, rumors obliged the alchemist to leave the town, and stories continued to grow around him: that the Devil accompanied him in the form of a black dog, and that he could summon the dead (such as King David and King Solomon) from the grave.

The details of the pact between the magus and the Devil may vary from one story to another. But there are recurrent themes whose echo can be found in the vampire tale. In Agrippa's story, one element is easily recognizable. The spirits of darkness are summoned by pronouncing their names, just as in "The Family of the Vourdalak," the vampire is summoned when his grandson utters his name. Equally important is the invitation theme. From Bram Stoker's Count Dracula to Buffy's foes, the vampires cannot enter a household without being invited in, just as Mephisto has to be asked to enter three times:

Faust: Who's there? Come in! Now who the devil's pestering me?

Mephisto: It's me.

Faust: Come in!

Mephisto: Just one more time, to make it three.

Faust: Well, come in then!

Mephisto: And here I am, you see.[5]

Carmilla, the beautiful young woman, is invited to stay with the family among whom she will find her victim, as her apparent innocence and frailty makes them feel protective towards her. In *Interview with the Vampire*, Lestat hears Louis wishing he was dead: "The invitation was open to anyone," and he is even given the choice between his despair and a life beyond the norm.

This brings us to another common point between the theme of the pact in magic and witchcraft, on the one hand, and vampirism, on the other, whether it appears in legend or literature. The pact is a result of a choice,

of a decision of the human partner. It is an allegory of the human spirit
that feels incarcerated in its own mortal destiny and tries to evade it:

> The God who dwells within me and who fires
> My inner self, my passionate desires,
> The God who governs all my thoughts and deeds,
> Is powerless to satisfy my outer needs.
> This weary life, this burden I detest;
> I long for death to come and bring me rest.[6]

The Dr. Faustus myth is its most powerful illustration, and one of the
most important motifs of all literature. It appeared in English literature,
first of all, in Marlowe's tragedy, which was inspired by a German legend
of Dr. George Faust, a fifteenth-century necromancer. The scientist invokes
the Devil and asks for a pact which would grant him 24 years of life and
the service of the Devil, in return for his soul at the end of that period of
time. Faustus is allowed to listen to both his guardian angel who speaks
of the possibility of redemption, and a bad angel who tells him that his
end will be eternal damnation. His final choice between the two is made
when he decides to ask for Helen of Troy to appear in front of him and he
embraces her. "Her lips suck forth my soul"—a vampiric illustration, if
ever there was one.

The choice is always there. It is, for example, the magician who has to
summon the spirits of darkness, it is he who has to invite them in, and
who always mentions the pact first. The motif of the pact borrowed by
the vampire story usually functions as a crucial element that triggers
the evolution of events. This is the "contract of immortality"; the choice
belongs to the individual, and they are offered an answer to their desires
for eternal youth and sexuality at the cost of happiness and love. One
moving interpretation of the vampire myth is in Coppola's film, where
Dracula is torn between his vampiric desire and his eternal love for Mina.
Half under his spell and half moved by a rediscovered love, she chooses
to give herself to him and to stand by him as he is attacked by van Helsing
and his companions. What is interesting in this case is that both the
vampire and the "victim" are faced with a choice.

But often, as is usually the case with vampirism, the concept of the
pact is distorted, for one of the participants is often an unwitting victim.
In return for their lifeblood, often given without their volition, they will
indeed receive what might appear to be a great prize, namely, immortality.
Count Dracula, and all the other vampires, represents the gate to an existence outside the norm. It is an offer that we can accept or reject, but once
accepted, there is no going back: "Welcome to my house. Come freely. Go
safely. And leave something of the happiness you bring."[7]

This choice is not always as free as it seems; it is often made with
imperfect knowledge. The hosts acts in ignorance of the true import of

what they are doing. Carmilla does not appear as an evil demon; she appears as a young, innocent, injured, and vulnerable girl. She tricks her host into inviting her in, an imitation of the traditional approach of Satan who appears in all kinds of forms liable variously to attract the sympathy, or often the lust, of his victims (as St. Dunstan discovered). So, too, with Count Dracula, a potential client to Jonathan in need of business advice. Jonathan enters his castle of his own free will, not knowing what is in store for him. It is an evil abuse of trust that touches something very deep within our emotions and our sense of fair play. Even more powerful is the scene in *Interview with the Vampire* where Claudia found out how she had been "made" and hated Lestat because he had turned her into a vampire. She is doomed to an eternal life trapped in the body of a child (when she is turned into a vampire, the aging process stops completely) even though, somewhat contradictorily, she develops the emotions of a woman.

This pact is often entered into under a form of duress. The victims of the vampire, whether the legendary victims of Arnold Paole or the literary ones of Dracula, Varney, Lord Ruthven, or Carmilla, are normally unable to resist their fate. Neither did Claudia know what she was letting herself in for when she became a vampire. They are either innocently lured into the power of the vampire, such as the young children who are attacked in "Wake Not the Dead!" or the vampire exercises some form of hypnotic power over them. There is no real concept of free choice in these cases; the victims are powerless to resist or do not see the danger that they are in. They are like insects lured unwittingly into the web of the spider.

Another element that accompanies the ancient pact with the forces of evil is the ritual aspect. This is, first of all, a pact of blood, "a very special kind of juice," as Mephisto calls it. The witch or the magus is requested to sign the contract with the Devil in blood:

Any scrap of paper here will do I think;
We'll use a drop of blood instead of ink.[8]

In the same way, the human being becomes a vampire when their blood is used to revive the undead. The scene in *Interview with the Vampire* when Lestat flies over the city with his teeth in Louis's neck, and the morning scene when the latter finally becomes a vampire himself are good illustrations. The moment when the vampire drinks its victim's blood for the first time is when the gates of doom are opened, when the living become part of the diabolical pact.

The seal of the pact, as described in old treatises on the works of the Evil One, is applied to the body of the witch. Such signs were often proof enough to send the accused to the flames. The Devil's mark, or *stigmata diaboli* (a perverted contrast to the stigmata of Christ), or *sigillum diaboli*, was described in many demonology books, such as *De Demonialitate:*

The demon imprints on [the witches] some mark, especially on those whose constancy he suspects. The mark, however, is not always of the same shape or figure; sometimes it is the likeness of a hare, sometimes like a toad's foot, sometimes a spider, a puppy, a dormouse. It is imprinted on the most secret parts of the body; with men, under the eyelids or perhaps under the armpits, or on the lips or shoulders, the anus or elsewhere; with women, it is generally on the breasts or private parts. Now, the stamp which makes these marks is simply the devil's talon.[9]

A form of *sigillum diaboli* appears as a recurrent image in vampirism. The mark that the vampire's teeth leave on the neck or chest of the victim is, as in the witch hunts, a sure signal that somebody is, or is about to become, a vampire. Dr. Seward notices it on Lucy's throat: "Just over the external jugular vein there were two punctures, not large, but not wholesome-looking. There was no sign of disease, but the edges were white and worn-looking, as if by some trituration."[10]

The mark on the neck has become a classic image, the sign that seals the dark alliance between the vampire and its victim. Modern stories emphasize this special link between the vampire and its maker—again, an inverted Christian symbol. The bond between Lestat and Louis, between Claudia, Louis, and Lestat, between evil Darla and the "ensouled" vampire Angel in *Buffy*, are only a few of many examples of the dark and secret link sealed by the mark on the neck and which may vary from a master–disciple relationship, to paternal feelings, and to sexual attraction.

In *Dracula*, Mina comes to bear a different sign which is a reminder that she has been touched by a vampire. When van Helsing touches her forehead with the sacred wafer, it hurts her skin: "There was a fearful scream which almost froze our hearts to hear. As he placed the Wafer on Mina's forehead, it had seared it—had burned into the flesh as though it had been a piece of white-hot metal." Realizing the meaning of this, she breaks into tears: "'Unclean! Unclean! Even the Almighty shuns my polluted flesh! I must bear this mark of shame upon my forehead until Judgement Day.'"[11] This mark reminds people of the famous trials of the witches, where the judges had the women accused of sorcery touched with the Host in order to see a sign from above that would prove their guilt. The same holy wafer keeps away the count and the vampire women at his castle, as they cannot break into the circle sealed by it.

The pact with the Devil also grants demonic help to master the elements. The accusations against the witches included:

1. The raising of storms and tempests, winds and weather, by sea and land
2. he poisoning of air
3. Blasting of corn
4. Killing of cattle, and annoying men, women and children.[12]

These accusations were brought all over Europe, even in Transylvania. One account from the year 1615 states the following:

Several magicians and witches gave themselves to Hades, and in their search it is said that they wished to bring hail over all Hungary and Transylvania, so that all the fruits and vineyards would be lost. This scheme was miraculously discovered when a girl of 10–12 years of age went with her father into the vineyard and when she heard him talking of the drought, she said 'Father, if you want, I can bring rain and even hail'. The father asked from whom she learned this, and she answered that her mother had taught her. Then the father in disbelief said 'if you can, bring hail, but in such a way that only our vineyard is touched but those of my neighbours remain untouched'. She did as she said, bringing terrible storms and hail, and her father's vineyard was almost destroyed.[13]

A famous British witchcraft case took place at North Berwick in 1590. One accusation against the witches there was that they had tried to wreck the ship carrying King James VI of Scotland to Norway by calling up a storm. Earlier, great medieval theologians such as Thomas Aquinas accepted that witches were capable of raising storms.[14] Reports from as far afield as Finland confirm that this was a widely held belief, one dating from 1577, telling how "they [witches] tie three knots on a string hanging at a whip. When they loose one of these, they raise tolerable winds. When they loose another, the wind is more vehement. But by loosing the third, they raise plain tempests, as in old time they were accustomed to raise thunder and lightning." Clearly, the thunderbolts of Thor survived on into Christian times!

In 1645, the 70-year-old Revd. John Lowes of Suffolk, England, confessed that he had summoned up a storm that sank a ship off Norwich, drowning 14 people, which made him "joyful to see what powers his imps had!" More examples can be found on the continent. One of the best-documented witch trials was that at Eichstatt, Germany, in 1637. Here, the accused was asked about her abilities to create storms. She said that "she had thought about storm-raising for a long time, and had helped cause eight tempests. The first storm she had made fifteen years ago, between midday and one o'clock, in her own garden, spurred on by the Devil to make the fruit drop so that it would not ripen. This happened."[15]

The magicians' powers made their way from legend into classical literature. Prospero became much more than a magus who was capable of commanding the spirits by use of magic. In time, he has become a literary motif. Shakespeare's Prospero had Ariel to help him:

Prospero: Hast thou, spirit,
                       Perform'd to point the tempest that I bade
                       thee?

Ariel: To very article ....
                       Jove's lightnings, the precursors

O'the dreadful thunder-claps, more momentary
And sight-outrunning were not: the fire, and the cracks
Of sulphurous roaring, the most mighty Neptune
Seemed to besiege, and make his bold waves tremble,
Yes, his dread trident shake.[16]

Such "talents" are not dissimilar to those ascribed to Dracula, who can "summon fog and storm and snow"[17] and who haunts his victims under the protection of the fog:

The mist grew thicker and thicker, till I could see now how it came in, for I could see it like smoke—or with the white energy of boiling water—pouring in, not through the window, but through the joinings of the door. It got thicker and thicker, till it seemed as if it became concentrated into a sort of pillar of cloud in the room, through the top of which I could see the light of the gas shining like a red eye. Things began to whirl through my brain just as the cloudy column was now whirling in the room, and through it all came the scriptural words 'a pillar of cloud by day and of fire by night.'[18]

In Mina Harker's journal, these symbols carry a terrible duality. The biblical smoke and fire, far from spiritual help, are part of the props of hell. And the guidance means blind, powerless surrender to a devilish force, which never lets its followers out of the desert.

The vampire acts under the protection of foul weather. Storms keep the enemies away, while fog and darkness offer shelter for the beings of the other world. We are again caught between opposites that delimit our mental patterns of good and evil. The sun and the light are associated with divine order and protection. This is why, in some variants, vampires are destroyed by light. The now classic *Nosferatu* is constructed around this very theme—the victim accepts her death in order to keep the vampire out of his tomb until dawn, when the first rays of sun destroy him. In *Interview with the Vampire,* the pact begins with Louis's last sunrise, his last moment of human existence, and his final, irremediable choice. The terms of the pact are clear when it comes to the sun; this is the last sunrise that he would ever witness. On the other hand, replacing fair weather with foul, the sun with darkness, and the brightness of day with fog is again one of the oldest fears known to man. Threatening the sun means threatening the universe, and only demons could wish to disturb the rightful laws of God's creation.

Another similarity between the vampire and the servants of the Devil is their extraordinary bodily strength. The pact with the Devil presupposes, first of all, power above the limitations of humans, power over the minds and the bodies of others, and ultimately, over their life and death. The vampire's strength, the result of their pact, is beyond the powers of humans. "One sign of the vampire is the power of the hand. The slender hand of Mircalla closed like a vice of steel on the General's wrist when he raised the hatchet to strike. But its power is not confined to its grasp; it leaves a numbness in the limb it seizes, which is slowly, if ever, recovered from."[19] This supernatural power reminds us of witches and their ability to provoke unexplainable weaknesses of the body.[20] Carmilla cannot be killed by weapons; Dracula can easily lift heavy trunks and even earth-filled coffins. The image of the count in *Nosferatu* getting off his ship and creeping around the streets of the town in broad daylight with his coffin under one arm remains a haunting (and now a slightly comical) one in the history of vampire film.

Together with everlasting life, the vampires have achieved the ability to fly (just as witches were deemed to be able to fly to the sabbat—a so-called reward for their allegiance to Satan), one of man's most ardent desires. Flight is one of the supreme symbols of freedom, of power beyond that of man, ultimately, of existence outside the norm. In *Interview with the Vampire*, the image of the vampire Lestat (Tom Cruise) carrying his new victim, Louis (Brad Pitt), high above the port, high above the world of mortals, is one that frightens and excites at the same time.

The "contract of immortality" of the vampire myth plays with the duality and the mystery surrounding love and sexuality. The breaking of a taboo stirs the imagination, and the vampire has become synonymous with the idea of trespassing boundaries, whether moral or physical (notice, for example. how many traditions equate vampirism with the breaking of sexual taboos, such as incest or illegitimacy). The pact with the Devil offers the key to an existence outside the norm and the promise of a life free from the constraints of society.

It is not a novelty in literature and thinking. The Faustian myth revolves around the same choice. The final choice of Marlowe's Faustus, the one that seals his fate, is the invocation of Helen of Troy. Helen is a complex figure of Greek mythology. Ancient Greeks valued beauty in body as well as mind, and from this point of view, she is an image of perfection. She is, above all mortal women, an ideal icon. At the same time, her beauty is indirectly a source of doom. Helen is herself trapped as the final reward in a pact she knows nothing about. She is offered to Paris as a reward for granting the supremacy of beauty to Aphrodite, the goddess of love and bodily passion. Helen becomes a representation of the duality of femininity, so powerful a theme in many vampire stories: the beauty and perfection that are inherent in her are an instrument of doom. It is this very theme that is used in the story of Faustus, who sells his soul to the Devil in order to achieve knowledge and power beyond human limits, and to obtain the supreme ideal of feminine beauty, even if this means eternal damnation.

In the modern world, the concept continues to sell. The vampire pact grants a perfect, desirable body and hypnotic power over the bodies of the victims. Jonathan falls under the deadly spell of the beautiful women in Dracula's castle:

All three had brilliant white teeth, that shone like pearls against the ruby of their voluptuous lips. There was something about them that made me uneasy, some longing and at the same time some deadly fear. I felt in my heart a wicked, burning desire that they should kiss me with those red lips…. I lay quiet, looking under my eyelashes in an agony of delightful anticipation. The fair girl advanced and bent over me till I could feel the movement of her breath upon me. Sweet it was in one sense, honey-sweet, and sent the same tingling through the nerves as her voice, but with a bitter underlying the sweet, a bitter offensiveness, as one smells in blood.[21]

Carmilla's vampirish desire is the doom of the young, innocent girls who accept her friendship. In her fits of anger and passion, she hints at love as a facet of death: "You do not know how dear you are to me. The time is very near when you shall know everything. You will think me cruel, very selfish, but love is always selfish; the more ardent the more selfish. How jealous I am you cannot know. You must come with me, loving me, to death; or else hate me and still come with me, and *hating* me through death and after."[22]

The vampire pact is a paradox. It offers the instrument for passion—the attractive, voluptuous body—but it forbids true love. Carmilla's passion is a desire full of hatred. Stoker's Count Dracula is presented in permanent antithesis with Arthur and Jonathan, who love Lucy and Mina, and are ready to sacrifice themselves for these women. The paradox of the vampire story lies in the dual images of love and sexuality. The vampire's embrace brings death, not life.

Eternal youth and bodily beauty is a recurrent image of the pact with the Devil. One of the most famous examples in literature can be found in Oscar Wilde's *The Picture of Dorian Gray*. Dorian hears Lord Henry's words: "Youth is the one thing worth having,"[23] and he comes to envy the picture that would preserve the beauty he is destined to lose. In his desire for beauty, "the wonder of wonders," he makes a wish that will open for him the gates of a doomed life: "If it were I who was to be always young, and the picture that was to grow old! For that—for that—I would give everything! Yes, there is nothing in the world I would not give! I would give my soul for that!"[24] In the end, people who realize that he has stopped aging believe that he has sold his soul to the Evil One "for a pretty face."

The pact with the Devil makes this reversal of nature's laws possible, just as the vampire pact offers the key to a world which is ruled by other norms than that of everyday existence. The paradox is that the vampire has obtained everlasting life; the body is not only maintained, it is enhanced (so this is not just a suspension of the laws of nature—it is an active reversal of them). New blood restores youth to the count, and his victims (Lucy, the women in the castle,) look more beautiful and voluptuous than when they were alive. Eternal youth is accompanied by exceptional strength and vitality, and it offers power over the elements and animals, as well as over other souls.

Yet the vampire himself is trapped. Once signed, the contract of immortality allows him no escape, and a further choice is impossible. Its existence is cursed, as it lives by the death of others, a perverse distortion of the central doctrine of Christianity. The pure blood of innocent victims leaves on their souls a stain of doom. More than anything, this is a juicy literary motif. If Mina's unforgettable words, "just think what will be his joy when he too is destroyed in his worser part that his better part may have spiritual immortality,"[25] are only a small example of the forced air of melodrama which dominates the novel, the idea in itself is interesting. The vampire cannot find peace in the grave, something terrible has happened which has destroyed the normal course of nature, transforming life after death into eternal doom. This motif is the construct around which the entire story is built in *Interview with the Vampire*. Louis is torn between his need to kill in order to survive and his awe for human life. His greatest punishment is that, unlike many other vampires, he still retains a conscience, as if something of his former self lives on. The pact, signed in blood, has as its price: everlasting damnation. The vampire story therefore offers not an answer to the desire for immortality, but rather a temptation into a world of illusion and destruction.

NOTES

1. *The Witchcraft World*, p. 75.
2. Children were more willing to testify in trials because they were less likely to be punished for their participation in the demonic rites and were also easier to manipulate.
3. *Reading the Vampire Slayer*, p. 277.
4. In *The Encyclopaedia of Witchcraft and Demonology*, under "Pact with the Devil."
5. *Faust*, p. 48.
6. Ibid., p. 49.
7. *Dracula*, p. 41.
8. *Faust*, p. 53.
9. In *The Encyclopaedia of Witchcraft and Demonology*, under "Devil's Mark."
10. *Dracula*, p. 139.
11. Ibid., p. 285.
12. In *The Encyclopaedia of Witchcraft and Demonology*, under "Maleficia."
13. *Auszug aus der Chronik von Simion Massa und Marcus Fuchs* in *Quellen zur Geschichte der Stadt Kronstadt, vol. v, Brasov*, 1915, p. 364, in *Istoria Romaniei in texte*, edited by Bogdan Murgescu, author's translation.
14. See entry on "Storm-Raising" in the *Encyclopaedia of Witchcraft and Demonology*.
15. Transcript of trial, see entry on "Eichstatt Witch Trial," *Encyclopaedia of Witchcraft and Demonology*.
16. *The Tempest*, I.II. 191–204.
17. *Dracula*, p. 345.
18. Ibid., p. 261.

19. *Carmilla,* p. 93.

20. This is the subject of one of Thomas Hardy's lesser known short stories, "The Withered Arm," a haunting love story.

21. *Dracula,* p. 61.

22. *Carmilla,* p. 41.

23. *The Picture of Dorian Gray,* p. 21.

24. Ibid., p. 24.

25. *Dracula,* p. 304.

CHAPTER 11

The Power of the Mind

Mortal eye... may not pierce the dark secrets of another world, or penetrate the deep abyss that separates earth from heaven.
—Johann Ludwig Tieck, "Wake Not the Dead!"

The vampire story, like the exotic, fascinating counts who are some of its main characters, changed its form and purpose over time. It emerged from the depths of popular burial and apotropaic rites and beliefs about the dead and their dark realm. The Age of Reason tried to smother the gods, but man's need for the supernatural resurrected the spirits of the Ancients in some of their most monstrous forms. A new science sprouted from the remembrance of the "dead" superstitions: teratology, the science of monsters and abnormal beings. The Romantic and Gothic movements transformed the need for the fantastic into amusement for the general public, and brought vampires increasingly into literature and theater. The undead thrived in this realm of fiction; they continued to grip the mind when the silver screen brought them closer to a public hungry for images that would thrill its imagination. Unfortunately, the vampires sometimes leave their fictive realm and step, in a more violent and dreadful manner, into the real world. As we have seen, there are still newspaper accounts of horrible murders committed by people who believe that the blood of their victims can grant them strength, youth, and longevity.

The fascination with vampirism works at several levels. Its folkloric basis is one that uses fear of death and of the dead as revenants, not only to thrill in a terrifying fashion, but also to transmit a type of teaching concerning the other world and its associated apotropaic rituals and a set of rules about everyday life and behavior. Fear is sometimes an effective teaching instrument. Religion brings to death an aura of sacredness, as it is seen as a rite of passage, a natural transformation. To break this rule means challenging the conventional, and it is considered to be an abnormal phenomenon—the dead are expected to rest peacefully in their graves, not to return as vampires, ghosts, *Nosferatu*.

Fiction, as opposed to folklore teachings, has to sell. The vampire, exotic and mysterious, eludes all explanations and therefore catalyzes a gloomy fascination. The vampire grips the reader with the same hypnotic force as its fictive neck-bitten victims, and our curiosity gives them as much life and strength as the fresh blood of their very innocent and good looking prey. Just as Varney, when appearing in front of his lovely victim, "holds her with his glittering eye," the undead bewitch the reader with their fascinating mystery. This power over the mind, the ability to manipulate fundamental fears, is an integral part of the vampire tale's effectiveness.

The main impact of the vampire story, no matter what form it may take, myth, legend, folklore, novel, or film, is due to one basic human reaction. There are no hidden, deep symbols to offer the reader a masterpiece of philosophical thought; the images that it uses and often abuses are meant to function on a stimulus-response basis. The vampire is primarily meant to provoke terror, not moral or theological debates. The vampire accesses some of our major fears: of pain, of strangers, of death, fear of the great Unknown which surrounds our cozy little world. Fear sells books. Why? Because, ultimately, it is our fears that represent the most fascinating part of our life. It is not the everyday journey to work that releases hordes of butterflies in our stomach, but the unique encounter with something we do not know or have not experienced before.

In *Dracula*, as well as many other stories about the undead, the vampire is not the central figure of the book, but rather a catalyst of fears and an inherent evil that makes all the other characters gravitate around this mysterious character. As readers, we find out very little about vampires, and it is precisely the seal of secrecy that retains our curiosity. So no one knows how Stoker's count first came to be a vampire, the antecedents of Lord Ruthven are undiscussed, and Carmilla cannot be destroyed until her true identity is revealed. Even in legends, the focus is generally placed on the struggle of the living to overcome the peril of the undead and to destroy the devilish being, which does not belong to our world, and can be neither tamed nor fully understood. The information that we gather from the other characters does not lift the veil that covers its existence, and every time we think we have found a key, there are other locked doors before us.

All that is different from us, from what we know, is frightening and, at the same time, fascinating. In spite of our fears, we find it impossible to escape the "fatal attraction" of all that has not been tamed into our frames of thought. Such emotions underlie the impact of the vampire on our minds in the same way that tales of demonic rites shocked and fascinated the villagers of seventeenth-century Salem, or any other place unfortunate enough to witness the horrors of a witchcraft trial.

The vampire is often portrayed as a Stranger, like Count Dracula or Carmilla, coming from a country existing on the verge of legend. We fear them above all because we perceive them as different, bearers of all the traits of alterity: the Foreigner, the one who comes from afar, who speaks with a heavy accent, whose ways are eccentric and actions difficult to understand. Often in history, they became the target of fear-born hatred and served as scapegoats. In the Würzburg witchcraft trials of the early seventeenth century, a significant number of the witches executed were "strangers." In one batch of executions, all seven put to death were described as such.[1]

The vampire epidemics were most powerful along the cultural borders between Eastern and Western Europe, areas where Catholicism clashed with the Orthodox Church. Stories of these far-off lands haunted by the dead seized the minds of westerners and real countries or regions became the fictional spaces of the undead.

"Transylvania is not England. Our ways are not your ways, and there shall be to you many strange things,"[2] Dracula tells Jonathan Harker, and in his words we can perhaps hear Stoker's explanation for choosing this setting, which over the years has become a sort of symbolic land of the vampire. This country, which to his (and many modern) readers seemed remote and isolated from Western influences, therefore outside Western culture and mentality, has all the exotic traits that turn it into a land of fantasy and magic. Being so little known in the West, it allowed the author to give it all the features of alterity that would create the perfect landscape for the vampire, a being that could not be understood.

Its very name, Transylvania, "the land beyond the forest," has an almost mythical ring to it. Stoker's Transylvania is not only a space between two civilizations, but between reality and legend. The fact that Jonathan could not find the count's castle on any maps could be an allusion to a place off the map of the real world. At the same time, maps represent the ordering power of knowledge. He enters a land that has not been subdued to "civilized and civilizing" ordering and reordering by means of rational measurements. In a way, he goes back in time, as modern man rediscovers one of the most powerful symbols of the medieval imaginary: *hic sunt leones*—the blank spot on the map, the land of the unknown.

Stoker presents Transylvania as a land where

all the forces of nature that are occult and deep and strong must have worked together in some wondrous way. The very place is full of strangeness of the geologic and chemical world. There are deep caverns… and fissures that reach none know whither. There have been volcanoes, some of whose openings still send out waters of strange properties, and gases that kill or make to vivify.[3]

The soil here is indeed varied and rich. There are volcanic formations in the northeast, in exactly the region where Stoker placed the castle. Transylvania is rich in oil and coal, and therefore so-called strange phenomena appear, such as the small blue flames like those that Jonathan sees on his way to the castle. There are undoubtedly legends that such places may be haunted or may hide ancient treasures. There are also deposits of gold and other metals that have been worked even in the pre-Roman period by Dacian tribes.

Therefore, this is a space of paradoxes. There is something frightening in the majestic beauty of the mountains, the legends speak of treasures and spirits protecting them against those who would try to steal them, the waters[4] may kill or bring life, the soils are rich, but at the same time, dangerous. This duality of nature is mirrored in the history of men and their life here. This land can indeed be seen as the gate between two worlds: Western Europe and its disparate regimes, on the one hand, and the East, which for centuries was flooded by Byzantine and Ottoman influences, on the other. It is also a place where very different types of population met and lived together.

The result was not only a complicated cultural mixture in a very small area, but often a cultural clash, a frequent source of misunderstandings between these populations. Each in its turn was perceived as the Other, thereby creating a second level of the image of alterity that pervades the novel. Such a mixture of populations made this crossroads of history a place where Eastern European, Roman, Saxon, and Asian traditions meet: "I read that every known superstition in the world is gathered in the horseshoe[5] of the Carpathians, as if it were the centre of some sort of imaginative whirlpool,"[6] Jonathan notes, as he meets Hungarians, Romanians, Saxons, gypsies, each with their beliefs and superstitions, each with a different attitude towards the feared Count Dracula and his powers. This "imaginative whirlpool" will lure Jonathan, and the reader, into a trap of fear. At the same time, it is Stoker's warning that the reader, together with the book's characters, will plunge into a swirl of nightmarish imagination, where our own fears will take the shape of the Other.

Transylvania may be the most famous "realm of vampires," but it is definitely not the only one. Orthodox Greece, the land of the ancient *lamiae,* but also a favorite place for Western holidaymakers, stirred the imagination of many writers. Goethe's "Bride of Corinth" and Keats's "The Lamia" are literary variations of the myth of the beautiful Phoenician woman (therefore a foreigner) who wants to devour the beautiful body of her lover. Polidori's hero, Aubrey, is advised by his Greek friends not to remain in a certain forest after dark, as "they described it as the resort of vampyres in their nocturnal orgies and denounced the most heavy evils as impending upon him who dared cross their path."[7] The French took Greek vampires very seriously in the nineteenth century. Polidori's "Vampyre" came back to life one year later, in the novel of a Frenchman, Bérard: *Lord Ruthven ou les vampires,* "a two-volume variation on the Ruthven theme...with long sub-plots which read like a bloody Grand Tour"[8] in Greece, Italy, India, and Eastern Europe. In 1821, Nodier published *Smarra ou les Démons de la Nuit*, a terrifying tale about a demon released by Méroé, a beautiful demonic woman from Thessaly.

The young girl telling the story in *Carmilla* is English, but she and her father live in Styria, an Austrian province partly inhabited by Slovenians, and consequently divided in 1919 between Austria and what was Yugoslavia. Initially, Bram Stoker himself had chosen Styria as the setting for his novel, but the discovery of the more distant and exotic realm "beyond the forest," with its bloody history and its numberless superstitions, turned out to be an even more sinister home for his Count Dracula. Mérimée places his story, *La Guzla,* in Illyria, where the Bey of Moina's victim is his bride, la Belle Sophie. Serbia is a propitious land for vampires, especially in legends.

Even now, the Carpathians remain a favorite spot for vampire stories and legends. Elisabeth Bathory, the Hungarian countess, was one resident who was a real example of the obsession with the rejuvenating powers of blood. But the vampires of literature and movies, whether they are Count Azzo von Klatka (Anon, *The Mysterious Stranger*), Dracula, Brunhilda, or Lestat, are simply fictive characters haunting both some half-invented realms and the very permeable imagination of people all over the world. And even the lands that actually do exist are merely the foundation on which semi-fictional landscapes are painted.

There is another instance where difference/otherness is a portent of evil. With Le Fanu's stories, a mysterious figure of darkness occasionally appears, connected with a terrible deed. In *Carmilla,* somebody notices that in the carriage of the countess there was "a hideous black woman, with a sort of coloured turban on her head ... nodding and grinning derisively towards the ladies, with gleaming eyes and large eye-balls, and her teeth set as if in fury."[9] The eyes and the teeth are hints of the terrible nature of the foe incarnated in the innocent looking Carmilla—the most distinctive features of the vampire, the gleaming eyes and the bare teeth.

But there is a similar case in a different story of his, "The Child that Went with the Fairies." It is the story of an Irish widow living near the Slieveelim hills. One of her boys was stolen by the fairies from Lisnavoura. The children were playing one evening when they saw a carriage, and inside, a beautiful young lady who asked the little boy to come with her. By her side there was "a black woman, with a wonderfully long neck, hung round with many strings of large, variously coloured beads, and on her head was a sort of turban of silk striped with all the colours of the rainbow, and fixed in it was a golden star. This black woman had a face as thin almost as a death's head, with high cheek-bones, and great goggle eyes, the whites of which, as well as her wide range of teeth, showed in brilliant contrast with her skin."[10] The image that Le Fanu uses can be linked to the image of the black servant, suppressed and feared at the same time, or with the gypsy witch, with black magic and the darkness. In the past, differences in race, color, or customs, in thinking or in language, were perceived as fascinating and threatening in equal measure.

Persecution is often directed towards groups that are different from what the majority perceives as mainstream society. One group that has been a target over the centuries is gypsies, and inherent prejudice is reflected in the legends that exist about their origins. In many of these, gypsies are forced to wander the earth because of the sins of their remote ancestors. Some myths assert that they are the descendants of Cain, the first murderer— here the Other is associated with violence. Further variants link gypsies with specific anti-Christian offences, in one version, by making the nails that crucified Christ, in another, by refusing to help the Virgin Mary when she fled with the Christ Child to Egypt. The thought process is a fairly transparent one: gypsies have historically had a nomadic lifestyle, their so-called difference makes them dangerous, and their unconventional way of life is sometimes perceived as punishment for their "evil" nature. [11] Given this background, it is no surprise to find that the people who carry Dracula's coffin in the climactic scene of the novel are gypsies.

In "For the Blood is the Life," by F. Marion Crawford, Cristina, a gypsy girl, is murdered by a couple of thieves whom she had discovered while they were burying their loot. From beyond the grave, she attracts the man she loved while she was alive and who had never returned her love. Now, trapped between his dread and the evil power that Cristina has over him, Angelo receives her vampiric kisses which drain his blood and his life for the deadly hunger of the gypsy girl. Even after she is unburied and "killed," her shadow continues to appear whenever moonlight shines over her tomb.

Another Angel is trapped between two worlds by a gypsy curse—this time in *Buffy the Vampire Slayer,* and this time, a vampire. As a punishment for having killed a gypsy girl, her family cast a spell on him through which his soul is returned to him. He is therefore obliged to live with the full memory and conscience of his evil deeds, unlike other vampires who are soulless and therefore unable to know the pain of remorse. The gypsy curse also means that if Angel finds one moment of true happiness, which he does as he makes love to Buffy, he loses his soul and is turned again into Angelus, the vampire.

Fascination can become literal in the vampire story, as the undead are often described as having hypnotic powers over their victims. In his "Fragment of a Novel," Byron describes his vampire as a trickster, a master of illusions (what else is any creator of fiction, whether an author or a filmmaker?): "He had a power of giving to one passion the appearance of another."[12] *Dracula,* for example, is such a powerful story because it uses certain psychological devices. It is highly manipulative, as it plays with our deepest fears and seems to offer a tempting alternative to the norm; it opens up the space where the two worlds of life and death touch. The vampire's existence is suspended between the two; it has access to both, but belongs to neither.

In the history of ideas, there are mythical creatures whose eyes ensnare those they look upon. The most famous of these are the Gorgons. There were three of these creatures, sisters who lived on the Atlantic shores of Africa. Significantly, the Greeks regarded the Far West as being the region of the underworld. They turn all those they gaze upon into stone. But Perseus attacks one of them, Medusa, while she sleeps. Her eyes shut, she has lost her power, though Perseus still does not dare to look upon her and uses the guide of her reflection in his shield. When he strikes off her head, the winged horse Pegasus flies forth from her body—again, suggesting the cycle of death and rebirth in nature, so vital to the concept of vampirism. There is power in the eyes, something also found in the legend of the basilisk, a serpent-like creature most recently famous for its appearance in *Harry Potter and the Chamber of Secrets*, the gaze of which will kill those it looks upon.

The vampire has two weapons at its disposal in its attempts to ensnare its victims: its eyes and its voice (although infrequent, there are some accounts in folklore of the undead "calling" their prey to their graves, though this might be metaphorical rather than literal—but in literature and films especially, the hypnotic effect of the voice is far more common). Many of the mythical creatures who hypnotized their victims were women, an obvious allusion to the seductress as a classic motif. The Sirens of Greek mythology used their voices to entrap passing travelers. Those who hear them are instantly entranced; there is no degree of choice in the bargain, the victim (invariably male) loses control over his senses, and is doomed to add to the heap of rotting cadavers surrounding the Sirens—not unlike the vampire temptress who bewitches her prey. The only defense available, adopted by Odysseus's crew, is to plug their ears with wax.

The game of illusions is one of the most interesting themes in literature. The difference between reality and illusion in the universe of fiction often escapes the norms of reality. The power of the mind is the ability to discern between the two. The trickster at the medieval fair, the sorcerer who whispered the destiny in the ear of a king, the magus in a novel like John Fowles's,[13] or the magus form behind the vampire story, all share the power of making others believe the unbelievable: "His eyes on mine, Conchis grimaced, as if he found death a joker. His skin clung very close to his skull. Only the eyes lived. I had the strange impression that he wanted me to believe *he* was death; that at any moment the leathery old skin and the eyes would fall, and I should find myself the guest of a skeleton."[14] Fowles's work may be a vampire-less novel, but the theme, and its goal, revolve around the enigma of reality melting into illusion. The games of the mind are the games of the unknown, terrifying, fascinating and, most of all, addictive. The victim of the vampire cannot and often would not escape the frightening grip that takes them beyond the frontiers of reason.

The vampire becomes the ultimate illusion in Coppola's movie, *Bram Stoker's Dracula*. The feeling that haunts us after we watch it is the sensation that Coppola's vision hints at the possibility that perhaps, beyond the story, beyond good and evil, there might be just a caricature. The characters appear in a completely new light, like Lucy, no longer the innocent girl in the novel, although probably many prefer this version to Stoker's very black and white model. The prince with his armor resembling a skinned body has little in common with the classical image of medieval heroes, although he is seen as one. The love story between the vampire and Mina as a reincarnation of a medieval princess, too, seems a long way from the spirit of the book. And yet the distance is not as great as it first appears, as the film only carries further the duality that is the constant underlying message of the novel. The book managed to hide this deep under the Victorian clichés, which may be one of Stoker's greatest literary achievements: to breach the limits between good and evil which normally work within a very constricted pattern.

Or perhaps it is simply the pure power of the image, luring the public into the world of show business and phantasms. The storyline is a pretext for the domineering images of the blood springing out of the cross, a pair of red eyes above the horizon, Dracula's shadow on the wall, the count's violet eyeglasses, Mina and the count dancing among thousands of candles, the red sun setting behind the jagged mountain ridges. Coppola's *Dracula* contains all the clichés of the movie industry: the confrontation between good and evil, the love story, blood, violence and eroticism, the death of one "good" character in the final confrontation and, of course, the grand finale. This could be a "metafilm." a hint of the true nature of all movies. On the one hand, it is fiction that mimics life, the deception of the filmed image; on the other, this world of magic lights which spring out in the darkness fascinates us with its (false) claim to immortality and eternal youth and beauty. Just like vampires, movies hypnotize us, offering a silver illusion for real life.

After all, the most effective and devilish feature of the vampire is not its physical strength, but its power over the mind of the victims. All descriptions emphasize the eyes, often gleaming with the flames of hell. The victim cannot move or cry for help: "Her eyes are fascinated. The glance of a serpent could not have produced a greater effect upon her than did the fixed gaze of those awful, metallic-looking eyes."[15] Carmilla's victims cannot perceive the danger they are in, as the vampire clouds their mind and spirit: "The narcotic of an unsuspected influence was acting upon me, and my perceptions were benumbed."[16] The Marquis d'Urfé reminisces about the first night in the house of the family of the Vourdalak, and how he sensed the vampire's visit during his sleep: "I felt his dead eyes trying to penetrate my deepest thoughts as they watched the movement of my breathing."[17]

Dracula can control his victims from a distance; Cristina in "For the Blood is the Life" holds Angelo in a trance "with the furious and unappeased physical hunger of her eyes that devoured him. They feasted on his soul and cast a spell over him."[18] This recurrent theme may have its origin in the hypnotic eye of the undead, in the fear that they raise, or even in the attraction of a demonic but sensuous being, a form that the vampire (whether an aristocratic Dracula or a very desirable Brunhilda) has borrowed in most of its literary appearances. As for the victim, "revelling in bliss, thou beholdest not the abyss that yawns beneath thy feet…"[19]

Mythology places Hypnos, Sleep, in the shadows of the underworld, together with his brother Thanatos, Death. People and gods alike can fall under his influence, as Hypnos can cast them into a deep sleep by waving his magic wand or by fanning them with his black wings. Terror is often hidden in the shadows of sleep, both in legend (where most vampire visitations take place at night) and in literature. In the world of dreams, reality loses its attributes and the frames of mind that shape our waking existence become blurred. The puzzle is reconstructed using new rules, which escape logic and understanding. In many ways, sleep, even more than death, is the realm of shadows. For the vampire's victims, sleep and all the states like it represent the gate that leads them into his power, as it paradoxically resembles, at the same time, death and madness.

Here is the border between life and death—when Mina is hypnotized by van Helsing, she enters this nowhere land: "Sleep has no place to call its own." This is where reality meets nightmare. The events are often referred to as "agony," preceding death. The entire story evolves in this shadowy atmosphere, which lures the reader into the realm of their own fears. The count's castle is a space dominated by fear and uncertainty, where logic is distorted; it "is old, and it has many memories, and there are bad dreams for those who sleep unwisely. Be warned! Should sleep now or ever overcome you, or be like to do, then haste to your own chamber or to these rooms, for your rest will then be safe,"[20] as Dracula warns Jonathan. The danger is both in sleep, as here the mind is under the influence of evil powers, but also in wakefulness, because lack of sleep pushes him down the road to madness. The men on the ghostly ship that carries Dracula to England cannot sleep, and it is at nighttime that they disappear.

Nighttime is the moment when the vampire is most often experienced in folklore for obvious reasons; it is after all the time of darkness, of shadows, when the light is hidden away from the world. So, for example, the visitations of William of Newburgh's Buckinghamshire vampire are, first of all, limited to the nighttime attacks on his wife. The night after his burial, "he suddenly entered the room where his wife lay asleep and, having awakened her, he not only filled her with the greatest alarm but almost killed her by leaping upon her with the whole heaviness of his weight and overlying her. On the second night, also, he tormented the trembling woman in such the same way. Wherefore in the extremity of dread she resolved that on the third night she would remain awake..."

On occasion, even the victims of vampire activity were unsure whether they were attacked while they were awake or during some dreadful nightmare. One of the vampire outbreaks during the eighteenth-century epidemics was centered on a man called Peter Plogojowitz. Shortly after his demise, there were further deaths in his Serbian village. Those affected had symptoms that "were complete exhaustion and a faintness as though from an excessive loss of blood. They complained that they had been visited by a fearful dream in which the dead Plogojowitz seemed to glide into the room, catch them by the throat biting hard and suck the blood out of the wound."[21]

There is an important contrast between folklore and literature as far as the hypnotic effect of the vampire is concerned. Folklore says little about the subject. In times past, vampirism was thought to be a physical disease, in the same way that plague and cholera are (with many symptoms in common). The vampire in literature is perceived as a fictional product, but the power of the mind has its greatest impact in the real world, because here, physical evidence filtered through the imagination repeatedly made history melt into fantasy. There is little doubt that those who were "victims" at the time were believed to have been attacked by "real" vampires. The vampire epidemics are for us, though, an image of mass delusion. With many victims describing how they were attacked while they slept, it is a clear clue to the mass psychotic origins of the epidemic.

The historical victims of vampire attacks might well have believed that they were being assaulted by a relative or a neighbor who had recently died. Given the contagious nature of epidemics, the newly dead could have been the physical cause of the ongoing deaths within the community. But in an age where the borders between the physical and spiritual realms were delineated differently from the way they are now, the analysis of the causes of death within the community would have led to conclusions that we, with the benefit of several hundred years of medical research to call upon, would not agree with.

The mind of the entire community was gripped during vampire infestations. When an exhumation took place, most people present "saw" the reactions of the vampire as it was exterminated. This often included the "corpse" going into spasm as a stake was driven into it, along with bloodcurdling screams and generous lashings of blood. No doubt many believed that they saw this, and some of the physical signs shown by the so-called vampire might actually have been present. It is, for example, quite probable that if you drove a stake into a corpse bloated by the gases formed during decomposition that there would be some strange sounds emanating from the body. But much of what was seen was distorted by the perspective of the viewer. They saw what they expected to see. It is significant that Tournefort, with a very different mental attitude from that of the inhabitants of eighteenth-century Mykonos, saw the same things that they did but interpreted them completely differently.

Sometimes, when folkloric versions are involved, the vampire attack is considered by the skeptics to have been just a nightmare following a rather heavy dinner. This developed in literature as the theme of doubt regarding the validity of the whole experience and a consequent delay in taking action against something that is considered an hallucination. Carmilla's victim does not realize that the danger lies in the vision that not only terrifies her, but also drains her blood and life away. Lucy and Mina are visited by Dracula during their dreams. Lucy is afraid to sleep as she perceives it as "a presage of horror." Later, Mina suffers from identical symptoms. Still, for a long time (sometimes, for the reader, too long), nobody manages to put two and two together and discover that there might be something significant in all those nightmares and the weakness that the girls suffer from. They actually need Renfield, the lunatic, to tell them that Mina is becoming a vampire. This could be seen as a tedious delay in building the plot to an appropriate climax, but also as a hint to the reversed perception in the upside down world where vampires' existence is accepted as reality.

Secondly, sleep is associated with vulnerability, physical and mental, whether it be in the realm of the vampire or that of the incubus and succubus in medieval demonology. The vampire attacks when sleep leaves his victims defenseless and their senses numbed. Mina cannot recollect the moment when the count entered her room, and she cannot fight his presence off: "I found a lethargy creeping over me." This incapacity to move or cry for help is a common theme, and it is the more effective as it is a sensation which is often experienced in real nightmares. The impossibility of action is more frightening than the fight itself. Panic and terror reach their peak when one cannot act, cannot do anything against the enemy which attacks. And thirdly, night is the time of sensuality, to which we dedicate the next chapter.

In this fictional space where reality and illusion are mingled, the characters share one obsession: the need to remember. The characters *have* to tell their story, as their experience must be shared, and the mists of mystery explored and re-explored in new company. Many stories are told in the first person singular (*Carmilla*, "The Vampyre," "The Family of the Vourdalak," "Dracula's Guest," *Interview with the Vampire*, among others), which is an incredibly good trick to give more life to the story and to make it more frightening, as the narrator is both directly involved and transmits to the listener/reader his or her own fears.

In *Dracula*, the diaries are, up to a point, very effective, as they describe the events almost as they happen, and so, at a first level of reading, they are a good auctorial device meant to create a gloomy, oppressive atmosphere. The plethora of detail, often exaggerated, weaves a net of hints and symbols that are the trusted props of the gothic novel. The shifting from the omniscient narrator to the subjective story of each character creates tension through the fragmentation of the point of view.

At a symbolic level, they represent an access to memory that provides evidence that the events are real and not invented. Doubt means fear and therefore vulnerability. Lucy cannot remember her dreams and this scares her. Sometimes, forgetfulness means peace of mind, but it is a passive defense. Van Helsing says that garlic is "like the Lotus flower, [it] makes your trouble forgotten," and she can sleep peacefully. Jonathan chooses to forget and gives away the diary, but action means remembrance of evil. Van Helsing insists upon the importance of the diaries and the count tries to destroy them, as they can be used as a weapon against him. Mina's scar is a constant reminder of her becoming a vampire. Memory is the key to understanding, and even when the vampire is destroyed, the characters need to remember their terrifying and extraordinary experiences—Mina and Jonathan have a child whose "bundle of names links all our little band of men together; but we call him Quincey."[22]

The need to survive through memories is an image whose impact on our consciousness should not be underestimated. It is, after all, why the great and the powerful so often build magnificent mausoleums for themselves. For those who become vampires, remembrance loses its human coordinates, but they have a need to return, always preying on their own kin or righting old wrongs. Dracula's castle holds the history of his ancestors' violent life. And he needs the earth of his fatherland to continue his existence: the wooden boxes contain earth "so sacred of holy memories, that he has brought from a far distant land for such fell use.". It is interesting that this evil entity needs "holy memories" to survive. Louis (*Interview with the Vampire*) needs to tell the world his story, how he was led on this path of blood by the seductive Lestat, and how he discovered the taste of blood and death. Carmilla needs to preserve her identity in the anagrams of her name: Mircalla–Carmilla–Millarca. In *Buffy*, the avatars of the ensouled vampire are preserved in the slight change in his name: Angel–Angelus.

The closest thing to vampires in *The Lord of the Rings* are the Black Riders, once humans, but whose souls had been drained by the evil of the rings that gave them unearthly power. Frodo himself, as Ring Bearer, almost begins to transform into one, to feel less and less human as the Ring make him lose his memories: "I know that such things happened, but I cannot see them. No taste of food, no feel of water, no sound of wind, no memory of tree or grass or flower, no image of moon or star are left to me. I am naked in the dark, Sam, and there is no veil between me and the wheel of fire. I begin to see it even with my waking eyes, and all else fades."[23]

The loss of memories represents the final loss of the self, of all identity and, therefore, absolute dissolution into the void. This is why people need to remember their dead, in all types of rituals, from the sharing of food and lighting of candles to Remembrance Day. This is because the souls of the departed need our memories to find their path, and we need to remember them as our roots, and our guidance into life. We cling desperately to our memories, our history, and folklore is one way of perpetuating the knowledge and recollection of old days. We need the past to sustain our existence.

The "cousins" of the Black Riders are the Dementors in the *Harry Potter* series, with their vampiric draining of memories from the humans around them. These soulless creatures feed on the souls of their victims, sucking out their happiness, leaving them in a hell composed of the most terrible memories. In this way, life becomes devoid of meaning as it becomes devoid of the senses of goodness and happiness on which it is normally based. Eventually, the victim will lose their soul, the ultimate fate of the prey of the vampire.

The loss of memories disrupts the normality of the world and plunges it into chaos. The vampire in literature is an embodiment of the Irrational, of all that is beyond reasonable explanation. The atmosphere around it seems to be infested with madness. We are afraid of all that escapes our logic and powers of comprehension. It is fear that opens the gates of a world where the laws of logical thinking are abolished and where the deepest, most unexplainable instincts rule supreme.

In *Dracula*, the first victim is Jonathan Harker himself. His "strange night-existence" at the castle makes him doubt his own self and throws him into a topsy-turvy world that he cannot believe and understand. And because he cannot fit the strange events around him into a frame of mind based on logical explanation, he does not see the frailty of the general thinking pattern, but rather starts to question his own sanity, to such an extent that he disbelieves his own experience: "Whilst I live on here there is but one thing to hope for: that I may not go mad, if, indeed, I be not mad already."[24] His constant allusions to *Hamlet* give us a key to his fears: uncertainty opens the path to madness. The dreamlike atmosphere makes it impossible for him to retain a palpable proof of his experience, which would help him preserve his sanity. As he escapes, he suffers from brain fever, and he needs proof that somebody else has met the vampire count in order to be able to admit the reality.

A similar maddening lack of evidence is used in "What Was It?" the story of an invisible vampire that attacks its victim in the night, written by an Irish-American author, FitzJames O'Brien, and published in 1859. It cannot be seen, though it is no less violent and bloodthirsty than the more showy vampires. No shape, no name, therefore a "Mystery," a "Horror," and a "King of Terrors," in the view of those who, in spite of catching this monster, are faced with the dilemma of not knowing what to do with it.

The impossibility of understanding, and therefore of action, is more dreadful than any fight, as doubts feed on the spirit just as vampires feed on the blood of their victims: "God grant that I am not mad, and that this is not an insane fantasy."[25] This story uses another device which directs us to the distorting power of the mind—the characters who catch this monster have the doors towards the world of phantasms opened by opium: "We enjoyed together that wonderful expansion of thought, the marvellous intensifying of the perceptive faculties, that boundless feeling of existence when we seem to have points of contact with the whole universe..."[26]

"Is it real, or some dream so like reality as to nearly overturn the judgement for ever?"[27] It is a leitmotif of all vampire literature, as writers exploit to the full the human need to doubt all that escapes logical, scientific explanation. The literary convention includes this game, giving it a deeper meaning. The characters of the book (and the reader) enter a warped reality, with a set of mental landmarks that differ from those that are considered normal, and are therefore considered signs of lunacy. One by one, the characters doubt their own senses and reject a reality that does not fit the regular pattern. The uncertainty is like a mist around them, making them unable to defend themselves. It is the acceptance of the existence of evil that gives them power to react. Van Helsing's power is in the knowledge that he holds, in his allowing the "unnatural" to exist as part of the world. He considers "madness easier to bear compared with truth like this," because the truth defies the accepted order where madness has its own place, marginal, but acknowledged.

Count Dracula spreads terror and panic around him, as people are afraid of his inexplicable, supernatural evil powers. The captain of the ship on which Dracula travels to England thinks that the Romanian mate is "mad, stark, raving mad," and reads his terror as lunacy: "He looked wild-eyed and haggard, and I greatly fear his reason has given way. He came close to me and whispered hoarsely, with his mouth to my ear, as though fearing the very air might hear."[28] And yet he is the only one who understands and, therefore, escapes the vampire by throwing himself into the sea.

There are allusions to madness throughout *Dracula*. Dr. Seward runs an asylum; van Helsing is his teacher. The characters fear that they might lose their minds even more than they fear the vampire. This, like many such stories, is not a novel about fear in the face of an accepted evil, but about our panic when faced by evidence that reality might have other reference points than the ones generally accepted. So, when something strange happens which defies the norms of our world, it is not the norms that we doubt but our own sanity. The novel questions the order of a world that thinks in terms of good and evil, real and unreal, sane and mad. The perpetual doubts of the characters, the game of reality and appearances (Renfield, for example, sometimes seems sane and sometimes acts like a lunatic; Lucy, the innocent victim, becomes a demon; Mina's comment that Dracula himself is a victim), everything casts a huge question mark over our understanding of the world.

The vampire poses questions about life and death and about the frailty and the strength of the human mind and body. The undead inhabit a strange hinterland where neither and both worlds exist. Mortality represents the central point of all forms of human belief, for superstition, for religion, and for vampirism. Death can be seen as a journey, a quest for immortality. Neither does it have the finality that might be thought. Reincarnation at one level; the prospect of eternal, albeit, spiritual rather than physical, life, at another, suggests that death is just a rite of passage, a metamorphosis from one mode of existence to another. The path of blood and of imagination leads the reader of the vampire story to a land where fantasy and nightmare reach their peak.

NOTES

1. "Würzburg Witch Trials," in *The Encyclopaedia of Witchcraft and Demonology.*

2. *Dracula,* p. 46.

3. Ibid., p. 316.

4. Romanian fairy tales often speak about "dead water" and "living water" with magical properties that can cure or even bring people back to life. Such springs are thought to be at the end of the world, or protected by fierce beasts or spirits, sometimes by two mountains that fight each other.

5. It is interesting to note that the horseshoe is a symbol of good luck in Romania as well as in Britain.

6. *Dracula,* p. 28.

7. In Frayling, p. 115.

8. Ibid., p. 45.

9. *Carmilla,* p. 18.

10. Le Fanu, *Madam Crowl's Ghost and Other Stories,* p. 55.

11. *Folklore, Myths and Legends of Britain,* pp. 322–323.

12. In Frayling, p. 127.

13. There is an interesting coincidence between the name of the Marquis d'Urfé, who tells about his encounter with the family of the Vourdalak in Alexei Tolstoy's famous vampire story, and that of Fowles's hero, Urfé, and his boast about his descent from the French writer, Honoré d'Urfé (1567–1625), in *The Magus,* the splendid fantasia on the limits of the mind in a vicious game of illusions.

14. *The Magus,* p. 99.

15. *Varney the Vampyre,* in Frayling, p. 150.

16. *Carmilla,* p. 49.

17. "The Family of the Vourdalak," in Frayling, p. 263.

18. "For the Blood is the Life," in *Great Vampire Stories,* p. 17.

19. "Wake Not the Dead!" in Frayling, p. 175.

20. *Dracula,* p. 57.

21. Ibid., p. 150.

22. *Dracula,* p. 368.

23. Tolkien, *The Return of the King,* p. 254.
24. *Dracula,* p. 60.
25. Frayling, p. 208.
26. Ibid., p. 211.
27. *Varney the Vampyre,* in Frayling, p. 151.
28. *Dracula,* p. 105.

CHAPTER 12

Beauty and the Beast

Why are the kisses which he gave betray'd
By the impression which his teeth has made?

—Ovid, *Amores*

Throughout history, eroticism has assumed a wide range of appearances, from the sacred ritual to the taboo that some civilizations have imposed on it. As the vampire myth developed in the literature of the Christian era, and the figure of the revenant represented a blasphemous contrast to the holiness of the God-created world, the creature became an extension of the image of the Devil. Eroticism was condemned by the Church as the work of Satan; its vampiric dimension as the interface between a living person and a supernatural, hellish apparition, was perceived as a deed against the laws of nature and perhaps even a twisted, devilish inversion of the Immaculate Conception. Without Christianity, the vampire would have died. It is the essential perversion of the phenomenon that keeps it alive. There is an interesting insight into the connection between Christianity, vampirism, and sexuality quoted by Ornella Volta in *Il Vampiro*, who boldly asserts that, "to paraphrase Kierkegaard, who accused Christianity of having introduced sexuality into the world by the simple fact of having isolated it under the label of 'sin,' we might say that vampirism can also be attributed to Christianity."[1]

The concept of vampirism is strongly built around the contrasting paradigms, particularly of women, held by many societies over the centuries. It is a truism that women are "different" from men, and these differences have created an ambivalence that goes to the core of the attraction of the vampire legend. One analysis holds that "when what is different and 'other' is also desired it may be resented, hated and feared as well as loved and idealized."[2]

This dual view is represented in vampire lore and literature, where almost every story revolves around one or another aspect of woman. In Bram Stoker's *Dracula*, Mina is very much an idealized figure, almost too good to be true; while in "Wake Not the Dead!" Brunhilda is an apocalyptic, demonic killer. Mina inspires the men around her to act as her protectors, preserving her innocence against the terrifying forces of the seductive vampire count. Brunhilda ultimately inspires nothing save an uncontrollable urge to obliterate her.

Woman is represented as the epitome of duality, good and evil, life and death, Heaven and Hell. In many cultures, she is the cause of man's fall from grace, her earthy sexuality distracting him from the pursuit of nirvana. The very act of love was often held to drain man of his life force, so even when new life is being created, it is as a result of the male suffering a diminution of his essential energies. It is therefore impossible to consider vampirism without examining the sexual undertones that the phenomenon encapsulates. The vampire story doesn't only evolve around the figure of the temptress. The male seducer plays a similar role, ranging from the dark nobleman to the figures of hell, preying on the innocent— an occult development of a well-known stereotype. The vampire is then often a seductive male with irresistible magnetic charm, or a voluptuous woman, threatening to explode with volcanic sexuality. It is a key motif that helps to grip the reader's attention.

This attractive imagery is very different from the classic description in historical accounts from the epidemics of the seventeenth and eighteenth centuries. Here, the vampire is quite simply horrific. The symptoms of decay and normal death may not be present, but the picture painted is still grotesque. The "corpse" of the vampire is bloated, its teeth prominent, its hair and nails long and still growing, though it is noticeable that some of the accounts from history suggest a link with sensuality. The corpse of males is sometimes described as being in a "wild" state, which is a euphemism for the fact that the penis is erect. There are also hints that they prey on young women in the search for sexual gratification rather than just blood.[3] But even in literature and cinematography, all is not quite as attractive as it initially seems. In the Coppola version of *Dracula*, the count is an irresistibly attractive personality, but also transmutes into the most grotesque of creatures at various times. This ability to change from a figure of beauty or charm into a beast, found in many different examples from the vampire corpus, is part of the essential horror of the myth, the continuous game of appearance and reality, of appeal and terror.

The seductive vampire is traditionally represented in two ways. The male vampire is a Byronic figure. The sexual attraction of the noble lord (a caricature of Byron, whose real-life exploits were, to say the least, controversial) was the inspiration behind Polidori's "Vampyre," and in time became a classic image, revolving around the exploitation of young, innocent women by the vampire. There is an obvious allusion to what really interests Lord Ruthven in this story. The experienced seductress, Lady Mercer, eager for a sexual liaison with the inexplicably magnetic lord, is rebuffed. He, instead, turns his attention to more difficult targets, women with no previous skeletons in their cupboards—in other words, virgins. This becomes the basis for future seductive lords, be it Sir Francis Varney or Count Dracula, or even the less well-known Count Azzo. This literary stereotype has two prominent features. The first is the complete control he exercises by a combination of latent sexuality and the sheer force of his magnetism over his victims. The second is the so-called noble blood of the vampire. The combination of class and sex is just too much for would-be victims to resist.

This has been exploited to the full by Hollywood, where the stereotypical male vampire possesses a predatory hypnotic power that makes any young girl (the more innocent the better) who comes within his orbit helpless, unless an older, van Helsing-like figure sees through the demon and destroys him. Through his manipulation, the virginal young woman is transformed, once she herself becomes a vampire, into a Lilith-like figure, luring the unwary into her arms and sucking the life out of them in payment. One of the most famous actors to portray the count, Christopher Lee, described the fascination in an interview thus:

He offers the illusion of immortality ... the subcons cious wish we all have of limitless power ... a man of tremendous brain and physical strength ... he is either a reincarnation or he has never died. He is a superman image, with erotic appeal for women who find him totally alluring. In many ways he is everything people would like to be—the anti-hero, the heroic villain .... For women there is the complete abandonment to the power of a man.

As Lee says, the combination of sexual domination and supernatural power provides erotic imagery that is almost impossible to resist, either by the vampire's fictional victims or the cinemagoer.

The image of the seductive aristocrat, resplendent in a black cloak and evening wear, was not a product of Stoker's imagination alone—some of the props were provided by the twentieth-century actor Hamilton Deane and taken up enthusiastically by Hollywood. However, there are interesting precedents elsewhere from the arts world. Mozart's operatic would-be seducer Don Giovanni, resplendent in his black cloak, prowls around in search of his unsuspecting victims in much the same way as the cinematographic count does.[4]

The reverse image sees the female vampire acting as the temptress, with sex-starved males as their victims. This is the case with the three female vampires in *Dracula*, the lesbian seductress Carmilla, or even

Lucy in Stoker's novel. Men find it difficult to resist their advances. The attraction of the young woman to the well-intentioned (but slightly dull) Jonathan Harker overwhelms him, and even the saintly van Helsing has problems fighting off his attraction to her. Lord Arthur, although he knows better than anybody that Lucy is dead, is very tempted when her vampire shade invites him to join her as her "husband." From beyond the grave, the rampant sexuality of Lucy—something of a shock, presumably, given her innocence in life—exercises an attraction over Arthur that he would be unable to resist were it not for van Helsing. So strong is the lure of sexual fulfillment, that it threatens to overcome Arthur's rational side.

Similarly, with Carmilla, there are obvious undercurrents so that her victims find it difficult to keep her away, even though her approaches, lesbian in nature, are anathema to the way that young women of that era were brought up. The implication is that sexual attraction, present even among the most innocent human beings, is so strong that, in the right (or maybe the wrong) situation, with a sexually irresistible encounter on offer, all other forces become powerless. It is a demonstration of just how frail our human weaknesses make us; if chance places us in certain situations, nothing is taboo.

This sexuality is evidenced, without much subtlety, in Charles Baudelaire's poem, "Metamorphoses of the Vampire" (1857). Anyone who doubts that sex is at the root of the literary vampire phenomenon need only read this extract to be convinced:

> Meanwhile, from her red mouth the woman, in husky tones,
> Twisting her body like a serpent upon hot stones
> And straining her white breasts from their imprisonment,
> Let fall these words, as potent as a heavy scent:
> 'My lips are moist and yielding, and I know the way
> To keep the antique demon of remorse at bay.
> All sorrows die upon my bosom. I can make
> Old men laugh happily as children for my sake.
> For him who sees me naked in my tresses,
> I Replace the sun, the moon, and all the stars of the sky!
> Believe me, learned sir, I am so deeply skilled
> That when I wind a lover in my soft arms, and yield
> My breasts like two ripe fruits for his devouring—both
> Shy and voluptuous, insatiable and loath—
> Upon this bed that groans and sighs luxuriously
> Even the impotent angels would be damned for me!'

Despite her apparent charms, the horror of the victim, when he seeks one last kiss from his lover, can well be imagined when he finds "nothing but a hideous putrescent thing, all faceless and exuding pus." When he wakes in the morning, he turns to see that the woman who "seemed to have replenished her arteries from my own" is now nothing but a skeleton. The necrophilic imagery is gruesome and cannot fail to horrify the reader.[5]

The vampire-seductress, although not found in accounts of the vampire epidemic of the eighteenth century, has, in fact, far older antecedents. She is a regular member of the folklore pantheons of many cultures. One such example is that of the *baobhan-sith*, a vampiric creature from Scotland, an attractive being who entices men with her sexual charms. She is invariably dressed in green, the color of the forest, but also, significantly, the color worn by prostitutes in the Middle Ages (the basis, incidentally, of the well-known sixteenth-century song "Greensleeves," which, rather than being a romantic lament as it is often popularly supposed to be, is a highly satirical complaint from a cuckolded lover). It is also the color associated with Venus, the goddess of love.

One story tells of a party of four young men who were out hunting in the wilds. They took shelter for the night in a remote shieling. During the hours of darkness, they are joined by four young women, resplendent in green dresses and beautiful with their flowing blonde hair. While one of the young men plays music, the other three dance. The musician eventually notices that there is blood dripping from his friends. Understandably terrified, he rushes off into the night. When he returns to the shieling in the morning, he finds his friends dead and completely drained of blood.

The *dearg-dul*—the "Red Blood-Sucker"—is the Irish cousin of the *baobhan-sith,* and one of the oldest of all vampires. One account of such a creature from Waterford has the vampire returning from the grave several times a year to lure unwary young men to their doom.[6]

Such phenomena are not just occidental in incidence, suggesting that there is a universal deep-rooted fear and longing, making us susceptible to the seducer/seductress in whatever form they might appear. A harrowing example is that of the *sundal bolong,* found in Java. A woman becomes one when she is raped and subsequently commits suicide. We find here two of the strongest taboos: the woman forced to have sex against her will and the human being who takes his or her life—both acts against the accepted laws of nature. This vampire dedicates her half-life to taking revenge against men. Once she has trapped them, she drains them of their blood.

A fifteenth-century story from Iraq tells of a wealthy young man from Baghdad, Abdul-Hassan. While wandering around the countryside deep in thought, he hears the beautiful voice of an incredibly attractive young woman. He is instantly besotted and marries the girl. They are at first very happy, but Abdul-Hassan is intrigued that his wife, Nadilla, never eats in the evening. When he discovers that she disappears at night, he is suspicious. Following her, he finds himself in a cemetery. His wife is before him, eating corpses. When he confronts her, she attacks him. He slays her with his sword. But after being buried, she returns from the grave, possessed of superhuman strength. Abdul-Hassan manages to escape and has her exhumed. Her coffin is found awash with blood, so her corpse is burned to ashes and the unfortunate young husband is bothered no more.

A temptress from the Philippines was known as the *mandurago* (blood-sucker). By day, the creature takes the form of a beautiful woman, but by night, it assumes the shape of a hideous flying monster. She uses her day-time beauty to ensnare a husband, young and virile, who subsequently supplies a regular stock of blood. During the night, she flies away from the domestic nest, returning at daybreak to her unsuspecting husband.

Another predatory seductress from the other side of the world (mainly Central America, but also parts of the United States) is *La Llorona,* the "Weeping Woman." She, too, appears in white and preys on men in revenge for the tragedy of her life. The story has been traced back to early colonial Mexico. She was originally a beautiful young woman who fell in love. Her lover deserted her, despite the fact that she had borne him three children. She, uninvited, attended his wedding, but was so overcome with grief that she fled from the church, went home, and murdered her children. She was subsequently executed. Her former lover was overwhelmed by remorse and killed himself. It is another classic tale, containing many motifs recurrent in the lore of the seductress. The most striking elements are, again, the breaking of taboos—in this case, a mother murdering her own children, themselves born out of wedlock; an abuse of trust—the lover who was disloyal—and the thirst for revenge. *La Llorona* is one of the many vampire seductresses found all over the world.

The legendary temptresses, as, for example, the *lamiae* of Antiquity, were revived in the literature of later centuries. She became a direct inspiration for Gothic-era writers. The image of the woman who breaks the taboos of innocence became connected with the shadowy figure of creatures from hell. The vampire tale plays on this theme. In "The Family of the Vourdalak," the young and formerly innocent Stenka, who had shared her family's vampiric doom, became a very different being: "her former timidity had given way to a strange wantonness of manner. She seemed more forward, more knowing. It dawned on me that her behavior was no longer that of the naïve young girl I recalled in my dream."[7]

This description could just as easily have been applied to Stoker's Lucy. More than that, Tolstoy's vampire has renounced her Christianity as her vampire state was no longer compatible with the holy relics and tiny icons which were supposed to protect her from harm. In *Buffy,* vampires are repulsed by the sign of the cross, except for Angel, who can approach Buffy when she is wearing her crucifix. As the gypsies' curse brings back his soul, Angel is able to feel not only remorse, but also true love, which breaks the boundaries between him and Buffy, between their apparently irreconcilable natures—vampire and Slayer. The motif of the cross emphasizes the relationship between Christianity and morality, on the one hand, and its inverted image in vampirism and sensuality, on the other. The modern vampire myth survives by sucking the blood out of Christian taboos.

Some of the most powerful taboos concerned sex itself, particularly incest. Such acts were deemed to cause disaster, as Oedipus would witness. Incest was also a way in which one could become a vampire (for example, the *pijaciva*, a Slovenian vampire). Illegitimacy was another taboo. Those born out of wedlock (especially those born to illegitimate parents) were particularly at risk of becoming vampires in some cultures. The theme of incest is one of many underlying the plot in *Interview with the Vampire*. Louis's relationship with Claudia, the child vampire, one which, in the movie, has barely concealed sexual overtones, threatens to break taboos in several ways. First, they are, in a vampiric sense, parent and daughter, therefore the relationship is incestuous. Second, although she has the emotions of a woman, the Lolita-like Claudia has the body of a girl, therefore the relationship is also pedophilic.

Interview also explores sexual taboos in other ways. It is based in part on the homoerotic relationship between Louis, Lestat, and Armand. The power of this movie may be connected to the timing of its release. It appeared when concerns about the AIDS epidemic was prominent, and the connections between homosexuality and a fatal illness spread through the medium of blood find a good metaphor in the vampire tale as represented in this film. The sex in *Buffy* (season 6) takes the perversions of vampirism to yet another level. Much of the sex in this—and there is a fair bit of it, implied, if not actually seen—involves pain and sadism.[8]

Another not very subtle hint at depravity can be found in Francis Ford Coppola's *Dracula*. In Stoker's novel, Lucy turns from angel into demon as she gives her blood to the count. Arthur, her fiancé, is shocked to see that his pure bride had, in death, turned into a lecherous monster. But the movie takes the sexuality of the plot much further. Lucy is, from the very beginning, a coquette who seems to understand more about the ways of the world than a woman of her station is supposed to know. Her encounter with Dracula, who assumes a shape resembling that of a werewolf, takes place in the cemetery at night, and leaves little doubt about the ways in which the vampire takes advantage of his victims. The attack on her resembles sexual intercourse of a bestial nature far more than anything else.

The danger of breaking taboos was a theme enthusiastically adopted by writers. The vampiric Brunhilda is a classic case in point. However well disguised the talented author makes his story, this is essentially a tale of necrophilia. The sexual hold that his wife had over Walter while she lived is so strong that it even survives the grave—in life they "abandoned themselves to the enjoyment of the passion that rendered them reckless of aught besides."[9] Predictably enough, once he breaks the laws of nature, rejecting in the process his second, more domesticated (and more alive!) wife, everything possible starts to go wrong. The Cassandra-like admonitions of the sorcerer not to proceed with his plan are, of course, ignored. Blinded by his own passion, Walter is oblivious as his world collapses around him like a house of cards. He loses everything, his second wife, his children and, most of all, his peace of mind to the lustful desire for that which he can no longer have.

The cataclysmic final scene is almost a parody. He becomes besotted by a woman closely resembling his second wife. Perhaps fed by feelings of guilt for the rejection of one who had never been anything but loyal to him, Walter finds a happiness with the stranger that he thought he had lost forever. She accepts his offer of marriage, but when they proceed to the nuptial chamber: "Oh horror! scarcely had he cast her in his arms, ere she transformed herself into a monstrous serpent, which entwining him in his horrid folds, crushed him to death."[10] This truly was the wedding night from hell.

The biblical connection is transparent. The snake (a phallic symbol) is synonymous with Satan, particularly in his Garden of Eden incarnation when he tempted Eve into Original Sin, and she, in turn, persuaded the weak-willed Adam to follow. For Eve/Satan combined, read Brunhilda; for Adam, read Walter. But there are other symbolic links, too. Keats's "Lamia" describes how the sensual star of the story was a serpent transformed by Hermes into a beautiful woman who tries to lure a serious student from his studies into her vampiric embraces. The snake and sensuality (and Christianity) are irrevocably entwined.

A similar necrophiliac theme underlies the storyline in "For the Blood is the Life." Angelo is lured by the vampiric gypsy girl, and he yields to her embraces although he knows that she is dead. In the daytime, guilt and fear tell him that the liaison is wrong. But come the night, he is powerless to resist "this dream of terror and delight." His amorous urges overcome his moral sensibilities, and the invocation of the girl's name—Cristina (derived from Christian)—is enough to create a breach with reality where "he could not tell whether her red lips burned his or froze them, or whether her five fingers on his wrists seared scorching scars or bit his flesh like frost; he could not tell whether he was awake or asleep, whether she was alive or dead, but he knew that she loved him, she alone of all creatures, earthly or unearthly, and her spell had power over him."[11]

In medieval times, the Church was obsessed with the carnality of Satan, warning that the incubus or the succubus preyed on young innocents in their sleep. The incubus was a male demon who visited women during the night and committed unspeakable sexual acts with them. There are similarities with the vampire. After these nocturnal attacks, the victim would feel weak and lethargic. In some beliefs, these creatures can actually father children, though such offspring are demonic. The succubus, the female equivalent, is equally voracious, denuding the victim of energy. Romanian legends speak of *Zburatorul*, a flying demon who would come down the chimney as a flame, transform itself into a physical entity, and deflower virgins. The victim would inevitably show signs of melancholy, wither, and eventually die. In his presentation of Moldavian customs, the eighteenth-century scholar Dimitrie Cantemir tells of the relatives of the victim sometimes waiting in her chamber to fight off the demon. This occasionally turned out to be a very real young man from the village who would subsequently get an equally real beating-up.

Belief in succubi and incubi was widespread in medieval times, and was extensively preached by the Church without the benefit of psychologists who would be well placed to see the evidence of sexual repression among those of an age who would be sexually active, but whose celibate lifestyle—many victims were nuns, for example—made them susceptible to visions of this nature.

Sex was a taboo for many people, particularly those living in a monastic environment. Visions of a sexual nature were visitations from the legions of Satan. The predatory instincts of these evil spirits found expression in several vampire forms. One was the *mara* (Slavic *mora*) found in many parts of Europe, and especially well known in Scandinavia, a nocturnal female visitor capable of crushing the life out of its victims. She can appear either as a beautiful young woman or a horrible old crone. She could also appear in the form of a horse that places its hooves on the chest of its victim.

In the Slavic version of the myth, the creature drinks the blood of a man. Here, however, there is an interesting role reversal. After she draws blood from a victim, she is besotted with him and not the other way round. She will never leave him, and remains a persistent nighttime visitor once this link has been formed. One form of protection against her unwelcome advances was to draw a knife and point it upwards. As she descended on to the body of her intended victim, she would be impaled and forced to withdraw. Other forms resembling the incubus/succubus phenomenon include the *veripard* (blood beard), who visits victims at night in a version of the nightmare, tormenting them until dawn.

Given the perverted nature of vampirism, where penetration is by biting into the body rather than sexual intercourse, and the ultimate pleasure is the drawing of blood, it is unsurprising that extreme examples of sexual depravity have been linked with vampiric tendencies. The best known of all sadists was the man who gave his name to the word, the Marquis de Sade. Two of his more infamous works, *Justine* and *Juliette,* contain scenes which allude to vampirism with leading actors who enjoy watching their victims bleed and others who display marked vampiric characteristics. This emphasizes the close connection between vampirism and extreme sexual behavior, the sheer horror of which proved captivating to audiences, particularly in Victorian times, when sexuality was so often kept under wraps.

The ritual defloweringof innocent young virgins by predatory demons, ravished in the apparent sanctuaries of their own boudoirs, proved irresistible to readers who had been brought up to deny expression to their own sexual tendencies, and instead found release in literature. The loss of innocence threatens the immortal souls of the literary victims, too. In *Dracula,* Lucy, an unmarried girl and therefore, to the readers of the Victorian era, a virgin, returns from the grave as a lustful, seductive temptress. In an allegorical statement that medieval theologians would have been proud of, her approaches to the naïve Arthur Holmwood also threaten his soul. In this instance, the wages of sin really are death.

Sexual "misbehavior" was an essential part of Satan's armory in his efforts to seduce mankind away from the path to Salvation. The witches' sabbat culminated in wild orgies of bacchanalian intensity, where the Devil himself played a supreme role. The obligatory rites were a distortion of normality, anything was permitted, provided that it was obscene and against the norms of nature as perceived by the Church. There are hundreds of accounts that survive describing how incest, bestiality, sodomy, and intercourse with demons took place. Many of the participants were novitiates, innocents exposed to corruption and depravity in a horrific display of occult perversion.

Despite the apparent willingness of the participants to engage in sexual activity with demons, there was, in many accounts, little pleasure derived from it. A 16-year-old girl, Jeanette d'Abadie, said that "she feared intercourse with the Devil, because his member was scaly and caused extreme pain; furthermore, his semen was extremely cold, so cold that she never became pregnant by him; in fact, she was never made fat by the other ordinary men at the sabbat."[12] This was, in common with vampirism, a potpourri of perversions; the laws of nature are reversed, the sexual act is both painful and fails to produce children, there is no pleasure experienced by the participants—all this in return for putting their immortal souls in peril. In the same way, the victim of the vampire is abused, and as a result of their actions, willing or not, the only outcome that can be expected from their involvement is physical pain, illness, and death, accompanied by the threat of eternal damnation.

But we can also find in other accounts (mostly earlier ones) further evidence of the existence of the duality of occultism. For in some versions, sexual relationships with the Devil are described as being extremely pleasurable. Italian accounts speak of such activity as being *maxima cum voluptate* ("great with sensuality"). This did not last, however, as the later accounts of demonic intercourse almost invariably state that the act was unpleasant and painful.

The physical appearance of Satan also shares common features with the vampire. In some accounts, he copulates with his partners even when he is in the form of an animal. Various writers told how he could assume the shape of a serpent, a goat, a raven, a stork, a bull, or a dog, and even a woodpecker. This is a similar ability to that possessed by the literary vampire that can change its shape into that of an animal in the pursuit of its depraved pleasure. But the Devil can take other, far more pleasing forms, also resonant of the vampire. A seventeenth-century account of a young girl called Agatha Southtell who was seduced by the Devil "in the shape of a very handsome young man." And there are many accounts of how Satan appears as a seductive "man in black." The analogies are clear; the connection between the figures struck by the demonic seducer and the Byronic epitome of the cinematographic vampire à la Christopher Lee are transparent.

The suggestive sensuality of the vampire and the acts it indulges in is one of the most striking aspects of the myth. The combination of sex and terror is one that is difficult to resist. Whether it be through the aristocratic seducer or the voluptuous temptress who we all know will turn out to be a femme fatale in every sense of the word, the vampire continues to exercise a lurid fascination. Terrifyingly, beneath the voluptuous exterior, there is only death and decay: "[I saw that] her features, though still beautiful were those of a corpse; that her eyes did not see; and that her smile was the distorted grimace of a decaying skull. At the same time, I sensed in that room the putrid smell of the charnel house."[13]

Beauty, they say, is in the eyes of the beholder. And most victims of the literary vampire, and its legendary "seductress"/demonic antecedents, do not see things as they truly are until it is far too late.

NOTES

1. Frayling, p. 388.
2. *Encyclopaedia of World Mythology,* p. 29.
3. See Barber, pp. 9, 22.
4. Alessandro Barrico: see BBC News Web site, July 7, 2003.
5. Extracts and translation from the entry for Baudelaire in *The Vampire Encyclopaedia.*
6. See p. 2 of this book.
7. "The Family of the Vourdalak," in Frayling, p. 274.
8. For further discussion, see the chapter on "Heterosexuality and Sex" by Justine Larbalestier in *Reading the Vampire Slayer.*
9. "Wake Not the Dead!" in Frayling, p. 166.
10. Ibid., p. 189.
11. *Great Vampire Stories,* p. 17.
12. See "Sab bat," in *The Encyclopaedia of Witchcraft and Demonology.*
13. "The Family of the Vourdalak," in Frayling, p. 276.

CHAPTER 13

The Undead

The dead travel fast.

—Bram Stoker, "Dracula's Guest"

Although death is seen as a final frontier, some of the most powerful images of the supernatural occur when the line between the world of the living and the realm of the dead blurs. The latter often sends its messengers among the living, whether in an angelic or hellish form. Norse myths say that, on stormy nights, the skies are ravaged by "the furious army" of the dead warriors, led by Woden-Odin, on their "savage hunt." Their gallop of death was even more terrifying than the fury of the elements. The vampire myth is linked to such traditions, its power to instill fear predicated on the belief that, in their case, the souls of those who should be dead continue to walk the realms of mortals in a horrible distortion of life. In this concluding chapter, we will consider in more detail the ways in which the undead come to exist and, in particular, what underlying beliefs explain their "existence." We will also investigate the various ways of eliminating the vampire, an area in which literature particularly mirrors folklore.

Before doing so, however, we feel it is important to give our view of why the vampire was such a powerful image, particularly in the Christian West. It was not only because the vampire was believed to inflict the worst of all possible fates, the damnation of the soul, on its victims. It was also because vampirism and other so-called marginal manifestations of the supernatural, such as witchcraft, were perceived as perverted parodies of Christianity. The former revolves around the obsession with the life-giving power of blood, a distorted reflection of the Mass, and an unwilling and often unknowing sacrifice. The resurrection, another concept at the heart of Christendom, is also included in this myth. But this is, again, just an evil charade, for the vampire is not really resurrected—it never truly dies. It is not a ghost that the victim encounters, but a demonic version of the body that was, a body that does not even decay. This will not, as Christian theology demands, be raised on the last day, because it has never died in the first place. The vampire only sleeps, the unhallowed, restless sleep of the damned.

Folklore describes different ways in which a vampire is created. Paul Barber[1] identifies four. The first he calls predisposition, in which an evil life is followed by an evil death. The second type is the vampire created by predestination, called so because the creature has no control over its destiny—for example, a child born out of wedlock or the seventh child of a family. Children born with a red caul or with teeth are marked out as vampires from birth in some cultures. The third general category includes vampires created as a result of some violent event, almost invariably as the result of a vampire attack (interestingly, folklore places the bite around the heart, while the neck is a favorite in literary creations). The last category is where rituals, particularly those of burial, are not followed to the letter.

There are widespread beliefs in many different cultures, not just Christian ones, that vampires were people who had been evil in life. Some quite mundane categories could be at risk of becoming vampires, for example, alcoholics in many parts of Eastern Europe, or even "deceitful and treacherous barmaids and other dishonourable people."[2] This particular belief lives on in the person of the so-called modern vampire, Angel, from *Buffy*, who was an alcoholic before he became a vampire.

A Chinese version of the undead, the *k'uei*, is the soul of a person who has led a bad life and is therefore unable to enjoy the benefits of the Afterworld. An evil life was also given much prominence in Christian theology as a cause of vampirism. Leo Allatius wrote an account of Greek vampires, *De Quorundum Graecorum Opinationibus*, published in Cologne in 1645. He recorded details of both the vampires and the Orthodox Church's way of dealing with them. In his view, the vampire was the body of a man who had led an immoral life. Often he would have been excommunicated, which condemned him to wander the earth with no hope of spiritual redemption. His body was taken over by a demon, and the vampire then walked the streets. He knocked on the doors, and if the inhabitants answered, then they were invariably dead by the morning. The residents of Chios dealt with this problem by waiting before answering the door, as the vampire did not knock twice.

In Crete, there was a particularly interesting variant of the myth. The vampire would be someone that had lived an evil life, often someone who had been excommunicated. The body of the deceased would be taken over by a demon, and the vampire infestation would begin. For 40 days the vampire's strength gradually increased—40 days comes up often in

Orthodox death lore; it appears to be a kind of magic number. It is the length of time that is deemed to have elapsed between the Crucifixion and Christ's ascension to heaven. In Romania, the belief that the soul is somehow tied to the earth for 40 days is still widely held. During this period, the vampire could be frightened off by the sound of gunfire. Afterwards, however, it was practically indestructible, and it required the services of a priest to destroy it. But if this could be done, the epidemic stopped at once because all those that the vampire had infected also lost their power.

The belief that evil men and women return to earth, cursed to wander without peace for eternity, is a very common motif. It underlies many ghost stories, and is a common theme in literature (for instance, the ghost of Jacob Marley in Dickens's *A Christmas Carol*) and in folklore. One of the more famous examples of an evil revenant was Caligula, the depraved Roman emperor. When he was assassinated, his body was hastily buried in a shallow grave after being semi-cremated. His violent death, the lack of attention to detail in the burial rites, his evil life, and the shallow grave are all classic ingredients likely to cause the dead to lie uneasily. Death meant no peace for the tyrant, and it was said that his body did not find rest in its grave and returned to haunt the living. Evil rumors surrounded the place of his burial for centuries.

There are many stories in folklore of evil men and women dying, yet continuing to walk the earth—Newburgh's story of the Squire of Alnwick is one example.[3] Another tale was of the lord of Passenham, Northamptonshire, Sir Robert Banastre. He had a reputation for cruelty and tyranny, and his villagers were therefore pleased to hear of his death. But the gravedigger preparing his tomb was terrified to find Sir Robert standing next to him, saying, "I am not yet ready." These comments continued even during the funeral service, this time from inside the coffin. But when it was opened, Sir Robert was confirmed to be well and truly dead. His spirit, though, continued to haunt the village until a service of exorcism was held.

One did not have to lead a wholly evil life to be at risk; committing one particularly awful act could be enough to sentence the offender to a restless Afterlife. The Shadowy Host in Tolkien's epic gives one example of how such people could be terribly punished. The Men of the Mountains swore an oath of valor to Isildur, King of Men, but they broke it when they fled before the enemy. Isildur then cursed them "to rest never until your oath is fulfilled. For this war will last through years uncounted, and you shall be summoned once again ere the end." No rest and no grave was granted to them and, in death, they still dwelt among the living, "and the terror of the Sleepless Dead lies about the Hill of Erech and all places where that people lingered."[4] The oath breakers were summoned again, by Aragorn, Isildur's heir of Gondor, and by following him into battle, they bought redemption and final rest.

The breaking of spiritual taboos would also jeopardize the immortal soul, even if the person involved was an innocent victim, such as illegitimate children or even, in some cases, children who were conceived during a holy festival when their parents should have been abstaining from sexual relations. So strong was this belief that in many cultures it was believed that the earth would reject those who had broken some such taboo in life (this was a particularly prominent belief in Russia). One story tells how the parents of a sick child contacted a witch who, by means of a pact with the Devil, restored him to health. But his recovery was only temporary, and after a few months he died. He was buried on three separate occasions, and each time the earth "threw him out." On the last occasion, the poor child's remains were found scattered across the cemetery.

Although many elements of this story might have a natural explanation—the fact that the remains were scattered in such a way suggests that animals had dug up the corpse and fed on it—this was at the time seen as an act of God. The earth had clearly refused to accept the body of one whose soul had been traded with Satan; it was consecrated ground and it would therefore reject something unholy. In some areas of Russia, the belief that the earth would not accept the bodies of those who were involved in the breaking of such taboos led to the construction of charnel houses on the surface where bodies could decompose above the earth.

The third way of "creating" a vampire that Barber identifies is as a result of a violent event, either when they are attacked by a revenant or they are the victim of a more mundane murder/accident, such as Cristina in "For the Blood is the Life." Often, the victim is entirely innocent and is attacked by an evil, predatory vampire precisely because their pure blood acts as an attraction for the creature (though innocence is not a prerequisite—Tournefort's vampire was "sullen and quarrelsome" and was also murdered: two prime qualifications to become a revenant). This is a particularly dreadful fate. Such a "punishment" for a person who is essentially good is one of the most horrifying aspects of vampire tales, as we have already seen. The condemnation of such beings to an eternity without peace was a terrible curse. Lucy and Mina are two examples from *Dracula:* young women leading good lives who fall under a spell that they have done nothing to encourage (though Mina does at least see the curse broken when Count Dracula is killed). Equally abhorrent to the imagination are child victims of such assaults.

But sometimes the violence is self-induced, as in the case of suicides. This reflects widely held beliefs that the way that a person dies can have an effect on the well-being of their soul. Suicides especially, but also those unfortunate enough to die before their time through either murder or accident can be fated to walk the earth searching for peace. In Romania, the young who die unmarried are buried in wedding clothes, as all essential stages of life have to be undergone if the soul is to rest in peace. In Russia, those who drowned were often not buried because the earth would throw them out again as they had died before they should have done; they would instead be buried in the charnel houses described above.

In the Christian world, life is a gift from God, and therefore suicide is seen as a great taboo. To kill oneself is to defy the laws of God. This resulted in the well-known injunction placed by the Church on burying the bodies of suicides in consecrated ground. Barber quotes an account from Roben in Eastern Europe where, in the eighteenth century, attempts by the Church to bury suicides in consecrated ground were so widely resented by the local populace that riots resulted.[5] In other cases quoted by the same source, armed guards had to be supplied to ensure that the burial of suicides in consecrated ground was not forcibly prevented.

Because of the taboo against taking one's own life, suicides were especially vulnerable to vampirism or similar manifestations—a good reason to include in *Dracula* a scene where Mina spends time in a graveyard, next to the tomb of a suicide. There are old legends which show how the souls of suicides were in danger (in Bulgaria, taking your own life was one way of becoming a vampire). A story dating back to 1591 speaks of a shoemaker from Breslau, Poland, who slit his own throat. His wife, realizing that he would not be buried in hallowed ground, disguised the cause of death as apoplexy. He was therefore buried according to ritual, but was unable to rest in peace and returned to the town, a variation on the belief that we have already alluded to that the earth would reject the bodies of those who had died in "unnatural" ways. His visits only stopped when he was disinterred, cut up, burned, and the ashes thrown into the river.

A more recent story from the eighteenth century comes from Dorset, England, and concerns William Doggett, squire of Eastbury House. Doggett's master spent much of his time away from home, giving Doggett ample opportunity to involve himself in fraudulent activities. When Doggett's master uncovered his dishonesty, rather than face the consequences, the squire killed himself. The local populace believed that Doggett then became a vampire. He could be seen waiting at the gates of the house where a coach and horses picked him up and carried him up the drive to the house. To add to the effect of the story, those who saw the vampire said that the coachman and the horses were all headless. It was said that when the local church was demolished in the nineteenth century, the squire's corpse had not decomposed and his legs were tied together to stop him from wandering the earth.[6]

All significant stages of human life have rituals associated with them—births, christenings, marriages, and deaths, for example. They were designed to protect the souls and well-being of the person involved at what were critical moments in their lives. The rituals of death were among the most crucial, because failure to comply with the required formalities at this point could condemn the soul to everlasting suffering. There were things that could, or should not, be done in order to ease the normal passing of a soul to the Hereafter. In Britain for example, right up until the twentieth century, doors and windows were opened so that the soul could make its way out of the house. In addition, animals would be placed outside until after the funeral so that the spirit of the departed could not take up residence in them. Care needed to be taken that grieving was not excessive, as too many tears would stop the spirit from leaving. This was a collective effort to ensure that the soul did not stay on this earth, but made its way safely to the next life. Many apparitions are connected with those who have not undergone appropriate burial rites. For example, a ghost once seen at All Saints' Church in York was believed to appear because she had been denied a Christian burial and was returning to try to correct this.

In Christian cultures, the observation of rites to protect the soul started even before death. During the seventeenth century, in particular, there was a whole industry created around the art of dying. It was not enough just to live well; the right passing was even more important for the reception of the soul into heaven. Books were published teaching the inhabitants of Christian England how they should die. Even if they had lived an exemplary Christian life, a lapse right at the last could sentence them to eternal damnation. Protecting the dying against evil spirits was therefore important. Lighting candles around them kept demons at bay. For right up to the time the dying breathed their last, their immortal soul was in danger of being stolen away by the forces of evil. A formal religious service conducted by a bona fide priest was essential. Those who died alone (especially without a priest in attendance) were particularly at risk of joining the ranks of the undead—a feature, for example, of both gypsy and Finnish folklore.

Once death had occurred, there was a whole host of rituals that had to be observed. These included the way in which the body was handled after death, and ensuring that certain rituals were observed to protect the soul before the funeral service. We have already mentioned, for example, the need to keep animals away from the body and the importance of covering pots of water in the house to ensure that the soul is not "stolen." In Romania, even today the floors are not swept when a coffin is in the house so that no member of the family will follow the deceased, and there must always be light. Coins are still placed in the pockets of the dead. When the dead are carried out of the house, a pot is broken to symbolically keep evil spirits away.

The rituals were followed through into the funeral service and then the burial. The importance of observing burial rites, and the strong likelihood of vampiric activities if the rituals of death were not respected, is demonstrated in the story of Theodore of Gaza, who lived in Italy in the fifteenth century. This has an unusual slant in that the creature that exhibits vampire tendencies is a ghost combining two supernatural forms in one. A tenant farmer of Theodore's unearthed an urn while plowing the land. It was unmistakably ancient, containing the ashes of someone who had died many centuries previously. The farmer took it home with him, but during the night he had an awful dream in which he was confronted by the spirit of the man whose ashes were contained in the urn. He threatened him with terrible consequences unless he reburied the ashes where he had found them. On waking, the man did nothing. Soon after, his eldest son, a strong, vigorous youth, fell ill. Within days he was dead. The spirit then appeared again. Previously, he had been thin and gaunt, but now he looked robust and healthy, having fed on the life force of the eldest son. He warned the man to rebury the urn where he had found it, otherwise his other son would meet the same fate. On waking, the farmer needed no further convincing. He hurried back to the field and replaced the urn. The spirit, having fattened himself up on the eldest son, was seen no more.

Despite all the preparations that could be taken to help ensure that the departed did not return to the earth, there was still often a perceived risk that someone might return as a vampire. In some cases, the view of the community was that prevention was better than cure. In regions whose inhabitants were haunted by a real fear of vampire attacks, corpses were often dug up after a period of time, normally about three years, to see if they had decomposed properly. If they had not, it meant that the deceased could be a vampire and the corpse was dealt with accordingly. The practice reflects a belief that, when the soul dies, it does not pass directly to the next life, but stays in a form of limbo for some time. In many areas, it was quite common, as a result, to have two burials: the initial one when a person dies and the second one when their disinterred bodies have decomposed and they can be reburied with all due reverence, often at another burial site.

In Jewish tradition, those deemed to be at risk of being an *estrie* were examined before burial. If their mouth was open, then it was believed that they would become a vampire. By placing dirt in the open mouth, the transformation could be stopped. In Finland, too, corpses were often staked at burial if it was felt that they could become vampires. More unusual remedies included the practice in parts of Germany of putting fishing nets in their grave. Vampires could not stop themselves from compulsively counting the knots in the nets, and they would be so preoccupied counting them that they would never be able to leave the tomb. A different approach was to scatter linen seeds around the tomb of a suspected vampire. When the creature left the grave, it was compelled to pick up the seeds. In some versions of the legend, it was allowed to pick up only one seed a year, presumably leaving the village in peace for a very long time.

A similar remedy involving nets applied to the *viesczy*, a vampire known to the Slavic nations of northern Europe, especially Poland. This variant is interesting as its name has the same etymological root as a witch or a wizard, making an explicit connection between the different branches of the occult. Another way of dealing with this creature was to put a brick under its mouth when burying it so that it could not open its jaws. The ultimate remedy was to strike off its head and bury it under the arm. Additionally, if a child was born with teeth (another indication of vampirism), simply removing them could be a cure. On death, it was easy to tell if someone was a *viesczy*, because their face would be bright red and their left eye would be open. Thorns placed in the mouth of the dead, even sometimes driven through the tongue, were deemed to prevent potential vampires from chewing on their shrouds.

A similar approach was to sprinkle thorns liberally in the grave, which stopped a vampire from leaving it as the thorns caught the material of the shroud. In Romania, as well as actually driving stakes into those corpses which showed signs of belonging to a high risk category, they were also placed in strategic positions over the grave, so the vampire would impale itself trying to get out. In many cultures, sickles were buried with the dead, sometimes, as in Yugoslavia, placed in the coffin in such a way that a vampire would be decapitated if he tried to escape from his tomb. Removal of the heart was also a way of stopping vampire activity, and Barber quotes an account of a Romanian prince in exile in Paris in 1874 who wished to have his heart removed on his death to prevent his return as a vampire.[7]

In Finland, the knees of the dead were tied together to stop them from walking. Tying the mouth shut was practiced in other regions. In Romania, ropes were used to restrain the corpse; they were cut shortly before burial and buried near the cadaver. However, there could be dangerous aftereffects. If the bonds were subsequently employed in a black magic ritual, then the dead would return as a breed of vampire known as a *strigoi*.

If these attempts at prevention failed, then a cure was clearly needed, and there were a range of measures that could be used to do this, often varying by region. It was important to know how to protect oneself against the attacks of vampires. The use of natural measures, such as garlic, has been mentioned elsewhere. But in Christian cultures, the use of religious symbols was a strong source of protection. This is because the vampire is an abomination, something undoubtedly unchristian. This is why, for example, the cross repels them, though in vampire lore this is often deemed to be much less effective against an "old" vampire (one that has been a revenant for some time) than against a "new" one. Therefore, a crucifix is often seen as a protection against evil, though the importance lies in its symbolism rather than its actual form, and also in the faith of the person using it.

One example in folklore of the power of the crucifix is found in the story of the Yugoslavian Carniola vampire. This first appeared in print in 1689, and concerns one Grando, a landowner, who died but returned soon afterwards as a vampire. He made a number of attacks, and the church was called in to deal with him. Digging up his corpse, they noticed that he had a smile on his face. However, when a crucifix was held over him, tears rolled down his cheeks. He was decapitated and the infestation stopped forthwith. Holy water can also be used as a protection. In the Stephen

King vampire novel, *Salem's Lot,* holy water is used to show the presence of the undead. In some parts of Europe, frankincense, clearly associated with the birth of Christ, was smeared on knives or stakes before disposing of a vampire. In Tournefort's account of vampire activity on Mykonos, the inhabitants sprinkled holy water around their doorposts as a way of protecting themselves against attack.

Such beliefs in the efficacy of religious objects in the battle against the forces of evil mirror far older ones. The great French house of Anjou, from which the medieval kings of England claimed descent, was rumored to have "come from the Devil" and would return to him one day. One story tells how the founding matriarch of the family, Melusine, was a beautiful woman of unknown origin. It was noticed that she would invariably disappear from Mass before the moment at which the Host was raised. One day, her husband forced her to stay until this sacred moment. The sight was too much. Melusine—who was in fact an evil spirit—flew out of the window and was never seen again. No demon could tolerate the presence of the signs of the Christian faith, a motif mined consistently by vampire literature. Dracula himself claims a devilish descent: "What devil or what witch was ever so great as Attila, whose blood is in these veins?"[8] So given these antecedents, it is no surprise that, in Christian lore, the creatures of the Devil are unable to stand against the symbols of Christ.

Another example of the importance of religious symbols in dealing with vampires was to be found in the tradition of bottling one. This dangerous exercise could only be undertaken by a very experienced and nerveless sorcerer. However, vital in his armory is the presence of a suitable Christian icon or relic. The sorcerer lies in wait for the vampire, complete with a bottle. He uses the icon to drive the vampire into this, encouraging the vampire by placing its favorite food in the bottle (in the case of the Bulgarian *ubour,* this is not blood, but manure). As soon as the vampire is inside, a cork is inserted. The bottle is then thrown on a fire and the vampire is accordingly destroyed.

This again reflects beliefs that can be found in spheres much wider than those including just the vampire. The symbolic power of icons as tokens of divine support encouraged people to take them into battle. In the Byzantine era, the icon of the Virgin in Constantinople was deemed to guarantee victory to the Byzantines against their enemies. For Catholic Christianity, relics rather than images were used, as they were deemed to retain elements of the saint's holy power, giving great strength to the person who owned them—though images, of course, still have their place in Catholicism. Those of the two saints, Cosmas and Damian, were believed to have specific powers in the battle with the hosts of the undead.

Yet it is reassuring to know that being quick-witted can also provide protection. A vampire in Armenia killed its victims by sucking the blood from their feet. Two travelers in the region, aware of the potential danger, buried their feet under each other's arms when they slept. When the vampire duly arrived, he was nonplussed. He went away muttering at the injustice of finding a creature with two heads and no feet, and was never seen again. Other remedies to protect against vampires were distinctly unchristian. Taking a pair of socks from a dead man was also believed to be efficacious.

A vampire, once its existence was suspected, must be destroyed. First of all, there was the practical problem of finding where its resting place was. If the creature had been identified, then this was rarely a problem, but when it had not been, various remedies were used to identify where the vampire lay. Using a white horse saddled by a virgin in the cemetery has already been referred to.[9] Other methods included spotting blue lights that sometimes seemed to emanate from a grave, a variation on the tradition that such flames mark the spot where treasure is buried (see *Dracula*). This in itself is an extension of a perfectly plausible phenomenon. Decomposing corpses emit large amounts of methane, which is a highly combustible material. Holes in the ground around the grave were another clue to finding the resting place of a vampire, as was merely noting those places where the ground had sunk and the crosses marking the tomb appeared to have moved. In Slavic culture, the very practical measure of strewing salt or ashes around the graves of the newly dead was used to mark the footprints of those who returned from their tombs.

Once discovered, the vampire can be eliminated. However, as we have already noted, this is not always an easy thing to do as a variety of measures are available and not all are invariably effective. Vampires had to be destroyed, regardless of their righteousness when alive. For what existed after "death" was not the same being as the person who had lived. Van Helsing says as much when he instructs his comrades to destroy Lucy. It is understandably a terrible task for Arthur, her fiancé in life. He must drive a stake through her heart, after which they will decapitate her. Her mouth will also be filled with garlic (all classic remedies from folklore). He asks, "Is this really Lucy's body, or only a demon in her shape?" to which van Helsing enigmatically replies, "It is her body, and yet not it," something that seemed like "a nightmare" image.[10]

It is the scenes where such creatures are destroyed that often provide the most terrifying moments in vampire literature (though it is perhaps even more horrifying when such scenes are missing: the vampire lives on at the conclusion of both Polidori's "Vampyre" and "Wake Not the Dead!" where it survives to claim untold other victims in the future). In *Dracula*, it is surprisingly not the death of the count which provides such moments. He dies in a rather unsatisfactory brawl on the road as the sun goes down. In both *Nosferatu* and Hammer's *Horror of Dracula*, film producers chose the more dramatic denouement of having the count struck down as the sun rises at the break of day.

The really eerie moments in Stoker's novel are rather when Lucy is "killed" and, later, when van Helsing destroys the three female vampires that are the count's companions. In the former scene, the setting provides part of the atmosphere; the lonely crypt in the churchyard, dimly lit by candles placed on other coffins. The tension is built by Stoker giving van Helsing several opportunities to kill Lucy himself, but eventually deciding that Holmwood, her fiancé, should do it. Similarly, van Helsing finds the three women in the castle chapel, beautiful in death, and destroys them by driving stakes into their hearts. The result, beloved of vampire moviemakers, is that within seconds the women are transformed into nothing save a pile of dust.

In *Carmilla,* we see all the trappings of the classic vampire finale, some of which could have been lifted straight from folklore. The corpse is that of a beautiful young woman, not someone who has been dead for 150 years (a distinction here perhaps; in folklore, the vampire is generally someone who has died quite recently, and feeds on the life force of its family and friends). The body is robust, there is no smell of decay. This is classic vampire symbolism. The lack of all the so-called normal signs of death is the mark of the vampire in many legends, together with the supple limbs and the presence of blood in the coffin—"all the admitted signs and proofs of vampirism." Carmilla is dispatched with a stake through the heart, and she lets out a horrible shriek. The head is struck off, the body burned, and the ashes scattered on the waters—all remedies from legend that we have seen throughout this book.

In folklore, the most consistent ways of destroying a vampire seem to have been staking, decapitating, or burning the body. These all had their rituals. When the vampire was dug up, it was important that no blood was spilled on those performing the act, be it staking or decapitation. If it was, then the unlucky onlooker would either go mad or become a vampire. And decapitation of a vampire was not as simple as it might seem. Care needed to be taken to ensure that the head did not come into contact with the neck again or the two might miraculously reattach themselves. In Lithuania, the head should be buried between the legs. The *nachzehrer,* a north European variant of the vampire, has a particularly nasty habit of eating its own funeral attire while buried in its coffin. It then moves on to its own flesh. As it eats this, the members of its family start to fade away. Eventually, the vampire makes its way out of the tomb and starts physically attacking its family and drinking their blood. Cutting off its head and burying it away from the body is one way of destroying it.

The act of decapitation was often performed merely with the use of a sexton's spade, and bearing in mind that the "vampire" corpse was quite probably in an advanced stage of decomposition, this would presumably be fairly easy to do. To prevent blood splashing on the onlookers, the corpse was often covered with a thin layer of earth or some kind of fabric before cutting into it. In some regions of Yugoslavia, gypsies merely drove a stake into the stomach of the supposed vampire while it was still buried, making it a completely risk-free process (an intimation, incidentally, of how shallow many burials must have been).

Cremation was usually only employed as a last resort. It was considered an undesirable act and was therefore avoided. The traditions of some branches of the Church, particularly the Orthodox, stated that the body must decompose naturally in the grave as God willed it. There were other reasons, too, even though on its own it was an important prohibition. Cremation involved a large amount of handling of the corpse, a taboo in many cultures. There were also practical problems involved in generating high enough temperatures to destroy a vampire—and even if the heat could be created, there are often practical problems that prohibit the complete destruction of a corpse.[11] Despite these difficulties, however, in Greece and Bulgaria, potential vampires were sometimes burned when they died as a way of preventing an infestation. Cremation rituals varied by region. Some said that the head should be removed first, others that the body should be cut up and then boiled in holy water or oil.

The measures taken to prevent a vampire being created, or destroying it if it had been, are conclusive evidence of the belief in the existence of the undead in many communities. We have seen that there are a number of reasons that explain how a vampire came into being. But there is one last psychological feature to consider. Underlying the effectiveness of the vampire tradition is a primeval fear: that of being buried alive. So terrible was this image that it became the most awful of all punishments, a fate that was, for example, meted out to Antigone and Ismene, the daughters of the ill-fated Oedipus.

The belief that some "corpses" were erroneously buried alive has sometimes been offered as a rational explanation for vampirism. Calmet, for example, listed premature burial as one possible cause of the phenomenon experienced during the eighteenth-century epidemics. Whether or not some vampires were merely people in a coma buried in error is contentious, though in our view this is unlikely to explain many cases of vampirism. What is irrefutable, however, is that the fear of being buried alive is a terrifying thought for many, and for some becomes obsessive to the point of paranoia. The fear this engenders helps to explain the impact of vampire stories on the human psyche. It is certainly the case that in the premodern world, many people were buried when they were not dead.

Legends are made of such topics. A woman in St. Saviour's churchyard, York, was buried wearing a valuable ring on her finger. The following night, the sexton disinterred her so that he could remove the ring. However, as her fingers were swollen, he used a knife in an attempt to cut the ring off. As he did so, blood flowed from her finger, and the woman—who had been in a coma—came round. She returned to her family, who must have been, to say the least, surprised to see her. And in Christchurch, Dorset, an eighteenth-century mausoleum was erected for Mrs. Perkins, a local woman who was so scared of being buried alive that she had it designed so that she would be entombed above ground, and with ways of escaping if she were erroneously interred before death—such as insisting that the coffin lid should not be screwed down and that there should be a door that could be opened from inside the mausoleum.

The Roman naturalist Pliny the Elder was convinced that many of those who were buried were actually still alive. In later times, in parts of Eastern Europe, cremation was used as a way of ensuring that the body was actually dead. In Bavaria, a death hut was provided so that the body could lie above ground for a while before burial. The most famous literary stories to take advantage of these terrifying motifs were, of course, those of Edgar Allan Poe, particularly "Berenice" and "The Premature Burial." It is also the theme of the Sherlock Holmes adventure, *The Disappearance of Lady Frances Carfax*. The title of this story is interesting, as Carfax is also the name of the house in London where Count Dracula takes up residence.

Whatever the causes of their supposed existence, the undead have exercised an influence over the imagination for thousands of years. To many early civilizations, death was definitely a region of terror, very different from the paradisiacal images sometimes seen in later religions such as Islam and Christianity. The Greek god Hades is "essentially a god of terror, mystery and the inexorable."[12] The souls of the dying were taken away by the *Keres*, vampiric creatures notable for their red robes, representative of blood, and their sharp teeth. They finished off the wounded in battle by sinking their teeth into their flesh and drinking their blood. In Etruscan mythology—the parent from which many Roman beliefs were the offspring—the soul was fought over by two groups of spirits, one evil, one beneficent, to decide on its ownership.

Later religions helped to perpetuate fear of the realm of the dead. Christianity, for example, while it preached that paradise would be a reward for the righteous, also developed the concept of hell where the wicked would suffer unimaginable agonies for eternity. It was important to protect the souls of the just from being punished in this way, hence the need for rituals. In a way similar to that in which the Etruscan gods fought over the souls of the dead did the Christian Church battle for them. So fear of the undead did not dissipate over the course of the centuries, rather it showed itself in slightly different ways.

The vampire has proved a stubbornly hard creature to destroy. Even given the secularization of society, the image lives on, constantly evolving through the medium of characterizations such as Buffy or Angel. But underneath this evolution there lie, in our view, some constants. Fear of death, still unconquered and inevitable, is as real as ever. Despite our efforts, the aging process might have slowed somewhat, but it is still inexorable. The undead might be a different species from those "known" by our forefathers several hundred years ago, but the fact they are still around at all shows just how deep-rooted the fears they live off actually are.

NOTES

1. See "Vampires, Burial and Death," chap. 5.
2. Barber, pp. 29–30.
3. See Chapter 1.
4. *The Return of the King,* p. 52.
5. Barber, p. 30.
6. *Mysterious Dorset,* p. 71.
7. Barber, p. 73.
8. *Dracula,* p. 53.
9. See p. 17 of this book.
10. *Dracula,* p. 221.
11. Barber, p. 76.
12. *Larousse Encyclopaedia of Mythology,* p. 165.

Bibliography

Ackroyd, Peter. *Hawksmoor*. London: Abacus, 1986.

Barber, Paul. *Vampires, Burial and Death. Folklore and Reality*. New Haven and London: Yale UP, 1988.

Biedermann, Hans. *Dictionary of Symbolism*. Translated by James Hulbert. Ware, Hertfordshire: Wordsworth, 1992.

Bunson, Matthew. *The Vampire Encyclopaedia*. New York: Random House, 2000.

Burton, Sir R. F. *Vikram and the Vampire*. London, 1893.

Byron, G. [*sic*]/Polidori, John. "The Vampyre—A Tale." London, 1819.

Byron, Lord. "The Giaour." In *The Works of Lord Byron*. Ware, Hertfordshire: Wordsworth, 1995.

Calmet, Dom Augustin. "Treatise on the Vampires of Hungary and Surrounding Regions." In *Vampyres: Lord Byron to Count Dracula,* edited by Christopher Frayling, 93. London: Faber and Faber, 1991.

Casaubon, Meric. *A True and Faithful Relation of what passed for many years between Dr. John Dee ... and some spirits*. London, 1659.

Copper, Basil. *The Vampire*. London: Robert Hale, 1973.

Crowe, Catherine. *The Night Side of Nature*. Ware, Hertfordshire: Wordsworth, 2000.

Davies, David Stuart,ed. *Short Stories from the Nineteenth Century*. Ware, Hertfordshire: Wordsworth, 2000.

Deane, Hamilton, and John L. Balderstone. *Dracula: The Vampire Play in Three Acts*. New York: Samuel French, 1933.

Doyle, Arthur Conan. *The Return of Sherlock Holmes*. Ware, Hertfordshire: Wordsworth, 1993.

Eliade, Mircea. *Istoria credintelor si ideilor religioase*. Translated by Cezar Baltag. Bucuresti: Univers Enciclopedic, 1999.

_____. *Sacrul si Profanul.* Translated by Brandusa Prelipceanu. Bucuresti: Humanitas, 2000.

Eliade, Mircea, and Ioan P. Culianu. *Dictionar al religiilor.* Translated by Cezar Baltag. Bucuresti: Humanitas, 1993.

Encyclopaedia of World Mythology. London: BPC, 1975.

English Fairy Tales. Ware, Hertfordshire: Wordsworth, 1994.

Foucault, Michel. *Anormalii.* Translated by Dan Radu Stanescu. Bucuresti: Univers, 2001.

Fowles, John. *The Magus.* London: Vintage, 1997.

Frayling, Christopher. *Vampyres: Lord Byron to Count Dracula.* London: Faber and Faber, 1991.

Frazer, James, *The Golden Bough,* Ware, Hertfordshire: Wordsworth, 1993.

Folklore, Myths and Legends of Britain. London: The Reader's Digest Association, 1973.

Gantz, Jeffrey, trans. *The Mabinogion.* London: Penguin Classics, 1976.

Great Vampire Stories. Reprint, London: Chancellor, 2002.

Goethe, Johann Wolfgang. *Faust, The First Part of the Tragedy.* Translated by John R. Williams. Ware, Hertfordshire: Wordsworth, 1999.

Grimm, J.L.C., and W. C. Grimm. *Grimm's Fairy Tales.* Ware, Hertfordshire: Wordsworth, 1998.

Haining, Peter, and Peter Tremayne. *The Un-Dead: The Legend of Bram Stoker and Dracula.* London: Constable, 1997.

Haining, Peter, ed. *The Witchcraft Papers.* London: Robert Hale, 1974.

Keats, John. *Selected Poems.* London: Penguin, 1996.

Knott, Olive. *Witches of Dorset.* Milborne Port, Sherborne: Dorset Publishing Company, 1974.

Lecouteux, Claude. *Vampiri si vampirism. Autopsia unui mit.* Translated by Mihai Popescu. Bucuresti: Saeculum, 2002.

Le Fanu, Sheridan. *Carmilla.* Edinburgh: Soft Editions, 2002.

_____. *Madam Crowl's Ghost.* Ware, Hertfordshire: Wordsworth, 1994.

Legg, Rodney. *Mysterious Dorset.* Reprint, Wincanton: Dorset Publishing, 1998.

The Life of Doctor John Dee. London, 1842.

Mackay, Charles. *Extraordinary Popular Delusions and the Madness of Crowds.* Ware, Hertfordshire: Wordsworth, 1995.

Matarasso, P., trans. *The Quest of the Holy Grail.* London: Penguin Classics, 1975.

McNally, Raymond, and Radu Florescu. *In Search of Dracula. The History of Dracula and Vampires.* Boston: Houghton Mifflin, 1994.

Muchembled, Robert, ed. *Magia si Vrajitoria in Europa din Evul Mediu pana astazi.* Translated by Maria Ivanescu and Cezar Ivanescu. Bucuresti: Humanitas, 1997.

New Larousse Encyclopaedia of Mythology. Translated by Richard Aldington and Delano Ames. Reprint, London and New York: Hamlyn, 1975.

Poe, Edgar Allan. *Tales of Mystery and Imagination.* Ware, Hertfordshire: Wordsworth, 1993.

Rice, Anne. *Interview with the Vampire.* London: Futura, 1977.

Robbins, Russel Hope. *The Encyclopaedia of Witchcraft and Demonology.* Feltham: Hamlyn, 1968.

Ronay, Gabrie. *The Dracula Myth.* London: Pan, 1975.

Ross, Anne. *Folklore of the Scottish Highlands.* London: Batsford, 1976.

Rowling, J. K. *Harry Potter and the Philosopher's Stone.* London: Bloomsbury, 2001.

————. *Harry Potter and the Chamber of Secrets.* London, Bloomsbury, 2001.

————. *Harry Potter and the Prisoner of Azkaban.* London, Bloomsbury, 1999.

————. *Harry Potter and the Goblet of Fire.* London, Bloomsbury, 2000.

Seligmann, Kurt. *Magic, Supernaturalism and Religion.* London: Penguin, 1971.

Shakespeare, William. *The Complete Works of William Shakespeare.* Ware, Hertford-shire: Wordsworth, 1998.

Simons, G. L. *The Witchcraft World.* London: Abelard-Schuman, 1974.

South, James, ed. *Buffy the Vampire Slayer and Philosophy.* Chicago and La Salle: Open Court, 2003.

Stoker, Bram. *Dracula.* Boston and New York: Bedford/St. Martin's, 2002.

Summers, Montague. *The Vampire in Lore and Legend.* Reprint, New York: Dover, 2001.

Tolkien, J.R.R. *The Lord of the Rings.* London: HarperCollins, 1999.

Wilde, Oscar. *The Picture of Dorian Gray.* Ware, Hertfordshire: Wordsworth, 1992.

Wilkinson, W. *An Account of the Principalities of Wallachia and Moldavia with... Political Observations Relating to Them.* 1820. Reprint, London: Wordsworth, 1998.

Index

About the Authors

WAYNE BARTLETT wrote *Taming the Dragon, God Wills It! A History of the Crusades, An Ungodly War: The Sack of Constantinople, Fourth Crusade*, and *Assassins: Medieval Islam's Secret Sect*. He is a management consultant, currently working in Romania.

FLAVIA IDRICEANU is a philologist in Bucharest, Romania.